Discursivity, Relationality and Materiality in the Life of the Organisation

The field of organisational communication has been rapidly transforming in the wake of the linguistic and discursive turns that have been sweeping across the social sciences since the mid-eighties. These 'turns' have prompted organisational communication scholars to look more closely at how they think about communication and its relationship to the organisation and the process of organising. What has emerged from these reflections is a perspective that proposes communication is not merely something that happens *in* organisations but *is the heart of organising* and therefore actually constitutes the organisation. This perspective, which embraces several sub-threads, is now commonly referred to as the Communication as Constitutive of Organization (CCO) perspective. This is itself evolving as scholars come to realize that organising does not just occur at the discursive level. It is inextricably coupled to the material and relational aspects of work – the discourse mutually constitutes relationships between human and non-human bodies that combine to create what we encounter when we participate in organisational life. This book examines the way these three dimensions combine to create organisational outcomes. In doing so, it advances CCO and sociomateriality scholarship and contributes to new ways of thinking about strategy and practice. The series of empirical studies should interest the widely interdisciplinary audience that seeks to understand work, organising and management.

The chapters in this book were originally published as a special issue of the *Communication Research and Practice* journal.

Colleen E. Mills is a Professor of Management at the University of Canterbury, New Zealand, and an International Faculty Affiliate at Audencia Business School, France. Her research interests include organisational communication, sensemaking, materiality and organisational change. She is an executive member and past president of the Australian and New Zealand Communication Association, board member of the International Communication Association and editor-in-chief of Communication Research and Practice (2018–).

François Cooren is a Professor of Communication at the Université de Montréal, Canada. His research interests include organisational communication, language and social interaction, and communication theory. He is a fellow and past president of the International Communication Association, Distinguished Scholar of the National Communication Association and former editor-in-chief of *Communication Theory* (2005–2008).

Discursivity, Relationality and Materiality in the Life of the Organisation

Communication Perspectives

Edited by
Colleen E. Mills and François Cooren

LONDON AND NEW YORK

First published 2018
by Routledge
2 Park Square, Milton Park, Abingdon, Oxon, OX14 4RN, UK

and by Routledge
711 Third Avenue, New York, NY 10017, USA

Routledge is an imprint of the Taylor & Francis Group, an informa business

© 2018 Australian and New Zealand Communication Association

All rights reserved. No part of this book may be reprinted or reproduced or utilised in any form or by any electronic, mechanical, or other means, now known or hereafter invented, including photocopying and recording, or in any information storage or retrieval system, without permission in writing from the publishers.

Trademark notice: Product or corporate names may be trademarks or registered trademarks, and are used only for identification and explanation without intent to infringe.

British Library Cataloguing in Publication Data
A catalogue record for this book is available from the British Library

ISBN 13: 978-0-8153-8461-8

Typeset in Minion Pro
by diacriTech, Chennai

Publisher's Note
The publisher accepts responsibility for any inconsistencies that may have arisen during the conversion of this book from journal articles to book chapters, namely the possible inclusion of journal terminology.

Disclaimer
Every effort has been made to contact copyright holders for their permission to reprint material in this book. The publishers would be grateful to hear from any copyright holder who is not here acknowledged and will undertake to rectify any errors or omissions in future editions of this book.

Contents

Citation Information	vii
Notes on Contributors	ix

Introduction   1
Colleen E. Mills and François Cooren

1 How things make things do things with words, or how to pay attention to what things have to say   6
Nicolas Bencherki

2 A communicative approach to sociomateriality: the agentic role of technology at the operational level   24
Nicolas Arnaud and Bertrand Fauré

3 Modes of design tools: sociomaterial dynamics of a horticultural project   45
Carole Groleau and Christiane Demers

4 The materiality of discourse: relational positioning in a fresh water controversy   68
Theresa Castor

5 A spatial grammar of organising: studying the communicative constitution of organisational spaces   85
Consuelo Vásquez

6 Making mundane work visible on social media: a CCO investigation of working out loud on Twitter   112
Viviane Sergi and Claudine Bonneau

7 A communication perspective on organisational stakeholder relationships: discursivity, relationality, and materiality   141
Matthew A. Koschmann

Index   167

Citation Information

The chapters in this book were originally published in *Communication Research and Practice*, volume 2, issue 3 (September 2016). When citing this material, please use the original page numbering for each article, as follows:

Introduction
Colleen E. Mills and François Cooren
Communication Research and Practice, volume 2, issue 3 (September 2016) pp. 267–271

Chapter 1
How things make things do things with words, or how to pay attention to what things have to say
Nicolas Bencherki
Communication Research and Practice, volume 2, issue 3 (September 2016) pp. 272–289

Chapter 2
A communicative approach to sociomateriality: the agentic role of technology at the operational level
Nicolas Arnaud and Bertrand Fauré
Communication Research and Practice, volume 2, issue 3 (September 2016) pp. 290–310

Chapter 3
Modes of design tools: sociomaterial dynamics of a horticultural project
Carole Groleau and Christiane Demers
Communication Research and Practice, volume 2, issue 3 (September 2016) pp. 311–333

Chapter 4
The materiality of discourse: relational positioning in a fresh water controversy
Theresa Castor
Communication Research and Practice, volume 2, issue 3 (September 2016) pp. 334–350

Chapter 5
A spatial grammar of organising: studying the communicative constitution of organisational spaces
Consuelo Vásquez
Communication Research and Practice, volume 2, issue 3 (September 2016) pp. 351–377

CITATION INFORMATION

Chapter 6
Making mundane work visible on social media: a CCO investigation of working out loud on Twitter
Viviane Sergi and Claudine Bonneau
Communication Research and Practice, volume 2, issue 3 (September 2016) pp. 378–406

Chapter 7
A communication perspective on organisational stakeholder relationships: discursivity, relationality, and materiality
Matthew A. Koschmann
Communication Research and Practice, volume 2, issue 3 (September 2016) pp. 407–431

For any permission-related enquiries please visit:
http://www.tandfonline.com/page/help/permissions

Notes on Contributors

Nicolas Arnaud is a Professor of Management at the Audencia Business School, France. His research looks at collective competence, managerial innovation, communication, human resources management, organisational behaviour and theory, and strategic management. His work has appeared in many journals, including *Communication Research and Practice*, *Management International* and the *British Journal of Management*.

Nicolas Bencherki is a Professor in the Department of Human Sciences, Arts and Communication at Université TÉLUQ, Canada. His research focuses on organisational communication among community-based organisations, in particular when it comes to collaboration between groups to achieve collective action. His work has been published in *Management Communication Quarterly*, *Journal of Communication* and *Communication Research and Practice*.

Claudine Bonneau is a Professor in the Department of Management and Technology at the Université du Québec à Montréal, Canada. Her research focuses on social media usage and technological collaboration in a professional setting, business information systems and qualitative social research. Her work has been published in journals including *Communication Research and Practice* and the *International Journal of Project Management*.

Theresa Castor is a Associate Professor of Communication at the University of Wisconsin – Parkside, USA. She conducts research on organisational decision-making, focusing on crisis and problem situations in meetings and governance groups. Her work has appeared in journals including *Communication Research and Practice*, *Management Communication Quarterly*, *Discourse Studies* and the *Electronic Journal of Communication*.

François Cooren is a Professor of Communication at the Université de Montréal, Canada. His research interests include organisational communication, language and social interaction, and communication theory. He is a fellow and past president of the International Communication Association, Distinguished Scholar of the National Communication Association and former editor-in-chief of *Communication Theory* (2005–2008).

NOTES ON CONTRIBUTORS

Christiane Demers is a Professor in the Department of Management at HEC Montréal, Canada. Her research focuses on theories of organisational change, strategic management and communication. Her work has been published in *Organization Science* and the *Journal of Organizational Change Management*; and she is the author of *Organizational Change Theories: A Synthesis* (2007).

Bertrand Fauré is a researcher in the Laboratoire d'Études et de Recherches Appliquées en Sciences Sociales, University of Toulouse III (Paul Sabatier), France. His work has been published in journals including *Communication Research and Practice*; *Accounting, Organization and Society*; *Human Relations* and *Management Communication Quarterly*.

Carole Groleau is a Professor in the Department of Communication at the Université de Montréal, Canada. Her research concerns the organisational dimension of materiality and the interactional dynamics supporting the process of technological change, starting from approaches such as situated action, distributed cognition, structuration and activity theory. Her work has been published in *Organization Science*, the *Journal of Organizational Change Management* and *Communication Research and Practice*.

Matthew A. Koschmann is an Associate Professor of Communication at the University of Colorado Boulder, USA. His research explores the communication processes of inter- and intra-organisational collaboration, with a particular emphasis on non-profit organisations, cross-sector partnerships and the civil society sector.

Colleen E. Mills is a Professor of Management at the University of Canterbury, New Zealand, and an International Faculty Affiliate at Audencia Business School, France. Her research interests include organisational communication, sensemaking, materiality and organisational change. She is an executive member and past president of the Australian and New Zealand Communication Association, board member of the International Communication Association and editor-in-chief of Communication Research and Practice (2018–).

Viviane Sergi is a Professor in the Department of Management and Technology at the Université du Québec à Montréal, Canada. Her research focuses on organisational management, leadership and new collaborative practices. Her work has been published in *Communication Research and Practice*, *Long Range Planning*, *Human Relations* and *International Journal of Project Management*.

Consuelo Vásquez is a Professor in the Department of Social and Public Communication at the Université du Québec à Montréal, Canada. Her research focuses on interaction analysis, process thinking in organisational change and theories of organisational communication. Her work has been published in *Communication Research and Practice*, *Qualitative Inquiry*, *Human Relations* and the *Scandinavian Journal of Management*.

Introduction

The field of organisational communication has rapidly transformed in the wake of the linguistic (see Alvesson & Kärreman, 2000) and discursive turns (Grant & Hardy, 2004) that have swept the social sciences over the last two decades or so. These 'turns' have prompted organisational communication scholars to question the appropriateness of the functionalist perspective, particularly the way it positions communication as something that happens *in* organisations rather than something that is intrinsic to the organisation and organising. From this questioning, a perspective has emerged that proposes communication as constitutive of the organisation – the so-called CCO (Communicative Constitution of Organisation) perspective (see Ashcraft, Kuhn, & Cooren, 2009; Cooren, Kuhn, Cornelissen, & Clark, 2011; Putnam & Nicotera, 2008; Taylor & Van Every, 2000). Those advocating for this perspective are united by the notion that organisations are created, maintained and altered in and by communication (Cooren et al., 2011).

This and related discursive perspectives have held such sway that it was not until relatively recently that communication (e.g. Ashcraft et al., 2009; Cooren, Fairhurst, & Huët, 2013; Putnam & Cooren, 2004), and organisational and management studies scholars (e.g. Arnaud, Mills, Legrand, & Maton, 2016; Jarzabkowski & Pinch, 2013; Leonardi & Barley, 2008; Orlikowski, 2007, 2010) became interested in questions of non-human agency and materiality and how these dimensions articulate with the discursive nature of organising. This interest has seen scholars move beyond Giddens' (1979, 1984) agency/structure dualism to seek ways to recouple the so-called 'material world' to the discursive processes of organising. This 'material turn' has highlighted the significance of the 'geosocial environment' (Mills, 2002, 2005), and yielded the now-familiar concept of 'sociomateriality' (Ashcraft et al., 2009; Orlikowski, 2007, 2010) to denote the coupling of the corporeal and the symbolic. There is now widespread acceptance among those who study organising that the social and material dimensions of organising are theoretically and empirically coupled (Jazabkowski & Pinch, 2013).

As the various CCO schools of thought (see Schoeneborn et al., 2014) and the concept of sociomateriality have risen to prominence, a highly imbricated and dynamic conception of communication's relationship to the organisation has emerged. Researchers have become more cosmopolitan and practice-oriented in their research designs as disciplinary distinctions have given way to boundary spanning collaborations and spawned new concepts that extend and enrich our theorising in organisational communication (e.g. Leonardi & Barley, 2008; Robichaud & Cooren, 2013).

This special issue has provided an opportunity to explore this boundary spanning scholarship, to reveal where organisational communication and management scholars are directing their attention as they seek to refine their portrayal of the interminable achievement of organisational life (Tsoukas & Chia, 2002). Each of the seven articles in this special issue has embraced this opportunity and used it to (re)consider how the discursive, material and relational dimensions of organisational life can be addressed conjointly and how a communication lens can help to do just that. Individually and collectively, they confirm the versatility of the CCO and sociomateriality perspectives and the capacious explanatory power that is harnessed when they are combined. The result is a noteworthy and original collection of contributions to the organisational communication (and organisation and management studies) literature that edges us closer to understanding the ecology of organisational life and also helps us answer the question of what next.

The authors have all valiantly sought to avoid reproducing the artificial divide between materiality and discourse or between materiality and practice (Orlikowski, 2007). They convincingly show how much more finely nuanced our understanding of aspects of organising can be when we question the very existence of a 'material world' (the one usually associated with tables, chairs, walls and computers) to which we would clumsily oppose an 'immaterial world' (the world of discourse, turns of talk, ideas and emotions). Discourse, turns of talk, ideas and emotions must have a material component in order to exist, which means that they are, in fact, part of this so-called 'material world' to which we tend to oppose them. Conversely, tables, chairs, walls and computers are capable of *telling us things* about who designed them, when and where, which means that they also enter the discursive world. In other words, the material world is, in fact, the world as we know it, composed of beings with various levels of concreteness (from a rock to the flash in someone's mind we call an idea). Immateriality, if there were such a thing, would be the equivalent of nothingness, as even a ghost or spectre has to materialise itself in order to be what it is or appears to be (Cooren, 2015; Derrida, 1994). As a collection, these articles move us closer to appreciating the singularity and plurality of organising and how these are achieved in the nexus created by materiality, discursivity and relationality. The articles underline how a relational approach provides the vehicle for acknowledging and *analysing* the material dimension of discourse and, at the same time, the discursive dimension of materiality.

Nicolas Bencherki opens the special issue with a paper that uses data from an ethnographic case study of the work of a tenants association advocating for improved housing to show how a CCO approach can accommodate the notion that objects can speak on their own, acting as 'spokesthings' for other objects. He shows how run-down buildings can tell us things about their condition using tools designed to represent their 'objective' state in words, without requiring humans to interpret for them. In doing so, this article provides an example that confronts the critique of the Montreal School of CCO scholarship, a critique that suggests this scholarship reduces the role played by objects to their interpretation by humans.

Nicolas Arnaud and Bertrand Fauré illustrate the utility of applying a CCO perspective to the explanation of how sociomaterial resources operate when they are distributed over time and space as they are in the inter-organisational collaborations that comprise a supply chain. Using data from a study of the French furniture industry, they show how workers' communication allows what matters to be discerned in the face of chaos created by a technological communication system.

DISCURSIVITY, RELATIONALITY AND MATERIALITY

Building on Activity Theory's notion of tool, Carole Groleau and Christiane Demer's study uses three modes – the projective, authoritative and instructional mode – to characterise the sociomaterial dynamics that support design work in a horticultural garden. They show how design tools allow ideas to be first concretised, then legitimised and finally operationalized in the process of creating a garden. In doing so, they provide a convincing illustration of how tools allow sociomaterial processes to attain coherence over time.

Theresa Castor's article applies a relational ontology to a fresh water management controversy to reveal how the materiality of discourse positions freshwater, communities and organisational texts in various and shifting ways in relation to each other. Not only does she show that relationships are discursively performed but that the physical resources that are entangled in these discursive performance are also.

Consuelo Vásquez's article explores how a spatial grammar is enacted in a Chilean scientific outreach programme. Specifically, she shows how the spatial images that are voiced and embodied by the staff in this organisation and the organisational spaces in which staff work construct each other, serving to foster the delineation of the organisation's boundaries. In doing so, she advances the argument that imagined spaces have agency.

Viviane Sergi and Claudine Bonneau explore the interesting phenomenon of 'working out loud' (WOL) on Twitter. They show that WOL tweets make visible things that would otherwise remain hidden, private or difficult to reveal in an explicit way. This tweeting materialises work, its practices and how it is perceived, and has the potential to actively participate in the constitution of work and the professional identities of the workers performing WOL.

Matthew Koschmann's article completes our set of articles exploring discursivity, relationality and materiality in the life of the organisation. He sets out to rethink the notion of stakeholder communication by applying a CCO perspective to key considerations within this field: stakeholder identification and salience, the separation of material and symbolic resources and the political production of meaning involved in stakeholder relationships. In doing so, his article represents an important response to the question we posed in the Call For Papers – where to from here? Matthew illustrates how a field of study that has largely remained isolated from the CCO perspective can be introduced to this perspective by systematically reframing its axiomatic foundations. As such, he models one way to advance the CCO perspective. The other articles do this in different ways, providing equally enriching new insights into how discursivity, relationality and materiality define each other.

We hope you enjoy uncovering the details of their contributions. We have certainly enjoyed the opportunity to gather them together in a single volume.

Acknowledgements

Colleen Mills and François Cooren, the editors of this special issue, would like to thank the wonderful team of reviewers who ensured the articles selected for this special issue were of the highest quality. Without their willingness to share their time and expertise this special issue would not have been possible.

Nicolas Arnaud, Audencia Business School, France
Jonathan Clifton, University of Valenciennes and Hainaut-Cambresis, France
Michael Etter, Copenhagen Business School, Denmark

DISCURSIVITY, RELATIONALITY AND MATERIALITY

Gail Fairhurst, University of Cincinnati, USA
Janet Fulk, University of Southern California, USA
Owen Hargie, University of Ulster, Belfast, United Kingdom
Matthew Koschmann, University of Colorado Boulder, USA
Tim Kuhn, University of Colorado Boulder, USA
Frédérik Matte, University of Ottawa, Canada
James McDonald, University of Texas at San Antonio, USA
Grant Michelson, Macquarie University, Australia
Amanda Porter, Free University Amsterdam, The Netherlands
Alex Wright, Open University, United Kingdom
Consuelo Vasquez, Université du Québec à Montréal, UQÀM, Canada

Disclosure statement

No potential conflict of interest was reported by the authors.

References

Alvesson, M., & Kärreman, D. (2000). Taking the linguistic turn in organizational research: Challenges, responses, consequences. *The Journal of Applied Behavioral Science*, *36*(2), 136–158. doi:10.1177/0021886300362002

Arnaud, N., Mills, C. E., Legrand, C., & Maton, E. (2016). Materializing strategy in mundane tools: The key to coupling global strategy and local strategy practice? *British Journal of Management*, *27*(1), 38–57.

Ashcraft, K. L., Kuhn, T. R., & Cooren, F. (2009). Constitutional amendments: Materializing organizational communication. *The Academy of Management Annals*, *3*(1), 1–64. doi:10.1080/19416520903047186

Cooren, F. (2015). In medias res: Communication, existence and materiality. *Communication Research and Practice*, *1*(4), 307–321. doi:10.1080/22041451.2015.1110075

Cooren, F., Fairhurst, G., & Huët, R. (2013). Why matter always matters in (organizational) communication. In P. Leonardi, B. A. Nardi, & J. Kallinikos (Eds.), *Materiality and organizing* (pp. 296–314). Oxford, UK: Oxford University Press.

Cooren, F., Kuhn, T. R., Cornelissen, J. P., & Clark, T. (2011). Communication, organizing and organization: An overview and introduction to the special issue. *Organization Studies*, *3*(9), 1–22.

Derrida, J. (1994). *Specters of Marx: The state of the debt, the work of mourning, and the new international*. New York: Routledge.

Giddens, A. (1979). *Central problems of social theory: Action, structure and contradiction in social analysis*. Berkley, CA: University of California Press.

Giddens, A. (1984). *The constitution of society: Outline of the theory of structuration*. Cambridge, UK: Polity.

Grant, D., & Hardy, C. (2004). Introduction: Struggles with organizational discourse. *Organization Studies*, *25*(1), 5–13. doi:10.1177/0170840604038173

Jarzabkowski, P., & Pinch, T. (2013). Sociomateriality is 'the New Black': Accomplishing repurposing, reinscripting and repairing in context. *M@n@gement*, *16*(5), 579–592. doi:10.3917/mana.165.0579

Leonardi, P. M., & Barley, S. R. (2008). Materiality and change: Challenges to building better theory about technology and organizing. *Information and Organization*, *18*, 159–176. doi:10.1016/j.infoandorg.2008.03.001

Mills, C. (2002). The hidden dimension of blue-collar sensemaking about workplace communication. *Journal of Business Communication*, *39*(3), 288–313. doi:10.1177/002194360203900301

DISCURSIVITY, RELATIONALITY AND MATERIALITY

Mills, C. E. (2005). Moving forward by looking back: A model for making sense of organisational communication. *Australian Journal of Communication, 32*(3), 19–43.

Orlikowski, W. J. (2007). Sociomaterial practices: Exploring technology at work. *Organization Studies, 28*(9), 1435–1448. doi:10.1177/0170840607081138

Orlikowski, W. J. (2010). The sociomateriality of organisational life: Considering technology in management research. *Cambridge Journal of Economics, 34*, 125–141. doi:10.1093/cje/bep058

Putnam, L. L., & Cooren, F. (2004). Alternative perspectives on the role of text and agency in constituting organizations. *Organization, 11*(3), 323–333. doi:10.1177/1350508404041995

Putnam, L. L., & Nicotera, A. M. (Eds.). (2008). *Building theories of organization: The constitutive role of communication*. Oxford, UK: Routledge.

Robichaud, D., & Cooren, F. (Eds.). (2013). *Organization and organizing: Materiality, agency and discourse*. Francis and Taylor: New York.

Schoeneborn, D., Blaschke, S., Cooren, F., McPhee, R. D., Seidl, D., & Taylor, J. R. (2014). The three schools of CCO thinking: Interactive dialogue and systematic comparison. *Management Communication Quarterly, 28*(2), 285–316. doi:10.1177/0893318914527000

Taylor, J. R., & Van Every, E. J. (2000). *The Emergent Organization: Communication as a Site and Surface*. Lawrence Erblaum Associates: Mahwah, NJ.

Tsoukas, H., & Chia, R. (2002). On organizational becoming: Rethinking organizational change. *Organization Science, 13*(5), 567–582. doi:10.1287/orsc.13.5.567.7810

Colleen Mills

François Cooren

How things make things do things with words, or how to pay attention to what things have to say

Nicolas Bencherki ⓘ

ABSTRACT

While organisational communication research has traditionally limited talk to human beings, a trend within the Montreal School (TMS) of the Communicational Constitution of Organizations (CCO) perspective acknowledges that 'things do things with words' as well, and criticises the 'bifurcation of nature' into two distinct realms: materiality and discourse. However, due to a preference for studying human discourse, many TMS studies still may give the impression that only human spokespeople can make objects talk. This paper uses data from an ethnographic case study to argue that CCO is well equipped to recognise that other sorts of objects may speak as well, and that they enter the realm of language through yet other objects (i.e. their 'spokesthings'). In doing so, this paper advances an argument that will counter critiques of TMS scholarship that propose it reduces the role played by objects to their interpretation by humans.

Research in organisational communication, and in particular studies concerning talk in organisational settings (Boden, 1994; Czarniawska-Joerges & Joerges, 1988; ten Have, 1991), has for the most part considered the conversations of humans as its starting point. After all, talk regularly has been considered the privilege of human beings. For instance, in the Communicative Constitution of Organizations (CCO) tradition of organisational communication research, two of the three 'schools' (Schoeneborn et al., 2014) explicitly limit agency and communication to humans. The Four Flows approach questions whether non-human agency can be meaningful, thus locating meaning within the realm of humans only (McPhee & Seibold, 1999). The Luhmannian trend of CCO, for its part, prefers to consider objects as being part of the environment of organisations, limiting the latter to meaningful human practices (Schoeneborn, 2011).

However, perspectives on (socio)materiality in organisation studies have insisted – in various ways – that materiality and, in particular, technology play a part in the constitution of organisational reality (Leonardi, 2012). For the most part, the perspectives that have been put forth recognise the role of artefacts, technologies, and devices but maintain a distinction between the social and the material domains, as if they can be separated. That is the case of affordance theory (Faraj & Azad, 2012; Fayard & Weeks, 2007), structuration theory (Orlikowski, 1992, 2007), situated action (Suchman, 1987), activity theory (Engeström, 2000; Engeström, Miettinen, & Punamäki, 1999), or distributed cognition (Hutchins, 1995a, 1995b), amongst a long list of others. Putnam (2015) differentiates five different perspectives, all but one considers discourse and materiality as distinct phenomena. The exception is Orlikowski and Scott's perspective, which borrows from Barad's agential realism (2007). The literature, whatever its theoretical bent, continues to understand the involvement of objects and technology in action/agency/activity mostly through the spectrum of their *use* by human beings. Nardi (1996, p. 76), for instance, speaks of 'One's ability – and choice – to marshal and use resources'.

This article uses data from an ethnographic case study to argue that CCO is well equipped to move us beyond this limited view of material agency and show that, not only can the objects humans use speak, but they also enter the realm of language through yet other objects who speak for them (i.e. their 'spokesthings').

This paper starts by describing the Montreal School's (TMS) CCO perspective on materiality in order to make the argument that this perspective provides the latitude to recognise that things make other things talk and, in so doing, move away from the view that things *only* participate in the world to the extent that we, humans, 'interpret' what they have to say. It then explores how things speaking for other things allow an 'objectivity' that is otherwise not possible, before presenting data from an ethnographic study to illustrate how this occurs in practice. It finishes by proposing a redefinition of objectivity and of the way things may gain access to language and participate in human sociality.

Materiality and TMS perspective

TMS flavour of CCO (Brummans, 2006) has borrowed from Actor-Network Theory (ANT) the recognition that the distinction between, on the one hand, a social world made of speaking humans, and on the other, a material and natural realm made of mute objects, does not stand (Ashcraft, Kuhn, & Cooren, 2009; Latour, 1993). Through the notions of textual agency (Brummans, 2007; Cooren, 2004, 2008) and the 'plenum of agencies' (Cooren, 2006), TMS researchers have acknowledged that things can do things with words (Cooren & Bencherki, 2010).

To this day, however, TMS has mostly limited its attention to cases where materiality is brought by humans into their conversations or writings. In this paper, I argue that this is an artefact of TMS's preferred methodological approach – the analysis of interactions, and conversations in particular. The TMS approach does, however, have the theoretical and empirical apparatus to recognise that things 'speak' in different ways, besides being mobilised in human talk. In fact, as I will show, from a TMS perspective there are cases when things' ability to speak on their own is crucial. For instance, we humans have delegated the job of making things talk to other things (i.e. phonation devices) like medical instruments and navigational devices.

DISCURSIVITY, RELATIONALITY AND MATERIALITY

Putnam (2015) classifies the 'plenum of agencies' perspective of TMS as giving privilege to the discourse side of the duality. I do not believe this is accurate, but I admit that the TMS literature has sometimes left misleading clues in that respect. For instance, Cooren and Taylor's (1997) argument for the constitutive power of communication focuses on the interplay between talk and text, with the result that the meaning of materiality appears to be solely constructed in human communication (Brummans, Cooren, & Chaput, 2009). This confusion has also been fuelled by the choice of cases. For instance, Vásquez, Schoeneborn, and Sergi (2016) studied project proposal forms, a technical template and a presentation slide; Cooren's (2015) example of a museum-related creative project focused on a participant's oral presentation. These different studies discuss cases where verbal language is present, but what makes a difference in each case is the material (i.e. physical) availability of text or speech in given situations.

The apparent tension between a more conventional sense of materiality (i.e. physicality) and a more semiotic one may be traced back to contentious elements within TMS's underlying theory of materiality, namely ANT. Indeed, while some ANT champions, such as Law (2009), embrace it as a 'material semiotics', the precise status of language and representation in the theory has been decried as ambiguous (c.f., Lenoir, 1994). Furthermore, some authors have called for greater acknowledgement of the non-discursive side of artefacts, in particular in the study of technology and its agency (Bardini, 2007).

In this paper, I argue that when TMS scholars denounce the 'bifurcation of nature' (i.e. the separation of reality of things from their representation), they are not merely bringing the 'real' world into the realm of talk (c.f., Cooren, 2015). They are in fact rejecting the very terms of this alleged opposition. The distinction between the two realms simply does not hold, as illustrated in Arnaud, Mills, Legrand and Maton's (2016) study of the way texts, furniture, visual displays, and geosocial arrangements – all material that can be read – translate an organisation-wide strategy in the context of local branches and allow resistance and negotiation between the branch and the senior managers driving the change. Such cases suggest we need to go past 'either/or' considerations and embrace the plurality of reality (Friedberg, 2000; Latour, 2000; Raffnsøe, Gudmand-Høyer, & Thaning, 2016). I will therefore attempt to extend Cooren's (2015) proposal that things speak by using a more conventionally 'material' case to show how the very process by which things are brought into talk, or given the power to talk, is itself a material process. I will use the example of run-down buildings, which are both the object and the setting of the work of a tenants' association in a large North American city.

The argument that the process by which things are brought into talk is a material process in no way implies that humans do not play a part in the process. First of all, when things speak, they also speak to humans, who can then act (or not) on the basis of what they understand. Also, the tools through which things talk were designed by humans (e.g. engineers and designers) who embed particular scripts into them (Akrich, 1992). This is, for instance, what Groleau and Cooren (1999) describe in the account of a graphic design firm's use of computerised tools, which implement routines and procedures that otherwise would need to be learned and remembered by the workers. These include 'constative/performative' (p. 138) procedures, which may include tools that pick up specific aspects of reality as relevant and propose specific programmes of action as appropriate.

My choice to focus on buildings and on the way they can tell about their condition, as opposed to managerial examples (such as the strategy case described by Arnaud et al., 2016), allows me to make my argument clearer by avoiding what some readers could view as a 'feedback loop' (i.e. humans reading tools that describe their own human activity). Of course, from the moment we are discussing human-made artefacts, we are, as Cooren (2015) rightly says, in the 'middle of things' or, to say it in another way, in a 'chain of agency' (Cooren, 2006) where humans and technology cannot be clearly distinguished. Even a building, in describing its own state of deterioration, is also saying something about the way its landlord or tenant have failed to care for it. The ability of speech is not limited to humans, nor do things only speak through humans, or about human activity. This is not at issue. What is less certain is the way things take part in the world they share with humans. Various typologies have been proposed for the relationship between things/technology/devices and the social/human/discursive (Leonardi, 2012; Nicolini, Mengis, & Swan, 2012; Orlikowski & Scott, 2008; Putnam, 2015). Many of them, though, suppose a distinction between a 'technical subsystem' and a 'social subsystem' (Leonardi, 2012). The problem is to re-link the two – something that would take considerable theoretical effort. A more productive approach, perhaps, may be ANT's and TMS's suggestion to accept that our reality, in fact, is already hybrid (Latour, 1993, 2008). Then, speech is not the a-priori prerogative of humans. Whether someone or something can speak is an empirical matter. Being objective, rather than attempting to get interpretations 'right', then refers to paying attention to what objects have to say.

The objectivity of 'spokesthings'

The ethnographic field study that I analyse in this paper was chosen because of its concern with the issue of 'objectivity'. For the workers of the tenants' association, objectivity is instrumental and determines their ability to convince city official and courts to take measures to solve the housing problems that they document. While the workers understand objectivity in the prosaic sense of 'fact-based' and different from personal judgement, it is interesting to note that this objectivity is achieved exactly by relying on objects.

In other words, objectivity consists of recognising the fact that we share our sociability with things (I use the term 'objectivity' for convenience, even though, of course, if we reject the socio-material duality, it makes little sense). The social and material participate in the constitution of so many links between our ideas, judgements, etc., and the reality that we, humans, claim to be representing (Latour, 1988, 1996; Martine, Cooren, & Bartels, 2015). Objectivity can therefore be said to be achieved when we, humans, can present ourselves as merely reporting what things are saying by themselves. The issue of objectivity, then, is figuring out 'how things do things with words' (Cooren & Bencherki, 2010), but also how things can speak through yet other things that translate their 'objective' language into a verbal language that we, humans, can make sense of and that suggests a particular course of action for us to take. In fact, because I believe we humans need objects to speak without our direct help if we hope to ever achieve 'objectivity', I would like to argue for a somewhat radical perspective on the participation of things to the social – a perspective that recognises things ability to 'talk'. Far from being esoteric, I propose that this ability rests on the many tools that we humans have devised to make such forms of talk possible – tools that I refer to as phonation devices (Latour, 2004; Taylor & Van Every, 2000) and that act as 'spokes-things' for other non-humans. I prefer the word spokesthings rather than 'spokes-artefacts' or 'spokesobjects' (Vásquez & Cooren, 2011), to acknowledge the fertility of the word 'things', which etymologically points to the idea of deliberation and meeting (Latour, 2005a). Things, interestingly, always already include talk. Beings, whether human or not, are in fact heterogeneous to begin with (Latour, 1993), and therefore any analytical language that researchers use to distinguish between them is necessarily provisional.

Indeed, the so-called 'material world' (Hardy & Thomas, 2015) – an expression I actually reject, given that it precisely amounts to alluding to another world (the world of discourse and communication) that would be, in comparison, immaterial, which is not the case – regularly tells us about itself using verbal language but research so far has failed to acknowledge that form of participation. Yet, as will be made obvious by the case in this paper, without those tools that allow non-human things to talk, a large portion of what goes on in and around organisations can remain unaccounted for. After all, as French sociologist Gabriel Tarde (1893) recognised over a century ago, things are societies too (see also Cooren, 2010).

Recognising that things make things talk allows moving away from a perspective where things would *only* participate in the world to the extent that we, humans, 'interpret' what they have to say. In fact, we have built those phonation devices, and regularly use them, exactly to avoid being accused of 'merely' interpreting what things have to say. Paradoxically, it is because we want unmediated access to the world that we add more mediators that help us gain such access (Latour, 2005b). Cooren and Matte's (2010) discussion of a measuring stick used by Doctors Without Borders workers to decide who, among African children, may get help from a nutrition centre, may be read as such an attempt from physicians to downplay their own interpretation of the kids' health situation, and to let the 'talking' be made by the stick.

This kind of argument will not appear new to those who are interested in the history of sciences or in sociotechnical controversies, in particular from a science, technology, and society (STS) perspective. Daston and Galison (1992), for instance, suggested that our current scientific obsession with objectivity has grown as we have developed technical means to 'visualise' data and to make facts speak for themselves. Borck (2008), for his part, has shown how the field of neurosciences has evolved along attempts to visualise the brain through various devices. Historical efforts at photographing ghosts may also be seen as technologically mediated attempts to bring otherwise invisible reality into our social world (Gunning, 2008). More broadly, the way technology has allowed access to 'reality' has been the object of many STS studies (Baigrie, 1996; Bloor, 1991). While TMS scholars regularly draw on STS authors (in particular in the ANT tradition), the full extent of ANT's suggestion concerning the participation of objects in our common world has yet to be grasped in organisational communication.

DISCURSIVITY, RELATIONALITY AND MATERIALITY

Recognising that things make things do things with words will allow organisational communication research to acknowledge this participation, not only because objects are being mobilised in human conversations but also because they have technical means to access human language. To point this out, I will use a case that illustrates human actors' reliance on phonation devices (i.e. things that allow other things to talk). Indeed, I will show that the workers of a tenants' association use moisture meters, hygrometers, thermometers, and, more prosaically, cameras to make the buildings in which they work 'say' things about their run-down condition, without relying on the workers' interpretation of the building's appearance. The ability of the buildings to speak on their own is crucial, as we will show, as the workers have to *prove* that the buildings are run down, i.e. that this judgment is not only their 'interpretation'.

The data were gathered through a participative ethnographic approach, throughout the 16 years I was involved with that organisation, including the last 10 as a researcher. Given my personal involvement in the field, I consider my approach to be a mix of 'at-home' ethnography (Alvesson, 2009) and organisational autoethnography (Anderson, 2006; Anteby, 2013; Boyle & Parry, 2007). Over that period, I visited buildings, helped prepare court cases for tenants, lodged complaints to city officials, and more generally became involved with the life of the organisation. As part of various special projects, I have adopted an action research perspective (Brydon-Miller, Greenwood, & Maguire, 2003) and helped the organisation apply for grants, organise various events, and review its work methods. I amassed a vast assortment of interviews, videos, pictures, documents of all kinds, both specifically for research projects and as part of my involvement in the organisation. In the preparation of this article, I have revisited some of the material I collected through the years, in particular three interviews explicitly addressing work tools, as well as many reports, pictures, and my own notes and knowledge of the organisation.

How things may speak: three perspectives

Current theorising on the way things may speak recognises three perspectives that account for how they may speak. The first consists in describing things that are already textual or discursive in nature, such as documents, signs, slide presentations, etc. The second consists in considering communication as the circulation of action, beyond linguistic action. The third is the one I put forward here. It consists in observing the precise ways through which things enter the linguistic realm.

The first perspective has been undoubtedly the most popular in CCO literature, and is the one that underpins the notion of textual agency. This approach rests mainly on a reworked view of speech act theory (Austin, 1962; Searle, 1979). Cooren's (2004) example of a note reminding someone of a meeting, or Brummans' (2007) discussion of a euthanasia declaration both concern documents with words written on them. The agency of the text, then, consists in its ability to transport those inscriptions so that they can be read, interpreted, debated, etc., again in another situation, somewhere else and at a different time.

In this perspective, things play a part beyond being mere surfaces for our human words. For instance, in their discussion of a blackboard on which a nurse inscribes vital signs of hospitalised children, Cooren and Bencherki (2010) show that the precise structure of the table he drew on the board and the prominence of the board in the room makes it easy for the nurse to see, at a glance, whether a child's condition is worsening or not. In other words, the blackboard becomes a computational device that turns singular inscriptions into a form of diagnosis, rather than a mere carrier of words and numbers. Groleau and Cooren (1999), for their part, show that computer software does not only convey signs and representations of work but also present the workflow (i.e. the programme of action) in ways that guide workers through the production process.

A second approach to the way things may participate in communication consists in redefining the latter word – communication – as the circulation of action, beyond linguistic action. Communication then consists in allowing something to act at a distance, which may be done through linguistic inscription or translation (that's the first perspective above), but also otherwise. Theoretically, this perspective may be related to Latour's (1999a) notion of immutable mobiles (i.e. things that manage to remain 'the same' while moving around). They remain the same because, pragmatically, they keep producing the same effect, even though they in fact do so thanks to under-going the changes necessary so that the effect is achieved in various situations.

Latour's example is that of a box with a matrix of cells in which soil samples from the Amazon are put, so that each cell represents a particular sampling site. This way, the reference between the soil and a particular geography is maintained, even though the soil sample is moved to a laboratory in France, thousands of miles away from the original site. A theoretical root of the second approach may be found in French philosopher Gilbert Simondon's (1958/2005) discussion of transduction, a notion through which he captures the fact that what circulates from one entity to the next is always action: through a push on a pedal, I communicate to my car my desire to move forward, and it is through further (mechanical or electric) action that this push is 'interpreted' and passed on to the engine and then to the wheels.

At no point does communication leave the firm ground of action. Simondon's originality consists in showing that even when we speak of 'messages' and 'signs', these are rooted in concrete action that circulates from kin to kin, from one being to the next (Bencherki, 2015a). Closer to our concern here, Simondon recognises that things not only communicate through language but researchers may want to take into account the variety of ways in which things contribute to our collective lives. TMS scholars have regularly been advocating for opening up analysis to those alternate modes of participation, whether as the establishment of relations between entities through intermediaries (Cooren, Bencherki, Chaput, & Vásquez, 2015), as affect (Bencherki, 2015b) or otherwise. As Cooren (2000, p. 66) pointed out, 'a semiotician would have no problem with the proposition that two rooms communicate with each another [...] communication is the creation of a link between two entities'.

The third perspective is the one that I want to put forward here, and which in fact has been implicitly present in TMS literature. It consists in looking at the ways in which the non-linguistic communication of things can be translated into a language we humans may engage with. This perspective is consistent with ANT's insistence on the notion of translation (Callon, 1986; Latour, 2005b; Vásquez & Cooren, 2011) where the term is taken both figuratively and literally. It may surprise researchers that things may speak, but in fact people make things speak as part of their daily work life, through their human language but also through further things, as shown in STS research, for instance. Engineers have created devices of all kinds to make things speak, and scientists in all sorts of fields have created standard tests and measurements to convert the 'objective' symptoms of things into actionable language (Latour & Woolgar, 1979).

This last perspective combines the first two: the devices we have invented turn the non-verbal 'language' of things of the second perspective into a language we, humans, can make sense of and which is the focus of the first perspective. People, as they carry out their work, are therefore routinely acknowledging that there are ways in which things speak to them. In fact, we humans have delegated the work of interpretation to yet other things. Many of the numbers that make a difference in our organisations (Fauré, Brummans, Giroux, & Taylor, 2010; Quattrone, 2004) come from spokesthings that measure aspects of our organisation's 'well-being' (e.g. sales, accounting ratios of all sorts, and employee leaves). Through those measurements, spokesthings make organi-sational reality available to us in a language that we understand and that helps us attend to our tasks.

The role of the taxi meter, for instance, may be understood to a large extent as replacing an improbable inter-subjectivity between the cab driver and the client regard-ing the distance travelled, by an 'objectivity' (i.e. by agreeing to delegate the decision concerning the total fare to an object). In a similar way, the time clock may be seen to establish an 'honest full day's work' (following the expression by Taylor, 1911) and resolve disputes over attendance. In this last view, discovering how things speak there-fore amounts to empirically looking at the different things that translate what things have to say into language as we understand it.

No single perspective is better or truer than another. Each corresponds to different aspects of what it means to say that things do things and speak. All three combined acknowledge that things speak in a variety of ways, and that we engage with things in various ways. Here, however, I would like to focus on the fact that even what we believe to be a 'human' language may be mobilised by non-human agents, and that this possibility, in fact, rests on yet other things that we have invented to make this possible. As will be obvious from the case presented below, this is what makes 'objectivity' possible.

The 'machines' of housing workers

The Bigville Tenants' Association (a fictional name) was founded in the early 1970s by a group of Bigville University students who sought a means to fight for social justice. Bigville being a French-speaking city, all the data presented below are translated. While the organisation has changed premises and personnel through time, it still offers the same three basic services: legal advice to tenants who show up at its walk-in clinic; an outreach programme that consists of knocking on apartment doors to survey housing problems and convince tenants to address them; and the monitoring of government and city decisions that impact housing rights.

I became involved with the Bigville Tenants Association in 2000, first as an employee, then as a member of the Board of Directors, and finally, since 2007, as a researcher. My research approach, however, has always retained an aspect of advocacy through (a loose interpretation of) action research (Brydon-Miller et al., 2003; Chandler & Torbert, 2003; Lewin, 1946). I have remained a volunteer, helped write grant applications, acted as an informal advisor, and continued to knock on doors occasionally. What I realised through all these years is that the organisation was in a unique position, at the intersection of architectural, urban planning, social, and legal concerns.

The community workers had the very unique exigency of making a seemingly mute thing – an apartment building – say something about its condition, so they could figure out what course of action to follow and, in many cases, to translate the building's condition into a language comprehensible to judges and city inspectors. To do this, the community workers I observed used hygrometers to measure humidity in ambient air, moisture meters to measure humidity in walls, thermometers, and regular digital cameras. As an older employee, Charles, reminded me, it is only in the past few years since I had left the organisation that they acquired so many 'machines' and changed their work practices. It used to be that, except for heating issues for which they already had thermometers, other problems would simply be visually observed by community workers, who could then serve as witnesses to the tenants should the case end up in court.

In an interview, another employee, Tamara highlighted that even to this day providing witness to what she visually observes remains a big part of her work. That is because in spite of the availability of other tools the Rental Board, which is the trial court for housing issues, is not used to other forms of proof. However, this is insufficient as another colleague, Sylvia, told me on a different occasion. 'We can get into a building and it doesn't look like there are leaks'. However, that may be misleading, as 'there is mold, but the wall can look neat and clean, because the landlord painted over it'. This is particularly an issue because city inspectors, who do not have the same tools as the community workers, may give a notice to the landlord about a situation, but when they come back for a follow-up inspection the situation has been concealed.

> 'What does the landlord do? He puts plaster, he puts paint, and it lasts a while. [...] It's really just a visual inspection. [...] If he sees mold, he'll write it down, and if he doesn't, then it's as if the problem was resolved.'

During the same interview, Sylvia gave a particularly poignant example of why such a visual inspection is defective: she told me the story of an apartment where, 'in the bedroom, there is a big spot of mold, and it's so important that the whole family, there are five of them and they need to sleep in the living room, and they locked up that room, because they can't breathe'. Indeed, mould has been associated with respiratory diseases (see e.g. Kercsmar et al., 2006), and any person who has worked in run-down buildings will know the strong smell of severe mould. However, this experience is not enough. As Sylvia further explains, 'You know it, you can tell it's humid, and usually it smells of mold too, but ... it [having the measurements] allows you to have another proof. [...] Usually, we already know'.

Unfortunately an individual's experience-based testimony may not be sufficient to convince a city inspector or the courts that a building is unhealthy because its condition has been concealed. That is why, when Bigville Tenants' Association began collaborating with the public health physicians and scientists, who can issue (non-binding) recommendations regarding the healthiness of specific buildings, the community workers adopted some of the tools of their public health partners (in particular the moisture meters).

Since adopting these tools, community workers take measurements in each room, and then photograph the meter (either the moisture meter on the wall, the hygrometer, or the thermometer), to have proof of what the reading was on that day. With the moisture meter, they need to first indicate on the meter what type of surface the wall is and its composition, and then take multiple readings, as the presence of an electric cable or a metal part behind the wall may affect the reading. The strategy of taking photographs also explains why they prefer a basic moisture meter, which uses a needle that moves across a colour spectrum (not unlike volume meter on old audio equipment), as opposed to the more sophisticated but less easy to read digital moisture meter (see Figure 1). As Sylvia explains, 'normally it stays in the green', but as soon as the needle moves further towards the red zone, this indicates that there is a problem. When it hits the red, the meter also emits a screeching beep.

Once back at the office, the workers organise the pictures into both computer and paper folders corresponding either to a tenant's case (if the person came to the walk-in clinic) or to a building (in the case of the outreach programme), with an indication of the room and, for moisture meter photographs, of the wall section where the measure was made. When building a court case, as Charles showed me recently, he includes in the paper folder a plan of the apartment, where he uses numbered stars to reference printed photos. The photos, as shown in Figure 2, include a general overview, and then a zoom to the meter reading.

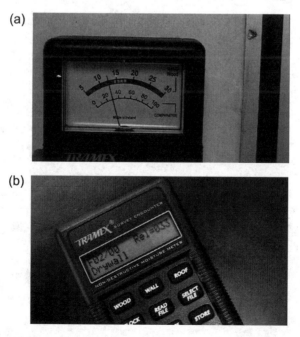

Figure 1. (a,b) The analogue moisture meter besides its more sophisticated digital counterpart.

Figure 2. A picture of a moisture meter included in a report, along with a close-up on the meter reading.

These documents are important in preparing court hearings. As Sylvia told me, 'if, say, the tenant gets to court and says "yeah, there's moisture in my room" and he's got nothing to prove it, he might as well just say anything [...] Everything you say in court has to be proven'. As I mentioned earlier, even readings from the community workers' meters are often not accepted as proof in court. A new strategy of the tenants' association is to request a report from the department of public health. Even though the tools they use are the same (remember that they are the ones who suggested them to the association), having a letter signed by a physician along with the rest of the evidence has greater weight than the pictures alone. Tamara explained, when I asked her about the way she built her proof, 'I don't know for the [court], but we can use that to convince the [public health administration] to visit the building'.

Besides convincing physicians and courts, an important challenge for the workers is to convince the tenants themselves there is a problem. Part of the community workers' job is to educate the district's tenants, many of whom are recent immigrants, regarding their rights and what constitutes acceptable housing conditions. This may be particularly important when some tenants require the organisation's help to initiate class actions, where each tenant's signature counts. As Tamara explains, speaking of one particular person, 'the tenant didn't want to do anything about it but, when I showed him the moisture meter and the needle went "beep, beep" in the red, he understood and agreed'. Sylvia also told me about tenants who were more willing to undertake action, 'and who will do like "oh yeah!" [when they see the readings on the moisture meter] and that will motivate them'.

Their anecdotes point to the importance of getting the right kind of translations. As Charles mentioned to me, the newer, more sophisticated model of moisture meter that the organisation acquired, while much more precise, produces more equivocal results. Indeed, the answer takes the form of a number on a black-and-green crystal liquid display or of a spreadsheet if the data are uploaded to a computer. The analogue moisture meter, while simpler, produces more obvious results. Convincing tenants is simpler because their colour code, as seen in Figure 1(a), provides a direct interpretation of the results, clearly indicating whether or not there is a problem, whereas the measures of the digital meter need to be translated by another human, perhaps by comparison with a chart. The thermometer does not pose the same problem. This has in part to do with the fact that people, including judges and city inspectors, know that, say, 16°C is cold for an apartment, but also because Bigville city regulations clearly require heating to be maintained at 21°C. It is relatively uncontroversial when measures taken with a thermometer indicate any lower temperature. The landlord knows they must fix the main heating system or provide auxiliary heating. Similarly, if a picture shows a broken door, a wall full of mildew or an obvious water leakage then the fact that the picture referentially points to an actual, 'objective' instance is not contested.

Discussion and conclusion

The devices that workers use provide many ways in which the 'objective' reality of things or structures – here, buildings – is made to speak and to 'say' things about itself through numbers, scales and categories of all kinds. The ethnographic case presented in this paper illustrates the ways by which physical communication (heat exchange between the thermometer and the ambient air; the effect of humidity on the hygrometer and the moisture meter) are turned into conventional language (e.g. 21, 70%, red, etc.). These codes are meaningful to humans, and can be transcribed and carried around to a city inspector, added to a report for the public health administration or to a file to be presented in court, and made comparable against the law, city regulations and other verbal artefacts. The building can speak through the meters. The building-with-meter hybrid can speak (see Latour, 1999b) to humans, but also, through those humans, in yet another translation, to the institutional/organisation reality with which they are dealing. These translations, as they are enmeshed in further discourse, then suggest concrete programme of actions to the workers, to their colleagues or to their clients – 'this wall needs repairs' or 'this room needs to be properly heated'. When the phonation devices provide the right kind of translation, the opinion of community worker is not 'just' his or her opinion; rather, it is the numbers or categories of the tool, sometimes paired with the law or other institutional realities, that tells the worker what she or he should think and do. This is not only a matter of justification, but also a practical necessity in order to get the work done. Recognising the work of 'spokesthings' implies that humans are not alone in doing the work of interpretation and in deciding what to do.

The perspective laid out here builds on Arnaud et al.'s (2016) idea that objects (i.e. physical) operate as translations. In their case, the translation was from broader organisational strategy to local situations. They showed that the layout of an office, compartments where paperwork was sorted, as well as tables and documents that embody procedures, made concretely present, but also more concretely negotiable, a nation-wide organisational strategy at the local office level. What I add to their work is that, besides strategy or other facets of the organisation, things also translate other physical things and make them relevant to people's work. Indeed, just as space and objects allow people to better engage with a seemingly abstract strategy or one that does not align with preferred ways of working, a similar translation is needed to engage with buildings that may appear merely physical and irrelevant to human activity. While objects have been mostly theorised as either the supports of human language, the objects of human conversations, or as exercising physical constraint on human activity, the fact empirically illustrated by the Bigville Tenants' Association case is that we humans create tools to listen to them and to translate what they have to say into a language we understand, and thus multiply the ways in which they participate in our actions. This has been hinted at in the extant organisational communication literature (Cooren & Matte, 2010), but has not yet been systematically discussed. The organisational communication literature needs to further acknowledge that things – whether seemingly abstract such as strategy or more concrete such as buildings – speak in a variety of ways, including by having their own way of communicating (the second way things may speak that I evoked earlier). Only when this occurs can we fully recognise the ways in which humans have been helping things enter the realm of human language, making them relevant to us (and commensurate to our laws, practices, etc.) and allowing them to let us know what they indicate or dictate. In fact, we have been creating tools to allow them to do these things.

A critique on the perspective proposed here could be that what I call 'spokesthings' are nothing but texts in the sense of textual agency. Of course, a hygrometer is also a set of human-made algorithms – but it is also much more. It is precisely because a human engineer made it, integrating into it some algorithm connecting all sorts of components, that it can, in its turn, connect the three perspectives described earlier. The hygrometer shows us numbers that humans can understand (first perspective), that translate a physical mode of communication (second perspective), and that therefore provide objects with the ability to 'speak' (third perspective). All three perspectives are better understood as empirically intertwined, even though I insisted here on the third.

As for TMS authors insisting on examining cases that are more specifically about text and talk, even such obviously 'linguistic' examples are not merely reminding us about what we agreed on earlier, or carrying out decisions to a different place and time. They are telling us what some other non-human is saying by converting a non-human action into a form of human language. My contribution, by taking the more obviously physical example of a building, insists, along with Arnaud et al. (2016), that TMS scholars have not simply brought things into the realm of discourse, but that they have actually rejected the bifurcation – a bifurcation that people, in their everyday work, routinely reject.

I also propose that understanding that objects may speak is particularly important in order to appreciate how objectivity is practically reached. Recognising the work of spokes-things makes it obvious that objects, in fact, have means to take part in our deliberations and disputes, and to provide their own perspective. This leads to a redefinition of 'objectivity' as the participation of objects in our conversations about reality (Latour, 1996; see also Martine et al., 2015). This is not to say that objectivity is not a 'construction', but this sociality includes objects whose voice must be heard. For instance, Hutchins (1995a) has shown how the objective achievement of the positioning of a warship on the waters, prior to the existence of a GPS, involved a work of translating landmarks and other physical objects into coordinates, thanks to visors, maps, rulers, and a variety of tools. The work of interpretation was shared among all of these participants, in what Hutchins called 'distributed cognition'. As long as there is, on the one hand, a material and natural realm, and on the other a bunch of humans attempting to understand it (Latour, 1993), then truth and objectivity are, in the words of American philosopher Richard Rorty (cited in Misak, 2013, p. 230), 'merely labels for what our peers will let us get away with saying'.

Acknowledgements

I wish to thank the participants to the 2015 EGOS 'Organization as Communication' special working group's sub-theme, as well as the guest editors and reviewers of this special issue, for their comments and suggestions. A special thanks to Bryanna Hebenstreit and James P. Snack for their insights and advice.

Disclosure statement

No potential conflict of interest was reported by the author.

ORCID

Nicolas Bencherki ⓘ http://orcid.org/0000-0003-3927-5346

References

Akrich, M. (1992). The description of technical objects. In W. E. Bijker & J. Law (Eds.), *Shaping technology/building society* (pp. 205–224). Cambridge, MA: MIT Press.

Alvesson, M. (2009). At-home ethnography: Struggling with closeness and closure. In S. Ybema, D. Yanow, H. Wels, & F. H. Kamsteeg (Eds.), *Organizational ethnography: Studying the complexity of everyday life* (pp. 156–174). London: Sage.

Anderson, L. (2006). Analytic autoethnography. *Journal of Contemporary Ethnography, 35*(4), 373–395. doi:10.1177/0891241605280449

Anteby, M. (2013). Relaxing the taboo on telling our own stories: Upholding professional distance and personal involvement. *Organization Science, 24*(4), 1277–1290. doi:10.1287/orsc.1120.0777

Arnaud, N., Mills, C. E., Legrand, C., & Maton, E. (2016). Materializing strategy in mundane tools: The key to coupling global strategy and local strategy practice?: Materializing strategy in mundane tools. *British Journal of Management, 27*(1), 38–57. doi:10.1111/1467-8551.12144

Ashcraft, K. L., Kuhn, T. R., & Cooren, F. (2009). Constitutional amendments: "Materializing" organizational communication. *The Academy of Management Annals, 3*(1), 1–64. doi:10.1080/19416520903047186

Austin, J. L. (1962). *How to do things with words.* Cambridge, MA: Harvard University Press.

Baigrie, B. S. (Ed.). (1996). *Picturing knowledge: Historical and philosophical problems concerning the use of art in science.* Toronto: University of Toronto Press.

Barad, K. (2007). *Meeting the universe halfway: Quantum physics and the entanglement of matter and meaning.* Durham, NC: Duke University Press.

Bardini, T. (2007). Retour sur une (d)ébauche: Une problématique communicationnelle du changement technique. *Tic&Société, 1*(1). doi:10.4000/ticetsociete.245

Bencherki, N. (2015a, May). *Organizational constitution of communication: How a CCO-specific theory of communication could be conceived, and how Gilbert Simondon may help.* Presented at the 65th International Communication Association Annual Conference, San Juan, Puerto Rico.

Bencherki, N. (2015b). Pour une communication organisationnelle affective: Une perspective préindividuelle de l'action et de la constitution des organisations. *Communiquer. Revue de communication sociale et publique,* (15), 123–139. doi:10.4000/communiquer.1701

Bloor, D. (1991). *Knowledge and social imagery* (2nd ed.). Chicago, IL: University of Chicago Press.

Boden, D. (1994). *The business of talk: Organizations in action.* Cambridge: Polity Press.

Borck, C. (2008). Recording the brain at work: The visible, the readable, and the invisible in electroencephalography. *Journal of the History of the Neurosciences, 17*(3), 367–379. doi:10.1080/09647040701348332

Boyle, M., & Parry, K. (2007). Telling the whole story: The case for organizational autoethnography. *Culture and Organization, 13*(3), 185–190. doi:10.1080/14759550701486480

Brummans, B. H. J. M. (2006). The Montréal school and the question of agency. In F. Cooren, J. R. Taylor, & E. J. Van Every (Eds.), *Communication as organizing: Empirical and theoretical explorations in the dynamic of text and conversation* (pp. 197–211). Mahwah, NJ: Lawrence-Erlbaum.

Brummans, B. H. J. M. (2007). Death by document: Tracing the agency of a text. *Qualitative Inquiry, 13*(5), 711–727. doi:10.1177/1077800407301185

Brummans, B. H. J. M., Cooren, F., & Chaput, M. (2009). Discourse, communication and organisational ontology. In F. Bargiela-Chiappini (Ed.), *The handbook of business discourse* (pp. 53–65). Edinburgh: Edinburgh University Press.

Brydon-Miller, M., Greenwood, D., & Maguire, P. (2003). Why action research? *Action Research, 1*(1), 9–28. doi:10.1177/14767503030011002

Callon, M. (1986). Some elements of a sociology of translation: Domestication of the scallops and the fishermen of St Brieuc Bay. In J. Law (Ed.), *Power, action and belief: A new sociology of knowledge?* (pp. 196–223). London: Routledge.

Chandler, D., & Torbert, B. (2003). Transforming inquiry and action: Interweaving 27 flavors of action research. *Action Research, 1*(2), 133–152. doi:10.1177/14767503030012002

Cooren, F. (2000). *The organizing property of communication.* Amsterdam: J. Benjamins.

Cooren, F. (2004). Textual agency: How texts do things in organizational settings. *Organization, 11*(3), 373–393. doi:10.1177/1350508404041998

Cooren, F. (2006). The organizational world as a plenum of agencies. In F. Cooren, J. R. Taylor, & E. J. Van Every (Eds.), *Communication as organizing: Practical approaches to research into the dynamic of text and conversation* (pp. 81–100). Mahwah, NJ: Lawrence Erlbaum.

Cooren, F. (2008). Between semiotics and pragmatics: Opening language studies to textual agency. *Journal of Pragmatics, 40*(1), 1–16. doi:10.1016/j.pragma.2006.11.018

Cooren, F. (2010). *Action and agency in dialogue: Passion, ventriloquism and incarnation.* Amsterdam: John Benjamins.

Cooren, F. (2015). In medias res: Communication, existence, and materiality. *Communication Research and Practice, 1*–15. doi:10.1080/22041451.2015.1110075

Cooren, F., & Bencherki, N. (2010). How things do things with words: Ventriloquism, passion and technology. *Encyclopaideia, Journal of Phenomenology and Education, 13*(28), 35–61. Retrieved from https://encp.unibo.it/issue/archive

Cooren, F., Bencherki, N., Chaput, M., & Vásquez, C. (2015). The communicative constitution of strategy-making: Exploring fleeting moments of strategy. In D. Golsorkhi, L. Rouleau, D. Seidl, & E. Vaara (Eds.), *The Cambridge handbook of strategy as practice* (pp. 370–393). Cambridge: Cambridge University Press.

Cooren, F., & Matte, F. (2010). For a constitutive pragmatics: Obama, Médecins Sans Frontières and the measuring stick. *Pragmatics and Society, 1*(1), 9–31. doi:10.1075/ps.1.1.02coo

Cooren, F., & Taylor, J. R. (1997). Organization as an effect of mediation: Redefining the link between organization and communication. *Communication Theory, 7*(3), 219–260. doi:10.1111/j.1468-2885.1997.tb00151.x

Czarniawska-Joerges, B., & Joerges, B. (1988). How to control things with words: Organizational talk and control. *Management Communication Quarterly, 2*(2), 170–193. doi:10.1177/0893318988002002003

Daston, L., & Galison, P. (1992). The image of objectivity. *Representations, *(40), 81–128. doi:10.2307/2928741

Engeström, Y. (2000). Activity theory as a framework for analyzing and redesigning work. *Ergonomics, 43*(7), 960–974. doi:10.1080/001401300409143

Engeström, Y., Miettinen, R., & Punamäki, R.-L. (Eds.). (1999). *Perspectives on activity theory.* Cambridge: Cambridge University Press.

Faraj, S., & Azad, B. (2012). The materiality of technology: An affordance perspective. In P. M. Leonardi, B. A. Nardi, & J. Kallinikos (Eds.), *Materiality and organizing: Social interaction in a technological world* (pp. 237–258). Oxford: Oxford University Press.

Fauré, B., Brummans, B. H. J. M., Giroux, H., & Taylor, J. R. (2010). The calculation of business, or the business of calculation? Accounting as organizing through everyday communication. *Human Relations, 63*(8), 1249–1273. doi:10.1177/0018726709355658

Fayard, A.-L., & Weeks, J. (2007). Photocopiers and water-coolers: The affordances of informal interaction. *Organization Studies, 28*(5), 605–634. doi:10.1177/0170840606068310

Friedberg, E. (2000). Going beyond the either/or. *Journal of Management and Governance, 4*(1/2), 35–52. doi:10.1023/a:1009977815841

Groleau, C., & Cooren, F. (1999). A socio-semiotic approach to computerization: Bridging the gap between ethnographers and systems analysts. *The Communication Review, 3*(1–2), 125–164. doi:10.1080/10714429909368576

Gunning, T. (2008). Invisible worlds, visible media. In C. Keller (Ed.), *Brought to light: Photography and the invisible, 1840–1900* (pp. 51–63). New Haven, CT: Yale University Press.

Hardy, C., & Thomas, R. (2015). Discourse in a material world. *Journal of Management Studies.* doi:10.1111/joms.12113

Hutchins, E. (1995a). *Cognition in the wild.* Cambridge, MA: MIT Press.

Hutchins, E. (1995b). How a cockpit remembers its speeds. *Cognitive Science, 19*(3), 265–288. doi:10.1207/s15516709cog1903_1

Kercsmar, C. M., Dearborn, D. G., Schluchter, M., Xue, L., Kirchner, H. L., Sobolewski, J., & Allan, T. (2006). Reduction in asthma morbidity in children as a result of home remediation aimed at moisture sources. *Environmental Health Perspectives, 114*(10), 1574–1580. doi:10.1289/ehp.8742

Latour, B. (1988). A relativistic account of Einstein's relativity. *Social Studies of Science, 18*(1), 3–44. doi:10.1177/030631288018001001

Latour, B. (1993). *We have never been modern.* Cambridge, MA: Harvard University Press.

Latour, B. (1996). On interobjectivity. *Mind, Culture, and Activity, 3*(4), 228–245. doi:10.1207/s15327884mca0304_2

Latour, B. (1999a). Circulating reference: Sampling the soil in the Amazon forest. In *Pandora's hope: Essays on the reality of science studies* (pp. 24–79). Cambridge, MA: Harvard University Press.

Latour, B. (1999b). *Pandora's hope: Essays on the reality of science studies.* Cambridge, MA: Harvard University Press.

Latour, B. (2000). On the partial existence of existing and nonexisting objects. In L. Daston (Ed.), *Biographies of scientific objects* (pp. 247–269). Chicago, IL: University of Chicago Press.

Latour, B. (2004). *Politics of nature: How to bring the sciences into democracy.* Cambridge, MA: Harvard University Press.

Latour, B. (2005a). From realpolitik to dingpolitik: Or how to make things public. In B. Latour & P. Weibel (Eds.), *Making things public: Atmospheres of democracy* (pp. 14–41). Cambridge, MA: MIT Press.

Latour, B. (2005b). *Reassembling the social: An introduction to actor-network-theory.* Oxford: Oxford University Press.

Latour, B. (2008). *What is the style of matters of concern?* Assen: Royal Van Gorcum.

Latour, B., & Woolgar, S. (1979). *Laboratory life: The social construction of scientific facts.* Beverly Hills: Sage Publications.

Law, J. (2009). Actor network theory and material semiotics. *The New Blackwell Companion to Social Theory, 3*, 141–158.

Lenoir, T. (1994). Was the last turn the right turn? The semiotic turn and A. J. Greimas. *Configurations, 2*(1), 119–136. doi:10.1353/con.1994.0014

Leonardi, P. M. (2012). Materiality, sociomateriality, and socio-technical systems: What do these terms mean? How are they related? Do we need them? In P. M. Leonardi, B. A. Nardi, & J. Kallinikos (Eds.), *Materiality and organizing: Social interaction in a technological world* (pp. 25–48). Oxford: Oxford University Press. Retrieved from http://papers.ssrn.com/abstract=2129878

Lewin, K. (1946). Action research and minority problems. *Journal of Social Issues, 2*(4), 34–46. doi:10.1111/josi.1946.2.issue-4

Martine, T., Cooren, F., & Bartels, G. (2015, May). *Assessing creativity through its degrees of objectivity: An actor-network approach to creativity.* Presented at the 65th International Communication Association Annual Conference, San Juan, Puerto Rico.

McPhee, R. D., & Seibold, D. R. (1999). Responses to the finalist essays. *Management Communication Quarterly, 13*(2), 327–336. doi:10.1177/0893318999132009

Misak, C. J. (2013). *The American pragmatists.* Oxford: Oxford University Press.

Nardi, B. A. (1996). Studying context: A comparison of activity theory, situated action models, and distributed cognition. In *Context and consciousness: Activity theory and human-computer interaction* (pp. 69–102). Cambridge, MA: MIT Press. Retrieved from http://books.google.com/books?hl=en&id=JeqcgPlS2UAC&oi=fnd&pg=PA69&dq=info:LOyVGvJ7PHEJ:scholar.google.com&ots=e_gaVztUCp&sig=aK_UwafKBksTJZkmesOr53AzZ3g

DISCURSIVITY, RELATIONALITY AND MATERIALITY

Nicolini, D., Mengis, J., & Swan, J. (2012). Understanding the role of objects in cross-disciplinary collaboration. *Organization Science, 23*(3), 612–629. doi:10.1287/orsc.1110.0664

Orlikowski, W. J. (1992). The duality of technology: Rethinking the concept of technology in organizations. *Organization Science, 3*(3), 398–427. doi:10.1287/orsc.3.3.398

Orlikowski, W. J. (2007). Sociomaterial practices: Exploring technology at work. *Organization Studies, 28*(9), 1435–1448. doi:10.1177/0170840607081138

Orlikowski, W. J., & Scott, S. V. (2008). Sociomateriality: Challenging the separation of technology, work and organization. *The Academy of Management Annals, 2*(1), 433–474. doi:10.1080/19416520802211644

Putnam, L. L. (2015). Unpacking the dialectic: Alternative views on the discourse–materiality relationship. *Journal of Management Studies, 52*(5), 706–716. doi:10.1111/joms.12115

Quattrone, P. (2004). Accounting for god: Accounting and accountability practices in the society of Jesus (Italy, XVI–XVII centuries). *Accounting, Organizations and Society, 29*(7), 647–683. doi:10.1016/j.aos.2004.03.001

Raffnsøe, S., Gudmand-Høyer, M., & Thaning, M. S. (2016). Foucault's dispositive: The perspicacity of dispositive analytics in organizational research. *Organization, 23*(2), 272–298. doi:10.1177/1350508414549885

Schoeneborn, D. (2011). Organization as communication: A Luhmannian perspective. *Management Communication Quarterly, 25*(4), 663–689. doi:10.1177/0893318911405622

Schoeneborn, D., Blaschke, S., Cooren, F., McPhee, R. D., Seidl, D., & Taylor, J. R. (2014). The three schools of CCO thinking: Interactive dialogue and systematic comparison. *Management Communication Quarterly, 28*(2), 285–316. doi:10.1177/0893318914527000

Searle, J. R. (1979). *Expression and meaning: Studies in the theory of speech acts.* Cambridge: Cambridge University Press.

Simondon, G. (1958/2005). *L'individuation à la lumière des notions de forme et d'information.* Grenoble: Jérôme Millon.

Suchman, L. (1987). *Plans and situated action: The problem of human-machine interaction.* Cambridge: Cambridge University Press.

Tarde, G. (1893). *Monadologie et sociologie* (J.-M. Tremblay, Ed.). Chicoutimi: J.-M. Tremblay.

Taylor, F. W. (1911). The principles of scientific management. Retrieved from http://www.gutenberg.org/etext/6435

Taylor, J. R., & Van Every, E. J. (2000). *The emergent organization: Communication as its site and surface.* Mahwah, NJ: Lawrence Erlbaum Associates.

ten Have, P. (1991). Talk and institution: A reconsideration of the "asymmetry" of doctor-patient interaction. In D. H. Zimmerman & D. Boden (Eds.), *Talk and social structure: Studies in ethnomethodology and conversation analysis* (pp. 138–163). Berkeley: University of California Press.

Vásquez, C., & Cooren, F. (2011). Passion in action: An analysis of translation and treason. In P. Quattrone, C. McLean, F. Puyou, & N. Thrift (Eds.), *Imagining organizations: Performative imagery in business and beyond* (pp. 191–212). London: Routledge.

Vásquez, C., Schoeneborn, D., & Sergi, V. (2016). Summoning the spirits: Organizational texts and the (dis)ordering properties of communication. *Human Relations, 69*(3), 629–659. doi:10.1177/0018726715589422

A communicative approach to sociomateriality: the agentic role of technology at the operational level

Nicolas Arnaud and Bertrand Fauré

ABSTRACT
When we talk about objects, their presence/absence *matters* during local conversations. So, how do sociomaterial resources come together in communication within networks of situated activities dislocated in time and space? How does problem-solving interaction accomplish that which is taken to be knowledge at a given technological site? How do communicative responses to heterogeneity influence resources for accountability? We answer these questions by applying a communication as constitutive of organisation approach to data from a qualitative study in the French transport industry during the implementation of a new interfirm information system. Our contributions are threefold: we (1) consider sociomateriality as, among other things, the expression of what matters in conversation, (2) argue that communicative practices, far from being residual talk, are at the core of the skilful achievement of (inter-)organisational collaboration and (3) assert that communication is at the heart of modern forms of work and organising and thus deserves more consideration by researchers and managers.

Introduction

This paper contributes to studies that have investigated the use of information technology as sociomaterial practices (Orlikowski, 2007; Orlikowski & Scott, 2008) by developing a communication as constitutive of organisation (CCO) approach to sociomateriality (Ashcraft, Khun, & Cooren, 2009; Cooren, 2015, 2016). While much of the recent interest in sociomaterial practices pertains to the use and implementation of digital technologies in organisations (Kallinikos, Leonardi, & Nardi, 2012; Orlikowski, 2007), this article emphasises the agentic role of digital technology as sociomateriality, the fact that these technologies often take the form of textual agents or artefacts that participate in sensemaking (Arnaud, Mills, Legrand, & Maton, 2016), as do human agents and physical (nondigital) objects.

One of the ways by which (digital) technologies make a difference (Cooren, 2010; Cooren, Fairhurst, & Huët, 2012) is by being performatively talked into existence (Ashcraft et al., 2009; Cooren et al., 2012; Martine, Cooren, Bénel, & Zacklad, 2016) in specific situations. Because we speak about them, they also end up speaking through us, which means that their presence/absence can come to *matter* a lot during local conversations. But how does this presence/absence come to matter or not in a given moment and, moreover, *what* does really matter when everything is entangled but at the same time dislocated in time and space?

The contemporary rise of digitalisation has fostered a situation where 'connectivity' is (too) often treated as a synonymous for 'interaction', making any digital tools/practice the 'magic bullet' (Markus & Benjamin, 1997) that will supposedly solve every single organisational issue. However, this overestimates the role of technologies and not only downplays the role of human agency but also the entanglement of humans and technology in practice (Orlikowski, 2007, 2009). Indeed, this information age (Taylor & Van Every, 1993) has given rise to abundant and complex technologies (Jones, Cline, & Ryan, 2006; Orlikowski, 2009) that 'dematerialise' information in the sense that information is communicated so quickly and so far that knowing where it is located has become irrelevant.

Although dislocated across time and space (Cooren & Fairhurst, 2008; Fauré & Arnaud, 2014; Orlikowski & Scott, 2008; Vasquez & Cooren, 2013), the materiality of information has, however, not disappeared. The simultaneous presence and absence of information technologies has become so profoundly evident in social life that it is sometimes hard to differentiate between the materiality of an object and the materiality of the information about this object. The map is not the territory, and the ticket is not the flight. But if you do not have a ticket, you do not fly. This drama happens every day at airline counters in airports. Of course, unfortunate travellers complain about missing their flight and having to fly later or elsewhere, but it is the missing ticket that is sought here and now.

What is manifested in these situations is a combination of matters of concern (Cooren et al., 2012) and the resolution of each drama depends on how these matters materialise themselves through words. Ultimately, how much the flight matters is materialised by how much the traveller can pay at the moment. A new sociomaterial agent then features the 'deus ex machina' response to the problem raised: the credit card. The absence/presence of the credit card then becomes what matters. If the cardholder can prove that he or she has sufficient income (salary, rent, profit, etc.), a credit card can cry 'Open Sesame' and magically open the plane's doors (by granting the traveller a last-minute ticket), at least if the plane is not full. All the process is about enabling a fluent materialisation of these dislocated encounters between humans, texts, cards, counters, seats, and tickets. They all matter as part of the process and are sometimes brutally materialised as crucial resources: the difficulty is to connect these dimensions during routinised interactions and conversations.

This article is specifically interested in how the sociomaterial agency of information technology is enacted through talk and how this entanglement comes to matter or not during hybrid and polyphonic conversations. Inspired by Ashcraft, Kuhn, and Cooren (2009), the paper addresses the following questions: (1) How do social and material resources come together in communication within networks of situated activities dislocated in time and space? (2) How does problem-solving interaction accomplish that which is taken to be knowledge at a given technological site? (3) How do communicative responses to heterogeneity influence resources for accountability? How do we not get *Lost in Translation* (Coppola, 2003) by information systems technologies by (re) giving sense and importance to very local and concrete operations, or acts of representation (Cooren, 2015, p. 12)?

The Technology, work, and organisation: material, social, or communicational section reviews research on technology-in-use and shows the relevance of a(n) (organisational) communication perspective on sociomateriality. The Methodology section presents the design of a qualitative field study conducted from 2010 to 2012 in the French transport industry during the implementation of a new Interfirm Information System (IIS). The Discussion section features an analysis that outlines the gap between the expectations of top management and the use of the software. It also analyses two successive phone calls between managers of different companies (a transporter and a customer) and shows how various textual agents of the delivery process (e.g. contract, order, and bills) organise the exchange and constitute the objects that *matter* for the participants (i.e. lost material).

It then demonstrates how an apparently superficial way of solving problems raised by the use of technology relies on a mutual understanding of respective constraints and accountabilities and on the capacity to make present/absent technologies and objects that matter through talk. The concluding section argues that such communicative practices, far from being residual talk, are central to the skilful achievement of modern collaborative practice at the operational level and discusses the implications and limits of this analysis for research interested in the entanglement of human and non-human agency. In an ever more complex and uncertain world, we argue that such sociomaterial richness is at the heart of modern forms of work and organising and as such requires more consideration by researchers and managers.

Technology, work, and organisation: material, social, or communicational?

The following paragraphs give an overview of literature on the relationships of technologies, materiality, and organisation and how it articulates with the notion of sociomateriality in recent works on communication and interaction.

From absent presence to sociomateriality accounts of technology

By examining every research article published over the past two decades in top organisational research journals, Orlikowski and Scott (Orlikowski & Scott, 2008, p. 433) confirm that '95% of the articles published in these management research outlets fail to take cognizance of the role of technology in organizational life. Recognition of this absence has spawned a growing literature on technology in organizations that can be characterized in various ways depending on the purpose, point of view, theoretical lens, and 'assumptions about the nature of technology and its role in organizations, the logical structure of theoretical accounts' (Orlikowski & Scott, 2008, p. 438). However, despite the variety of characterisations, two perspectives have emerged since the seminal work of Orlikowski (1992): a techno-centric perspective and a human-centred perspective.

The techno-centric perspective tends to consider technology as an exogenous force, 'a powerful driver of history having determinate impacts on organisational life'

(Orlikowski, 2009, p. 3). For instance, some studies, based mainly on investigations about the implementation and use of IIS, have explored how formal collaborative tools enhance the speed and reliability of activities and processes (see for a few examples Gallivan & Depledge, 2003; Grover & Saeed, 2007). Such works constitute examples of a larger field of study that seeks to 'theorize the relationship between technology and organization sufficiently generally so that predictions about technology effects may be made across types of organisations and technologies' (Orlikowski, 2009, p. 5).

This literature looks at the effect of technology on organisational structure and practice. Here, technologies generate contradictory pressures with the construction of a common framework for sharing information and make operators responsible for each situated enactment of their relationships, thus helping to generalise urgent depersonalised relationships. A strong limitation of these works is that they underestimate the power of human practice in organisations and organising processes.

In contrast, the human-centred perspective looks at how people interact with technologies and how such interactions contribute to organising as an emergent process (Orlikowski, 1992; Prasad, 1993). This literature, often based on Giddens' (1984) structuration theory, postulates that technology is socially constructed by users (see for a few examples DeSanctis & Poole, 1994; Orlikowski, 1992; Walsham, 2002) and, as such, is not deterministic. One contribution of the human-centred perspective is that it demonstrates that problems of different natures (organisational, technological, economical, and efficiency) are often interconnected in practice and present partially defined solutions that lead to unanticipated and undesired effects (Luff, Heath, & Hindmarsch, 2000). Unlike the techno-centric perspective of technology, this approach argues that people's behaviours influence organisational change (Griffith & Dougherty, 2001).

These two perspectives on technology and organisation are now considered 'ill equipped' to address the entanglement of practice dislocated in time and space in contemporary organisational life (Orlikowski, 2009; Orlikowski & Scott, 2008). Indeed, while the techno-centric perspective reifies technology, which precludes the consideration of human agency, the human-centred perspective tends to downplay specific technological properties and affordances, focusing primarily on human interpretations and social actions (Faulkner & Runde, 2009).

The notion of 'sociomateriality' (Mol, 2002; Orlikowski, 2007) aims to reconcile these two perspectives by focusing on how the entanglement of social and material is performed. Clarifying questions about their ontological assumptions (Leonardi, 2013; Mutch, 2013), or about their vocabulary/jargon (Kautz & Jensen, 2013), works about sociomateriality posit materiality as constitutive of everyday social life and practice (Leonardi & Kallinikos, 2012; Pentland & Singh, 2012). This entanglement perspective positions the organisational world as being both social and material (Barad, 2003; Latour, 2005). As Orlikowski (2007, p. 1437) argues, 'the social and the material are considered to be inextricably related – there is no social that is not also material, and no material that is not also social' (p. 1437).

This notion of sociomateriality is very much about the enactment of organisation and organising process (Orlikowski & Scott, 2008, p. 460) and, as such, has to be linked to the notion of performativity (Barad, 2003, 2007; Orlikowski & Scott, 2008). Being or acting performatively (Austin, 1962) concerns, among other things, discourses and linguistic practices considered as contributing to the constitution of reality and what it is supposed to be about. Latour (1987, 1996) has long argued that agency is a capacity realised through the associations of actors (both human and non-human), which implies accepting a relational ontology (Cooren et al., 2012).

An organisational communication perspective on sociomateriality

By presuming that 'situations, organizations, and environments are talked into existence' (Weick, Sutcliffe, & Obstfeld, 2005, p. 409), a performative approach to organising analyses language, talk, discourse, and communication not simply as reflecting but also as constituting organisational phenomena and actions: 'talk at work' (Boden, 1994; Drew & Heritage, 1992); 'organizations as discursive constructions' (Alvesson & Karreman, 2000; Fairhurst & Putnam, 2004), and 'CCO' (Putnam & Nicotera, 2008) represent variations of this performative approach.

For instance, Cooren, Taylor, and Van Emery (2006, p. 11) write, 'Agency is not a "capacity to act" defined a priori. On the contrary, it is "the capacity to act" that is discovered when studying how worlds become constructed in a certain way' (p. 11). Therefore, researchers should not study communication inside organisations or any organisational situation, but rather should 'find the organization in the communication' (Taylor & Robichaud, 2004).

Taylor, Groleau, Van Emery, and Heaton (2001) also argue explicitly for abandoning the dualism of 'technology' and 'organisation', and replacing it with a perspective that rigorously concentrates on social processes and interaction. In this perspective, work is seen as an imbrication of human and non-human agencies in organisational context. The process, because it is ongoing and continually (re)constructed or enacted, is what they called 'computerisation' (Groleau, 2002; Taylor et al., 2001). According to Taylor et al. (2001, p. 26), computerisation implies that patterns of agency emerge from the necessity of co-orientation in response to a complex environment. Co-orientation is then understood as the building block of all organisational processes and structures.

In this perspective, analysts are invited to look closely at non-human agency as a bearer of structure and as a means to 'trigger organizing processes and make salient interface contradiction' (Taylor et al., 2001, p. 24). It is thus possible to understand what is done on behalf of such devices and artefacts (Brummans, 2007; Cooren, 2010). As Cooren et al. (2012, p. 298) and Taylor and Virgili (2008) point out, organisational communication is thus always material because any interaction always has to be incarnated or *materialised* in specific circumstances, texts, technologies, artefacts, intonations, and preoccupations.

This view also conveys the idea that communication permanently mobilises effects of *presence/absence*, where certain questions, issues, beings, and realities come to materialise themselves in specific circumstances. Such reflection invites us to focus our attention on what seems to count or matter to participants of a conversation, but also what does not count or matter to them. This means that 'something whose materiality appears a priori unproblematic (an artifact, for instance) can lose a part of its materiality – etymologically, the substance from which it is made – because it does not appear to ma(t)ter(ialize itself) or count in what is said or done' (Cooren et al., 2012, p. 298). Thus, conversations also support or underlie (i.e. substantiate) what exists or not.

DISCURSIVITY, RELATIONALITY AND MATERIALITY

Assuming that communication is the site of organisation (Taylor & Van Every, 2000), where the interplay of material and ideational aspects of the world is continually 'realised' (Ashcraft et al., 2009, p. 36), a CCO perspective on sociomateriality raises the following research questions concerning technology in use: How do social and material resources come together in communication within networks of situated activities dislocated in time and space? How does problem-solving interaction accomplish that which is taken to be knowledge at a given technological site? How do communicative responses to heterogeneity influence resources for accountability? According to Ashcraft et al. (2009), 'addressing these questions entails studying how situated problem-solving communication confronts and actualizes the social-material elements of a given site' (p. 39). This is what the following section aims to do.

Methodology

Context of the study

To provide insight into the communicative practice through which these co-orientation and negotiation are performed, this research investigates collaborative practices between one of the main transporters in Europe (1200 employees, 7 business units, and 100 million euros turnover) and one of its key partners in the transportation process (Manuf.Co). This industry appeared highly relevant for investigating how sociomaterial resources come together in communication within networks of situated activities dislocated in time and space because it faces major transformations through the implementation of an IIS.

The study took place within a leading European transport company (OuesTranport) and a prominent French manufacturer (Manuf.Co). Their collaboration was one of the first to be defined in a contract stipulating that the transport firm had to carry the manufacturer's goods from the factory to the retailer. This contract also described the broad outlines of how the partnership had to operate. Texts such as faxes, delivery orders, delivery forms, and best practices were gradually integrated into meta-texts and meta-conversations (Robichaud, Giroux, & Taylor, 2004) such as contracts and information systems, which increased the entanglement of practice (Orlikowski, 2009). In the early 2000s, each company had formalised its own way of dealing with inter-organisational issues. However, the interfirm interface remained to be organised.

Data collection

The present study forms part[1] of a longitudinal ethnographic study (Spradley, 1979). Over a 2-year period, the first author worked as a non-participant observer within one of the teams of OuesTranport, then a leading European transporter. Three types of qualitative data (Yin, 2009) were collected and used to identify the sociomaterial dimensions of talking routines. Documentation about the industry, its evolution, and practitioners (e.g. academic journals, professional and government surveys, and specialised press), as well as internal company documents (e.g. procedures, general policies, profitability indicators for each trip, quality indicator sheets, and forms recording malfunction codes), were collected.

DISCURSIVITY, RELATIONALITY AND MATERIALITY

Table 1. Evolution of operational managers' daily interaction.

Type of interaction	Before (2004)	After (2006)	Evolution
Technology in interaction	13	25	+12
Tracking system	–	12	+12
Internal tools	9	5	−4
Delivery notice	4	8	+4
Face to face interaction	24	17	−7
Colleagues	12	10	−2
Managers	8	5	−3
Assistants	4	2	−2
Phone calls	19	33	+14
Drivers	10	15	+5
Customers	9	17	+8
Subcontractors	–	1	+1

Second, in-depth interviews with 42 individuals were conducted within transport and manufacturing companies (top managers, operational managers, and employees) to investigate general issues about the inter-organisational relationship system and strategy. Third, observations of onsite operations related to the inter-organizational collaboration (IOC) between transport and manufacturer were made over 2 years. During these observations, the first author carried out full days of observation with one operational manager in OuesTranport both before and after the IIS implementation. He noted each interaction (tools, face to face, and phone calls) and its purpose (information transfer, reporting, and dealing with a situation). Some results of this data collection are presented in Tables 1 and 2.

Data analysis

The material used in this article was collected, transcribed, and analysed as part of a previous study about how collective mind could be enacted in conversation (Fauré & Arnaud, 2012). This paper builds onto the insights gained from this previous research by identifying how certain entities and beings (e.g. texts, employees, managers, tools, documents, technologies, concerns, and substances) gained more weight and influence over the course of the IIS implementation and during interactions 'by speaking to, with, for, through, or against other entities and beings' (Martine et al., 2016). We also endeavoured to identify the heterogeneous entities that really matter in collaborative practice (i.e. interaction). Following Martine et al. (2016), the episodes that we analyse below 'epitomise' what appeared to matter (i) in this situation in particular and (ii) in (IOC) interactions in general. We focus our analysis on data that allow us to study the transformation of day-to-day work before and after the implementation of an IIS designed to manage daily IOC situations.

Analysis

How to capture the way objects, technologies, and pieces of information come to *matter* and *be materialised* through communicative practice in a context of technological change? Indeed, such situations are not so frequent and it is uncanny to realise how difficult it is to make things matter when everything is simultaneously dislocated and entangled (Vasquez

DISCURSIVITY, RELATIONALITY AND MATERIALITY

Table 2. Discussion between an operational manager at OuesTranport (Bill) and a manufacturer operator at Manuf.Co (Monique)[a].

1 Monique	Good morning. This is Monique of Manuf.Co
2 Bill	Good morning
3 Monique	How are things?
4 Bill	Fine. And you?
5 Monique	Very well, thank you. Tell me: I sent you an urgent delivery this week. I sent you a fax and I wanted to know whether you'd dealt with it... *because I don't have any information about it on IIS!*
8 Bill	Er, I don't know anything about it. In any case, I sent everything out for delivery on the 6th. What was it? Lele stuff?
10 Monique	Yes
11 Bill	But are you sure we've got the goods?
12 Monique	Yes
13 Bill	When was it sent? (begins searching on his computer)
14 Monique	It was sent on the 22nd, in the morning
15 Bill	(2) The 22nd?
16 Monique	Yes
17 Bill	Monday?
18 Monique	Yes
19 Bill	Where was it sent?
20 Monique	To OuesTranport! ((Laughs)) I've got an order number. That should help you, shouldn't it? (silence)
23 Bill	But, er – It's – I don't understand; it was sent on Monday. But you came to bring it to us on Monday?
25 Monique	Well – Look, I – the delivery notice, dated the 22nd at 08.45. Now – afterwards, I don't know ...
27 Bill	But I haven't got a delivery notice, see? (after looking for it on his computer) Because, with us, we never pick up anything from you on a Monday
29 Monique	Oh! You never pick up from us on a Monday?
30 Bill	Er, no. And also, this week, we loaded everything on Monday, for delivery before Thursday. So, we weren't loaded at your place on Monday. Was it for Nice? (For whom?)
33 Monique	[Yes, that seems to be right.]
34 Bill	(Consults his computer for Nice) No, I haven't got anything for Nice.
35 Monique	*Right! Well, there we are*: just the sort of day I like!
36	(silence)
37 Bill	Oh, hang on! – (10) But if it's like that, it was re- – That's weird: I'm sure it's still at your place. Can you find out from...? (continues looking on his computer)
39 Monique	Well yes – Yes – Of course, I'll ask everyone
40 Bill	Because, I haven't seen it. When did you send the fax: last week? (Looks at his log, where he has made a note of all the problems in loading)
42 Monique	Well, yes
43 Bill	Also, I was on holiday. (Consults his computer). No, I haven't got anything. I haven't got anything entered
45 Monique	O.K., fine. Thanks, anyway
46 Bill	If it's still at your place, and we can take it this week, er, I can deliver it, in a pinch, next Wednesday
48 Monique	Well yes, that would be fine. Yes, fine
49 Bill	Keep in touch and let me know if anything happens. Thanks
50 Monique	Thanks

[a]Most of the data collected used in the study were reported in a previous publication (Arnaud & Mills, 2012). In this article, we use some unused data from that study and some that has already analysed through a different lens in Fauré and Arnaud (2012).

& Cooren, 2013). Most of the time people make big deals of things they do not really care about or do not pay attention to things that should matter. Stuck at the entry door of the information age (Taylor & Van Every, 1993), they are like the characters in the movie 'Lost in translation' (Coppola, 2003). They do not know what matters for them as well as the others and thus fail to re-represent or materialise things that really count for all.

Hypnotised by hyper-organised times and spaces, they do not really communicate with others, do not really decide anything by themselves. As in the trial at the end of Alice's dream (in Lewis Carroll's *Alice's Adventures in Wonderland, 1865*), organisations sometimes lose their way in a world where everything is within everything, where no evidence and no authority appears to make sense anymore and where the 'orders of magnitude' change permanently. 'Not everything that counts can be counted and what is counted does not always count', Einstein used to say and the only right way to communicate when this paradox becomes epileptical is to assume being at each moment *in media res* (Cooren, 2015), that is, *in the middle of things.*

As Cooren (2015) points out,

> Any conversation, any oral presentation, any act of writing is also an activity of mediatisation, that is, an activity by which a plethora of beings can, by proxy or at a distance, express and reveal themselves. While media studies and interaction studies have historically and politically been estranged from each other, I think there is room for some sort of reconciliation. However, this reconciliation has a price, as we need to stop reducing media to technologies and start including humans as well as their conversations, discourses, and expressions in this category. In a relational world where there is no absolute point of origin, any being also always already is an intermediary, a middle ground, a channel of communication, that is, a passer. (p. 12)

The next subsection briefly shows the unintended consequences that follow the implementation of the IIS in order to provide a global context of what is *passing* – in the sense of Cooren (2015) – during the conversations analysed. Then, our analysis focuses on telephone interactions between the main transporter in Europe and of one of its key partners in the transportation process (Manuf.Co). This industry clearly illustrates how the materiality of objects and the materiality of information about these objects end up coexisting by interplay. It is not only delivering goods in time and to the right place that matters but also materialising where the product is and when it will be delivered.

In this context, we will see that the distinction between what is material and what is materialised through words becomes unclear. The anonymous and distant participants to the phone calls analysed spend considerable time talking about products, sites, and destinations they may never see physically. What is material for them at this moment is the missing information in the delivery tracking system, and not only the product not delivered. This is what matters, this is the problem to be solved, and this is what materialises through their words.

Background information: from mechanizing 'poor' communication to producing entanglement of practice

In 2009, OuesTranport launched an IIS project called the IIS. One year later, a tracking system was implemented that allowed collaborators (manufacturers and retailers) to access a web interface and follow forecast and completed deliveries and statuses throughout the delivery process. The objective was to reduce so called 'poor' communication. Seen as a 'magic bullet' (Markus & Benjamin, 1997) by top managers of both OuesTranport and Manuf.Co, the tool was thus designed and implemented to formalise, optimise, and mechanise information transfer in a very deterministic way. However, the ability to track the delivery process in the IIS was not sufficient to improve the IOC. IIS helps design or formalise IOC, but the result is never guaranteed. In the case studied, sharing direct information about the delivery process led to an increasing number and frequency of calls 2 years later (see Table 1).

DISCURSIVITY, RELATIONALITY AND MATERIALITY

Because operational managers had the opportunity to know in real time where their products were (or were supposed to be) and when they would be delivered, new practices emerged: manufacturers and retailers called more often, with more complex and urgent problems. In other words, with the materialisation of the product itineraries (since they could now be easily tracked down by the customers on their respective computer screens) came new questions that could not have been posed before.

Before the IIS, customers were only able to appraise the final performance of OuesTranport (delivered or not), whereas now they could question the company's response to situations at each step of the delivery process. Because of an increased materialisation of product itineraries, basic interactions were replaced by more demanding, complex, and detailed questions. Interviews suggest that interaction with customers changed from 'When will my product be delivered?' (operational manager à OuesTranport, 2012) to 'How are you/we going to deal with this situation?' (operational manager à OuesTranport, 2012).

Table 1 provides a quantitative view of an operational manager's daily interactions before and after IIS implementation in OuesTranport.

To ensure internal validity (Creswell & Miller, 2000), these tables have been post-validated by operational managers as representatives of the quantitative evolution of IOC routines: an increasing volume of interactions with customers (e.g. phone calls) or with the tracking system (e.g. recording, requesting, searching). This quantitative evolution gave rise to qualitative changes in the nature of the interactions, which became more and more entangled.

Given the unexpected use of the IIS and an increasing need for strengthened inter-organisational relationships, the company introduced two changes in IOC management: (1) visits/meetings with manufacturers to enhance a 'mutual understanding of respective constraints' (OuesTranport CEO, 2012) and (2) designation of a single contact person for the main manufacturers, to guarantee 'privileged communication in some areas' (Manuf.Co Sales Director). However, despite these attempts to improve IOC through technologies, an important issue remained – the co-production of agreement in problem solving based on such sociomaterial practices.

This context of IOC provides a relevant background for analysing how technology acquires an agentic role and affects sensemaking in organisations in general and between inter-organisational collaborators in particular. The following section analyses the communicative practices and skills through which such performative practices (co-producing agreement in problem solving) could be enacted.

Analysis of interactions: operational managers' matters in vivo

The exchange selected is representative of an important, growing category of inter-organisational interactions: two successive phone calls between OuesTranport and Manuf.Co's operational managers dealing with a recurrent type of problem raised by the delivery process – missing information in the IIS. Such problems, which were supposed to be reduced by the IIS, instead increased in volume and frequency. The inter-organisational interactions between the manufacturer's delivery services and the transporter are now divided into several specific sub-activities: validating, verifying, and reporting all the operations realised at each step of the delivery (ordering, discharging,

DISCURSIVITY, RELATIONALITY AND MATERIALITY

Table 3. End of the conversation.

Monique calls back half an hour later	
51 Monique	Yes, it's fine. It's been delivered
52 Bill	Good. So that one delivered. (Crosses it off from his 'to do' list.)
53 Monique	Sorry, I didn't know anything about it. Thanks, anyway, for your help
54 Bill	No problem. Speak to you soon

loading, and delivering) and more formalised than ever. Rather than reducing the need for information during IOC, this attempt to formalise uncertainty has unveiled previously invisible complications and delays related to the transport of goods (e.g. accidents, breakages, and shortages) or to information processing (e.g. breakdowns of the database; misplaced, incomplete, or false data).

The following transcripts (Tables 2 and 3) of the phone calls (translated from French) have been validated by interviewees as accurate accounts of how they deal with such problems. They illustrate (1) how the social and material come together in conversation, (2) a situation of problem-solving interaction, and (3) how people clarified their respective constraints and accountabilities to each other based on what really *matters*.

How do social and material resources come together in communication?

After the usual pleasantries, the interaction begins with an imperative question from Monique (operator at Manuf.Co) to Bill (operator at OuesTranport): 'Tell me', 'I want to know'. Bill searches for relevant information in the IIS but cannot answer Monique's request. He then asks for clarifications about the problem (from whom, when, to whom, and for what?). From lines 5 to 21, the whole conversation is structured by this question–response conversational pattern (Cooren, 2004) and ends with a situated recognition and acceptance of mutual ignorance.

Here, each participant accepts a priori any response from the other (whether informative or not) as a positive contribution to the exchange: what has been said can be repeated elsewhere to other interlocutors (Monique can now say: 'I've asked Bill. He doesn't know. So who has the information?'). Communication is not 'useless'. Indeed, the worst case scenario is not a non-response to a question or request, but a non-response to the call (i.e. no one answers the phone).

How does problem-solving interaction accomplish that which is taken to be knowledge at a given technological site?

Such a starting point is not a natural, taken-for-granted outcome of IOC conversational routines. For example, recognising/proving ignorance may, as we know, endanger self-presentations (Goffman, 1959). However, most of the recorded interactions were characterised by mutual comprehension (based on free and easy talk) and acceptance of ignorance about 'missing information in the database'. This excerpt is one of several that illustrate how this comprehension is conversationally enacted and could constitute a premise for co-producing agreement on how to solve this type of problem.

Another implicit agreement arises from the conversation: Monique not only has to call the retailer (Nice) but also to call Bill back 'to let him know if anything happens'. If she had not made the call in the first place, she would not have been given this responsibility. Far from the grand strategic discourse about 'reducing poor communication', a routinised communicative practice is emerging: enacting a distant yet concerned attitude that leads to agreement on how to deal with such problems. The following excerpt presents the callback from Monique half an hour later (see Table 3).

In this second call, we see Monique (1) informing Bill that 'it's been delivered' and that 'Everything is OK', (2) apologising for her unnecessary question, and (3) thanking him for giving her information about non-formalised sub-steps of the delivery process. Bill graciously accepts the information and apologies. The two tasks agreed on at the end of the previous call were effectively performed: Monique called Nice, got her answer, and called Bill back.

How do communicative responses to heterogeneity influence resources for accountability?

Such exchanges could be interpreted as a perfect example of 'poor communication'. Several phone calls between manufacturer, transporter, and retailer are made. The product is at the right place; only the information is missing. The analysis shows that despite the apparent superficiality of the exchange, participants indeed try to take into account the validity of any information they have, such as the time required to find specific information and the possibility of their having to report to their respective supervisors. When dealing with all these constraints, they also permanently negotiate agreements on how to solve the problem, which definitely helps to maintain collaboration between their respective companies.

This interaction shows how the social and material makes sense because of the entanglement created during the delivery process by the tracking system of the company studied. Indeed, most of the exchanges recorded during the immersion period are shaped by information processing rules and constraints. During these interactions, the IIS is enacted in different ways. While often clearly relying on what the software says, middle managers also know how to put the information provided by the software into perspective to attain different performative effects, depending on the situation. Sometimes, the software is seen as etched in stone ('The IIS says it is not possible') or the source of ultimate truth ('It is not in The IIS'). Nothing can be done without its authorisation (e.g. pickup, loading) and many things can be authorised on its behalf (e.g. ordering). However, we have shown that the software is also a source of unnecessary queries, allowing apparently meaningless interactions that effectively stabilise the IOC.

In the context of this study, the entanglement between the social and the material (i.e. the sociomaterial dimension of this conversation and the sociomaterial dimension of the delivery process during daily IOC) often takes the form of discontinued and flexible short turns following a question-and-answer conversational pattern. Instead of asking 'questions' in the strict sense, they state problematic facts, such as 'There is a bill I cannot find', which indirectly asks the question 'Do you know where it is?' It is not only an implicit request ('Please tell me where it is!') but also a form of prior acceptance of a possible incomplete response. It is not interrogatory. Non-answers are permitted and politely agreed on as contributing to positive problem solving, with mutual understanding for the respective constraints and accountabilities of each party (Frow,

Marginson, & Ogden, 2005). The speakers thus make sense of formal tools and co-produce agreement.

The following section discusses the extent to which such communicative practices contribute to the skilful enactment of IOC.

Discussion

This research has implications for theory and practice. It first confirms the value of a CCO perspective for studying the presence/absence of various matters (Cooren et al., 2012; Martine et al., 2016) in conversation. It then discusses the extent to which the communicative practices enacted in the analysed IIS context (Orlikowski, 2009; Scott & Orlikowski, 2014) represent the skilful enactment of (inter)organisational collaboration (Arnaud & Mills, 2012; Jørgensen, Jordan, & Mitterhofer, 2012) in modern forms of work and organisation.

A CCO perspective for studying the presence/absence of materiality in conversation

Our analysis provides insight into how absent/distant objects matter (or not) during conversations in IIS context. If lost material can become a mutual matter of concern for the operational managers Bill and Monique, it is because their conversation is shaped by a plenum of technological agencies (including phones and IIS) (Cooren, 2006) that draw attention to *missing information*, and possibly a *missing object*. In this case, the material being delivered has not disappeared, but exists independently of how it is accounted for in the software. In other words, its actual location does not materialise itself in the system.

This is precisely what matters: how the presence/absence of something materialises itself, in an act of re-presentation (Cooren, 2015, p. 12). Ironically, in the case analysed, the object has always been at the right place at the right moment. Only the materialisation/representation fails and it is this failure that concerns or pre-occupies the participants. What is thus constituted through talk is a polyphonic 'combination of material and symbolic' (Ashcraft et al., 2009, p. 39) that becomes a trans-locatable matter of concern (Barad, 2007; Cooren et al., 2012). It is the material delivered, the delivery process, and the delivery tracking software that all matter in here and now, that is, a combination of them made present though talk (phone calls, meetings, and interactions) and texts (orders, bills, information on a screen, etc.).

What is interesting in the case analysed is how this sociomateriality (Brummans, Cooren, Robichaud, & Taylor, 2014; Orlikowski, 2007) is not only enacted here and now but also continues to exist there and then. This re-enactment across time and space is a polyphonic performance because what is reconstituted, one interaction after another, is not a single object or a single symbol, but a multivocal concern for the relationship between the object, its re-presentation/materialisation and those present in the interaction.

In between Monique and Bill's two phone calls, successive and maybe simultaneous phone calls and direct interactions took place involving other participants (e.g. the

DISCURSIVITY, RELATIONALITY AND MATERIALITY

customer and the loader) in another time and space (e.g. Nice or the holidays). Despite this diversity, all these interactions tend to be linked by the same matter of concern, the same issue: determining if the order has been delivered to where it was supposed to go. Solving this problem is simultaneously material (to the extent that this order has to somehow materialise itself) and symbolic (to the extent that this materialisation expresses itself through a series of re-presentations). We argue that making such sociomateriality exist, giving it a durable existence during conversations, is not a peripheral skill in modern forms of organising characterised by the permanent dislocation/recomposition of organisational boundaries (cultural, hierarchical, and technical) (Vasquez & Cooren, 2013).

Inter-organisational relationships indeed provide a relevant field for analysing how these performances are achieved through texts and talks (Arnaud & Mills, 2012; Jørgensen et al., 2012). The first performance concerns how distant accountabilities are rendered present though talk. At least in appearance, the participants are concerned by what they are talking about. They assume their responsibilities and the interdependencies with other actors (Fauré & Rouleau, 2011; Frow et al., 2005). This is why the process can unfold, because the actors *matter* in it. The performance also concerns how the parties communicatively collaborate to achieve their accountabilities in practice.

Technology in use often generates endogenous problems (i.e. problems related to *how technology is used*, not about *what technology is used for*) that seem to matter in themselves at the moment, but that indeed matter durably only if they are related to other sociomaterial concerns. Trying to know *where the information about an object is* can make sense only if it is possible to know and materialise *where the object is* and if mutual concern about this issue exists. For the dialogue to be meaningful, participants must take an interest in this heterogeneity of knowing (Ashcraft et al., 2009, p. 40).

Emergent communicative skills in collaborative change

During the interactions analysed, sociomateriality is shown to be enacted in different ways (Orlikowski, 2007). While often clearly relying on what the software says, middle managers also know how to manipulate its results depending on the situation. This analysis confirms that IISs are powerful agents of (inter)organisational (re)structuring, a topic widely explored in the information systems literature (Gallivan & Depledge, 2003; Grover & Saeed, 2007). Indeed, most of the exchanges recorded during the immersion period were shaped by information processing rules and constraints.

However, one could argue that Bill and Monique's performance (mindful co-orientation, negotiated accountabilities) relies on very incomplete mutual knowledge and that nothing is done to address this. The operational manager in Manuf.Co's delivery department (Monique) calls her counterpart in OuesTranport (Bill) to find out if a 'loading order' she sent one week ago 'has been dealt with'. Despite a series of more than 10 question–answer turns (involving numerous consultations of the IIS's database and available contractual documents related to the delivery process), they cannot solve the problem and Monique is motivated to 'find out from Nice (the retailer)' what is going on.

A few hours later, Monique calls Bill back to confirm that the goods have been delivered. The managers spent ample time seeking the information in the tracking system, and a solution was found and agreed upon. However, nothing is known about what really happened: Who picked up the goods at the warehouse? How were they packaged? When were they delivered? Who did not record the pickup and the reception and why? Bill still has a blank space in his database (i.e. no traces of any operations) and does not try to find out why. Monique agrees with this despite the fact that she has wasted considerable time on a non-existent problem (i.e. the product had been physically delivered). The problem arose from an unrecorded process, which represents a dysfunctional use of the IIS. Nothing has been learned about how to solve similar problems should they arise in the future.

Such situations are not exceptional (Ashcraft et al., 2009; Cooren et al., 2012). Although designed and implemented to control the delivery process without requiring physical displacement (Orlikowski, 2009), the interfirm collaborative software often generates unnecessary problems like the one described above. Phone calls dealing with information-processing problems represent an important part of operators' day-to-day work, and few such calls are immediately resolved. During their interactions, the managers deal with missing information and evaluate the extent to which the problem can be attributed to the software or to the delivery process itself.

Knowing whether or not a product is at the right place at the right time (Cooren et al., 2012) is sometimes essentially a question of whether or not its delivery was properly recorded/materialised/presentified in the database. Physical checks to verify the presence of the product are considered a last resort after all the other potential solutions have failed. To deal with such issues, IOC is thus performed despite a lack of mutual knowledge through this form of minimal co-orientation (Cooren, 2004; Taylor, 2006).

Both transporter managers and operational managers, their counterparts at manufacturers, are responsible not only for the entire delivery process but also for each step therein. As part of their close collaboration with the process through the IIS, employees develop a practical knowledge of how, when, and with whom in order to balance between a strict compliance with information processing and a mindful understanding of the situation and resources it creates. In the interaction analysed, both managers know that the problem might be irrelevant. However, they also know that the routinised treatment of such small failures (Weick & Sutcliffe, 2006) is indispensable for managing the delivery process reliably.

This tedious process of validation, control, reporting, and other steps can only be achieved through close collaboration. Although the problem appears to be solved, participants in the exchange have knowingly addressed it by co-producing a situated agreement based on a mutual understanding of their respective constraints and accountabilities (Fauré & Rouleau, 2011; Frow et al., 2005), instead of placing the blame on the other person. We thus argue that these communicative practices are pivotal to dealing with what matters during (inter)organisational collaborative practices.

Inter-organisational relations as a paradigm of organisational transformation?

Contemporary societal and organisational transformations can be characterised in many ways – as individualism, globalism, or technicism, for example – but evolution about the way time and space are impacting our lives, work and organisation on a daily basis is a topic to which academic works are gaining increasing attention (Lorino, 2014;

Orlikowski & Scott, 2008; Vasquez & Cooren, 2013). This, it could be argued, is because organisations, through their representatives, technologies are penetrating more and more intimate aspects of our lives and orient, structure, and influence every single act and choice (Deetz, 1992).

Modern times are characterised by the extreme diversity, multiplicity, and volatility of both organisational forms and ways of doing work. More than ever, to respond to changes in markets, goods, technologies, governance, and the environment, one of the most challenging issues for contemporary business and organisations is to 'organize uncertainty' (Power, 1997) rather than to implement permanent rules. Thus, they strive to maintain a fragile and temporary coherence between fragmented activities, dislocated in time, and space rather than to build a 'vulnerable fortress' (Taylor & Van Every, 1993).

Consequently, organising activities pertains to time (deadline, time limits) and space (movement, localisation) of action with, about, for, or by something (e.g. the presence/absence of buildings, pieces of furniture, documents, texts, and technologies). In such a process, technology evidently matters, as it renews the forms and space-times of interactions through a 'synthetic world' (Castronova, 2008; Malaby, 2006), ERP (Jones et al., 2006), IISs (Rai, Pavlou, Im, & Du, 2012), collaborative systems (Grover & Saeed, 2007), and immersive environments for workplace collaboration (Orlikowski, 2009). Granted, they make time go faster and reduce space between people and organisations, but how do they come to matter in organisational settings and transform the profound nature of interaction, work, organisations, and organising?

Although such issues are marginal in a context of clear and stable organisational boundaries (e.g. internal/external; hierarchical/functional), they become much more important in a context characterised by layered organising processes (Tsoukas & Chia, 2002) and by networks of activities dislocated in time and space (Cooren & Fairhurst, 2004; Orlikowski & Scott, 2008). More than ever, modern organising practice involves articulating, coordinating, and co-orienting communities of practices with different skills, cultures, and objectives.

In this context, collaboration using technologies with unknown colleagues shifts from a mere property of inter-organisational relationships to become a paradigmatic issue for intra- and inter-organisational relationships alike. More specifically, we argue that in a context characterised by the systematisation and institutionalisation of organisational change and restructuring (Angwin & Vaara, 2005), IOC might no longer be a subcategory of previous forms of organisational collaboration, but rather represent the generic model of what organisational relationships will look like in the future, even more than they do today.

Therefore, analysts first need to understand how interaction/communication imbricate and co-orient (Taylor, 2006; Taylor et al., 2001) both human and non-human agency, which constitutes the 'entanglement' or 'sociomateriality' of practice (Orlikowski, 2007; Scott & Orlikowski, 2014; Suchman, 2007). Then, we have to evaluate/analyse whether or not such imbrications are fruitful or neutralising for co-orientation in practice (i.e. interaction). In other words, are they organising/constitutive? Our analysis demonstrated that they are.

Conclusion

This article aimed to contribute to studies that have investigated the use of technological systems as sociomaterial practices by developing a CCO approach to sociomateriality. It provides insight into the skilful communicative practices enacted during IOC routines using two interactions selected from a 2-year investigation of a leading European road haulage contractor and one of its main customers (Manuf.Co).

The analysis shows how employees of the transporter and the manufacturer collaborate to prevent potential physical disruption and glitches in information processing. The analysis also demonstrates that IOC does not consist of trying to find, at any cost, the missing information or why this information is missing. Instead, it also takes the form of mutual comprehension and acceptance of ignorance. Given that each participant's (human and non-human) performance relies on the performance of others, no one can be considered solely responsible a priori for any single problem. This implies minding and understanding in case of ignorance. What is important is not the solution agreed on per se based on hypothetical shared meaning, but rather the process whereby this agreement is constructed to sustain minimal co-orientation and to negotiate shared accountabilities.

This article illustrates how this kind of situation between organisations is sometimes lost in translation by the operation routines of information systems as well as the extraordinary ability of the people who handle institutionalised mess and make things matter despite routinised sociomaterial chaos.

Note

1. Most of the data collected used in the study were reported in a previous publication (Arnaud & Mills, 2012). In this article, we use some unused data from that study and some that have already been analysed through a different lens in Fauré and Arnaud (2012).

Disclosure statement

No potential conflict of interest was reported by the authors.

References

Alvesson, M., & Karreman, D. (2000). Varieties of discourse: On the study of organizations through discourse analysis. *Human Relations*, *53*(9), 1125. doi:10.1177/0018726700539002

Angwin, D., & Vaara, E. (2005). Introduction to the special issue.'Connectivity'in merging organizations: Beyond traditional cultural perspectives. *Organization Studies*, *26*(10), 1445–1453. doi:10.1177/0170840605057066

Arnaud, N., & Mills, C. E. (2012). Understanding the inter-organizational agency: A communication perspective. *Group and Organization Management*, *37*(4), 452–485. doi:10.1177/1059601112451125

Arnaud, N., Mills, C. E., Legrand, C., & Maton, E. (2016). Materialising strategy in mundane tools: The key to coupling global strategy and local strategy practice? *British Journal of Management*, *27*, 38–57. doi:10.1111/1467-8551.12144

Ashcraft, K. L., Khun, T. R., & Cooren, F. (2009). Constitutional amendments: "materializing" organizational communication. *Academy of Management Annals*, *3*(1), 1–64. doi:10.1080/19416520903047186

Austin, J. L. (1962). *How to do things with words*. Cambridge, MA: Harvard University Press.

Barad, K. (2003). Posthumanist performativity: Toward an understanding of how matter comes to matter. *Signs, 28*(3), 801–831. doi:10.1086/345321

Barad, K. (2007). *Meeting the universe halfway: Quantum physics and the entanglement of matter and meaning.* Durham, NC: Duke University Press.

Boden, D. (1994). *The business of talk: Organizations in action.* Cambridge: Polity Press.

Brummans, B., Cooren, F., Robichaud, D., & Taylor, J. R. (2014). Approaches to the communicative constitution of organizations. In L. Putnam & D. K. Mumby (Eds.), *The SAGE handbook of organizational communication: Advances in theory, research, and methods* (pp. 173–194). Thousand Oaks: Sage.

Brummans, B. H. (2007). Death by document: Tracing the agency of a text. *Qualitative Inquiry, 13*(5), 711–727. doi:10.1177/1077800407301185

Castronova, E. (2008). *Synthetic worlds: The business and culture of online games.* Chicago, IL: University of Chicago Press.

Cooren, F. (2004). The communication achievement of collective minding: Analysis of board meeting excerpts. *Management Communication Quarterly, 17*(4), 517–551. doi:10.1177/0893318903262242

Cooren, F. (2006). The organizational world as a plenum of agencies. In F. Cooren, J. Taylor, & E. J. Van Every (Eds.), *Communication as organizing: Empirical and theoretical explorations in the dynamic of text and conversation* (pp. 81–100). London: Lawrence Erlbaum Associates.

Cooren, F. (2010). *Action and agency in dialogue: Passion, incarnation and ventriloquism.* Philadelphia: John Benjamins Publishing Company.

Cooren, F. (2015). In medias res: Communication, existence, and materiality. *Communication Research and Practice, 1*(4), 307–321. doi:10.1080/22041451.2015.1110075

Cooren, F. (2016). Ethics for Dummies: Ventriloquism and responsibility. *Atlantic Journal of Communication, 24*(1), 17–30. doi:10.1080/15456870.2016.1113963

Cooren, F., Fairhurst, G., & Huët, R. (2012). Why matter always matters in (organizational) communication. In P. M. Leonardi, B. A. Nardi, & J. Kallinikos (Eds.), *Materiality and organizing: social interaction in a technological world* (pp. 296–314). Oxford, UK: University Press Oxford.

Cooren, F., & Fairhurst, G. T. (2004). Speech timing and spacing: The phenomenon of organizational closure. *Organization, 11*(6), 793–824. doi:10.1177/1350508404047252

Cooren, F., & Fairhurst, G. T. (2008). Dislocation and stabilization: How to scale up from interaction to organization. In L. L. Putnam & A. M. Nicotera (Eds.), *Building theories of organizing: The constitutive role of communication* (pp. 117–152). New York: Routledge.

Cooren, F., Taylor, J. R., & Van Emery, E. J. (2006). *Communication as organizing. Empirical and theoretical exploration in the dynamic of text and conversation.* London: Lawrence Erblaum Associates, Inc.

Coppola, S. (Director). (2003). *Lost in Translation.* San Francisco, CA: American Zoetrope & Tohokushinsha Film (prod).

Creswell, J. W., & Miller, D. L. (2000). Determining validity in qualitative inquiry. *Theory Into Practice, 39*(3), 124–130. doi:10.1207/s15430421tip3903_2

Deetz, S. A. (1992). *Democracy in an age of corporate colonization: Developments in communication and the politics of everyday life.* New York: State Univ of New York.

DeSanctis, G., & Poole, M. S. (1994). Capturing the complexity in advanced technology use: Adaptive structuration theory. *Organization Science, 5*(2), 121–147.

Drew, P., & Heritage, J. (1992). *Talk at work: Interaction in institutional settings.* Cambridge: Cambridge University Press.

Fairhurst, G. T., & Putnam, L. L. (2004). Organizations as discursive constructions. *Communication Theory, 14*(1), 5–26. doi:10.1111/comt.2004.14.issue-1

Faulkner, P., & Runde, J. (2009). On the identity of technological objects and user innovations in function. *Academy of Management Review, 34*(3), 442–462. doi:10.5465/AMR.2009.40632318

Fauré, B., & Arnaud, N. (2012). Contribution-representation-subordination as conversational patterns. Manifestation of collective mind during routinized talk at work. In F. Cooren & A.

Letourneau (Eds.), *(Re)presentation and dialogue* (pp. 213–235). Amsterdam: John Benjamins Publishing.

Fauré, B., & Arnaud, N. (2014). *La communication des organisations*. Paris: Repères, La Découverte.

Fauré, B., & Rouleau, L. (2011). The strategic competence of accountants and middle managers in budget making. *Accounting, Organizations & Society, 36*(3), 167–182. doi:10.1016/j.aos.2011.04.001

Frow, N., Marginson, D., & Ogden, S. (2005). Encouraging strategic behaviour while maintaining management control: Multi-functional project teams, budgets, and the negotiation of shared accountabilities in contemporary enterprises. *Management Accounting Research, 16*(3), 269–292. doi:10.1016/j.mar.2005.06.004

Gallivan, M. J., & Depledge, G. (2003). Trust, control and the role of interorganizational systems in electronic partnerships. *Information Systems Journal, 13*(2), 159–190. doi:10.1046/j.1365-2575.2003.00146.x

Giddens, A. (1984). *The constitution of society*. Cambridge: Polity Press.

Goffman, E. (1959). *The presentation of self in everyday life*. New York, NY: Garden City.

Griffith, T. L., & Dougherty, D. J. (2001). Beyond socio-technical systems: Introduction to the special issue. *Journal of Engineering and Technology Management, 18*(3), 207–218. doi:10.1016/S0923-4748(01)00034-0

Groleau, C. (2002). Structuration, situated action and distributed cognition. Rethinking the computerization of organizations. *Systèmes d'Information et Management, 7*(2), 13–36.

Grover, V., & Saeed, K. A. (2007). The impact of product, market, and relationship characteristics on interorganizational system integration in manufacturer-supplier dyads. *Journal of Management Information Systems, 23*(4), 185–216. doi:10.2753/MIS0742-1222230409

Jones, M. C., Cline, M., & Ryan, S. (2006). Exploring knowledge sharing in ERP implementation: An organizational culture framework. *Decision Support Systems, 41*(2), 411–434. doi:10.1016/j.dss.2004.06.017

Jørgensen, L., Jordan, S., & Mitterhofer, H. (2012). Sensemaking and discourse analyses in interorganizational research: A review and suggested advances. *Scandinavian Journal of Management, 28*(2), 107–120. doi:10.1016/j.scaman.2012.01.007

Kallinikos, J., Leonardi, P. M., & Nardi, B. A. (2012). *The challenge of materiality: Origins, scope, and prospects*. Oxford: Oxford University Press.

Kautz, K., & Jensen, T. B. (2013). Sociomateriality at the royal court of IS: A jester's monologue. *Information and Organization, 23*(1), 15–27. doi:10.1016/j.infoandorg.2013.01.001

Latour, B. (1987). *Science in action*. Cambridge, MA: Harvard University Press.

Latour, B. (1996). On interobjectivity. *Mind, Culture, and Activity, 3*(4), 228–245. doi:10.1207/s15327884mca0304_2

Latour, B. (2005). *Reassembling the social: An introduction to actor-network-theory*. Oxford: Oxford University Press.

Leonardi, P. M. (2013). Theoretical foundations for the study of sociomateriality. *Information and Organization, 23*(2), 59–76. doi:10.1016/j.infoandorg.2013.02.002

Leonardi, P. M., & Kallinikos, J. (2012). *Materiality and organizing: Social interaction in a technological world*. Oxford: Oxford University Press.

Lorino, P. (2014). From speech acts to act speeches: Collective activity, a discursive process speaking the language of habits. In F. Cooren, E. Vaara, A. Langley, & H. Tsoukas (Eds.), *Language and communication at work. discourse, narrativity, and organizing (perspectives on process organization studies)* (pp. 95–124). Oxford: Oxford University Press.

Luff, P., Heath, C., & Hindmarsch, J. (2000). *Workplace studies. Recovering work practice and informing system design*. Cambridge: Cambrigde University Press.

Malaby, T. (2006). Parlaying value capital in and beyond virtual worlds. *Games and Culture, 1*(2), 141–162. doi:10.1177/1555412006286688

Markus, M. L., & Benjamin, R. I. (1997). The magic bullet theory in IT-enabled transformation. *Sloan Management Review, 34*(2), 55–68.

Martine, T., Cooren, F., Bénel, A., & Zacklad, M. (2016). What does really matter in technologiy adoption? A CCO approach. *Management Communication Quarterly, 30*(2), 164–187. doi:10.1177/0893318915619012

Mol, A. (2002). *The body multiple: Ontology in medical practice.* Durham, NC: Duke University Press.

Mutch, A. (2013). Sociomateriality—Taking the wrong turning? *Information and Organization, 23*(1), 28–40. doi:10.1016/j.infoandorg.2013.02.001

Orlikowski, W. J. (1992). The duality of technology: Rethinking the concept of technology in organizations. *Organization Science, 3*(3), 398–427. doi:10.1287/orsc.3.3.398

Orlikowski, W. J. (2007). Sociomaterial practices: Exploring technology at work. *Organization Studies, 28*(9), 1435–1448. doi:10.1177/0170840607081138

Orlikowski, W. J. (2009). The sociomateriality of organisational life: Considering technology in management research. *Cambridge Journal of Economics,* 1–17. doi:10.1093/cje/bep058

Orlikowski, W. J., & Scott, S. V. (2008). Sociomateriality: Challenging the separation of technology, work and organization. *Aademy of Management Annals, 2*(1), 433–474.

Pentland, B. T., & Singh, H. (2012). Materiality: What are the consequences. In P. M. Leonardi, B. A. Nardi, & J. Kallinikos (Eds.), *Materiality and organizing: Social interaction in a technological world* (pp. 287–295). Oxford, UK: University Press Oxford.

Power, M. (1997). *The audit society: Rituals of verification.* Oxford: Oxford University Press.

Prasad, P. (1993). Symbolic processes in the implementation of technological change: A symbolic interactionist study of work computerization. *Academy of Management Journal, 36*(6), 1400–1429. doi:10.2307/256817

Putnam, L. L., & Nicotera, A. M. (Eds.). (2008). *Building theories of organizing: The constitutive role of communication.* New York, NY: Roultedge.

Rai, A., Pavlou, P. A., Im, G., & Du, S. (2012). Interfirm IT capability profiles and communications for cocreating relational value: Evidence from the logistics industry. *MIS Quarterly, 36* (1), 233–262.

Robichaud, D., Giroux, H., & Taylor, J. R. (2004). The metaconversation: The recursive property of language as a key to organizing. *Academy of Management Review, 29*(4), 617–634.

Scott, S. V., & Orlikowski, W. J. (2014). Entanglements in practice: Performing anonymity through social media. *MIS Quarterly, 38*(3), 873–893.

Spradley, J. P. (1979). *The ethnographic interview.* New York: Rinehart and Winston.

Suchman, L. (2007). *Human-machine reconfigurations: Plans and situated actions.* Cambridge: Cambridge University Press.

Taylor, J. R. (2006). Coorientation: A conceptual framework. In F. Cooren, J. R. Taylor, & E. J. Van Emery (Eds.), *Communication as organizing: Empirical and theoretical exploration in the dynamic of text and conversation* (pp. 141–157). New York, NY: Lawrence Erlbaum Associates.

Taylor, J. R., Groleau, C., Van Emery, E. J., & Heaton, L. (2001). *The computerization of work: A communication perspective.* Thousand Oaks, CA: Sage Publications.

Taylor, J. R., & Robichaud, D. (2004). Finding the organization in the communication: Discourse as action and sensemaking. *Organization, 11*(3), 395–413. doi:10.1177/1350508404041999

Taylor, J. R., & Van Every, E. J. (1993). *The vulnerable fortress: Bureaucratic organization and management in the information age.* Toronto, ON: University of Toronto Press.

Taylor, J. R., & Van Every, E. J. (2000). *The emergent organization. Communication as site and surface.* Mahwah NJ: Lawrence Erblaum Associates.

Taylor, J. R., & Virgili, S. (2008). Why ERPs disappoint: The importance of getting the organisational text right. In B. Grabot, A. Mayère, & I. Bazet (Eds.), *ERP systems and organisational change* (pp. 59–84). Cardiff, UK: Springer.

Tsoukas, H., & Chia, R. (2002). On organizational becoming: Rethinking organizational change. *Organization Science, 13*(5), 567–582. doi:10.1287/orsc.13.5.567.7810

Vasquez, C., & Cooren, F. (2013). Spacing practices: The communicative configuration of organizing through space-times. *Communication Theory, 23*(1), 25–47. doi:10.1111/comt.12003

Walsham, G. (2002). Cross-cultural software production and use: A structurational analysis. *Mis Quaterly, 26*(4), 359–380. doi:10.2307/4132313

Weick, K. E., & Sutcliffe, K. M. (2006). Mindfulness and the quality of organizational attention. *Organization Science, 17*(4), 514–524. doi:10.1287/orsc.1060.0196

Weick, K. E., Sutcliffe, K. M., & Obstfeld, D. (2005). Organizing and the process of sensemaking. *Organization Science, 16*(4), 409–421. doi:10.1287/orsc.1050.0133

Yin, R. K. (2009). *Case study research, design and methods*. Newbury Park, CA: Sage.

Modes of design tools: sociomaterial dynamics of a horticultural project

Carole Groleau and Christiane Demers

ABSTRACT
Our study of sociomaterial practices investigates design tools by drawing on activity theory. This framework examines how interactions among organisational members as well as with their material environment shapes and are shaped by past interactional patterns. The empirical investigation of a horticultural project allows us to build on activity theory's concept of tool to develop three modes to characterise sociomaterial dynamics supporting design work. We present the projective, authoritative, and instructional modes through which ideas are concretised, legitimised, and operationalised in concrete settings.

Sociomateriality and relationality

Orlikowski (2007) in her pioneer study on sociomateriality has opened up a fruitful dialogue among researchers regarding the place of materiality in organisations. Our objective is to contribute to this literature by building on the concept of tool from activity theory to understand entanglements linking social and material dimensions as artefacts are designed and deployed.

Jones (2014) provides an interesting categorisation contrasting notions of materiality, inseparability, and relationality to unsort this literature. He identifies a first group of authors that adopt a relational ontology. According to them, materialisation only takes form in instances of practice. These authors equate inseparability with mutual constitution, meaning that the social and the material are wholly relational. Furthermore, regarding relationality, they focus on relations that bring material and social into being. This first group is led by Orlikowski (2007, 2010; Orlikowski & Scott, 2008) who was inspired by Barad (2007).

We share the position defended by the second group of authors identified by Jones, who believe that there are different materialities that provide distinct conditions for their enactment. Unlike proponents of the first group, these researchers argue that materiality can be considered beyond instances of its enactment. Regarding inseparability, this second group of authors frames it as interdependence. They are interested in understanding artefacts as sociomaterial constructions. Finally, regarding relationality, they take into consideration form, attributes, and capabilities that exist beyond the scope of the studied situation to understand how material and social are entangled. Numerous authors have contributed to this view of sociomateriality including Faulkner and Rund (2012) and Leonardi (2012a, 2012b, 2013), an organisational communication scholar, who has become a leading figure in this second stream of research.

This second group of researchers has been confronted with the difficult challenge of conceptually capturing the entanglement through which material and social come together. The use of concepts, such as affordances (Faraj & Azad, 2012; Leonardi, 2012b) that are inspired by the work of Gibson (1986), has been criticised for being too materialistic and too deterministic (Jarzabkowski & Pinch, 2013; Putnam, 2015). In our study, we propose to build on the concept of tools from activity theory to overcome problems encountered by these authors because, like Jones (2014), we feel that activity theory remains too often overlooked in the literature on sociomateriality.

Within this approach, tools such as computers or drawings are understood as artefacts from which humans draw means and methods that orient the conduct of their daily activities (Groleau & Demers, 2012). This conceptualisation emphasises the potential tools have to mediate historically grounded constructs, providing a variety of means that can be enacted or not by those who manipulate them as activities unfold. We will further examine tools and the analytical ramifications of this concept to refine our understanding of sociomateriality by presenting an empirical investigation of design tools.

Design tools are of particular interest because they are created to materialise ideas, putting the concrete reality of projects in the centre of interactions. Furthermore, design tools are integrated into various social configurations as designs are developed, approved, and enforced. These multiple encounters provide different sociomaterial configurations in which drawings evolve and change status as actors gather around them to think, legitimate, and execute design projects. Because of their concrete dimension and the participation of multiple social configurations throughout projects, we believe the creation and deployment of design tools offer a fertile ground for our study.

In the next section, we will review existing studies on design tools to allow us to position ourselves using activity theory. In the subsequent sections, we will present our empirical study conducted in a botanical garden. Our analysis will lead us to identify different modes through which material and social dimensions of tools come together. We will present these modes by developing their distinct contributions to action.

Design tools: a sociomaterial outlook of design from its inception to its operationalisation

Our study of design tools will focus on drawings commonly used by a variety of occupations, such as architects, engineers, and horticulturists. Drawings, like other types of documents, are mundane material tools that have been explored only in a limited number of studies (Arnaud, Mills, Legrand, & Maton, 2016). We will now turn to the literature to see how past studies can help us analytically capture sociomaterial dynamics taking form in the different phases of design work.

Most studies within this literature study the conceptualisation process through which future projects and drawings are simultaneously formalised. Some of them focus on the process through which designs materialise. For instance, Corner (1992) sees design

DISCURSIVITY, RELATIONALITY AND MATERIALITY

drawings as projections because they are 'productive of a reality that will later emerge' (p. 245). These drawings embody the designer's ideas to be realised or ideational projections. Accordingly, he writes: 'a drawing that proposes a new and as yet unrealised landscape acts as the mediator between the designer's vision, or ideational project, and the actual construction of that project on the site' (Corner, 1992, p. 252). These drawings, which project ideas on paper, have codes and conventions that vary from one occupation to the other (Corner, 1992; Henderson, 1995). As we will see, the projective qualities of drawings described by Corner are of particular interest to us because they make design ideas concrete and accessible to individuals who engage with them through various interactions.

These interactions are investigated by authors such as Henderson (1999) and Ewenstein and Whyte (2007). Inspired by Latour (1986), Henderson (1999) conceptualises visuals used in engineering design as thinking tools. She studies iterations between seeing and thinking as ideas develop through drawings. She states:

> the interaction becomes collective as two or more people sketch to one another as a form of visual conversation, generating tangible representations of their mental concepts, giving first approximate shapes to ideas and then together combining and modifying them so that both the collective drawing and their own mental images of the design are modified. (Henderson, 1999, p. 205)

Interactional patterns around evolving drawings are also at the centre of Ewenstein and Whyte's (2007) analysis of the learning experience of junior architects working with senior colleagues to acquire aesthetic knowledge. The study of interactional patterns provided by Henderson (1999) and Ewenstein and Whyte (2007) adds a social dimension to Corner's (1992) characterisation of drawings as projected ideas taking material form.

These studies limit themselves to the exploratory phase during which ideational projects are tested and developed, often in a collaborative atmosphere. They exclude the decision process leading to the selection of a concept, its presentation to clients and its execution. We feel there is an interesting synergy between these phases as the same tool evolves from an exploratory artefact to one upon which a decision is taken and enforced. We argue that the process extending from inception to execution is a fertile ground in which to study a variety of interactions involving drawings, particularly as this remains largely unexplored in the literature.

Bechky (2003), in one of the rare studies that has addressed the execution phase of a design project, provides a particularly enlightening analysis of sociomaterial practices that differ from those described in studies of the development phase. She (Bechky, 2003) shows how workers from diverse occupational communities brought together to operationalise a design project each develop differentiated interpretations of tools such as drawings and prototypes. She notes that each of these communities possess their own codes and conventions that have developed over time within these occupations, leading workers to develop divergent outlooks on drawings. Interactions she describes also provide interesting instances in which workers co-create common ground to overcome these divergences. In contrast to the developmental phase, we see in Bechky's work various occupational communities coming together around drawings in a dynamic that is more complex than the collaborative participation among peers described by Henderson (1999) and Ewenstein and Whyte (2007).

Beyond illustrating interactional patterns that differ from those in the development phase of design projects and tools, Bechky (2003) ties situated practice with various divergent occupational traditions that analytically extend her study into a much broader historical context. Following Bechky, we reiterate our belief that materiality can be considered well beyond instances of its enactment to argue that numerous historically grounded constructs, like occupational conventions, can be enacted in situated practices involving design tools.

As stated earlier, we sought to integrate the different steps of the design process in a study considering the multiple historically grounded traditions that surface as situated sociomaterial practices unfold. We felt it would be pertinent to extend our investigation beyond the occupational realm to integrate other historical constructs, such as traditions specific to organisations to enrich our analysis of design tools (Groleau, Demers, Lalancette, & Barros, 2012). The confluence of these traditions in actual interactions extending from design inception to its execution will guide our investigation of sociomaterial practices. To further conceptualise these sociomaterial interactional patterns, we will build on the conceptualisation of tools taken from activity theory.

Framing tools in sociomaterial practices using activity theory

Activity theory stems from the work of Vygotsky (1978) in the 1920s and was further developed by researchers such as Leontiev (1976) and Engeström (1987) over the past century. Adopting a sociohistorical lens, this framework examines how interactions among organisational members as well as with their material environment shape and are shaped by past interactional patterns. This mutual influence between local and extended patterns of interactions is shared with other frameworks that are influential in organisational communication such as Giddens' structuration theory (1984) and Leonardi's conceptualisation of imbrication (2012b).

But activity theory distinguishes itself analytically by its concept of mediation through which it captures how situated practices are embedded in wider historical contexts. As such, this framework conceptualises human practices as a series of mediations through which humans access means and methods that orient the conduct of their daily activities. To think of practices as a series of mediations offers an opportunity we want to grab to frame activities in a communicational perspective.

We are particularly interested in tool mediation as originally developed by Vygotsky (1978). His conceptualisation was subsequently enriched by Leontiev (1976) and Engeström (1987) who added a social dimension to tool mediation.

In his pioneer work, Vygotsky (1978) argues that tools intervene in the relationship humans have with their environment. According to him, tools mediate means and methods developed through past human experience, to act upon that environment. These tools, which are passed on from past generations, constitute the cultural resources from which humans draw in their everyday practices. Vygotsky (1978) identifies two types of tools. Technical tools used to act upon things and psychological tools used to act upon humans. The distinction between these two types of tools has been often questioned. In this regard, we adopt Kaptelinin and Nardi's (2012) position, arguing that the barrier between the two is far

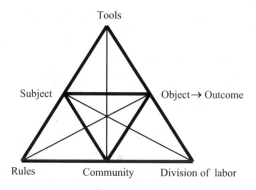

Figure 1. The activity system according to Engeström (1987).

from being clear-cut and that artefacts often possess the characteristics attributed to the two types of tools.

Following Vygotsky, Leontiev (1976) defines tools in the following way: 'Tool is the product of material culture that carries with it the most obvious and material evidence of human creation. It is not only an object possessing a particular format or specific properties. Tool is at the same time a social object in which historical work operations are integrated and fixed' (p. 260, our translation).

One of Leontiev's contributions to activity theory is to emphasise the social nature of tools. According to him, tools are mastered through collective know-how. It is together that humans learn to understand and manipulate them as well as to determine how they will be used to act upon their environment. This is one of the social dimensions of tools that Leontiev (1976) puts forward. He also observes various divisions of labour as individuals come together, adopting diverse configurations to create and manipulate tools. By focusing on humans interacting with tools in the conduct of collective work practices, Leontiev enriches Vygotsky's understanding of tools.

A few decades later, Engeström (1987) further develops the collective dimension of human activity with his revision of activity theory (Figure 1).

Moving away from an intersubjective logic, Engeström extends the model of past theorists by formalising the place of collectives influencing the conduct of activity with his concept of 'community'. Division of labour previously discussed by Leontiev (1976), is formally introduced in Engeström's model. As the meeting point between community and object, the division of labour refers to how collectives come together to meet the object. His model is concerned with the 'doing' as a collective accomplishment. More concretely, it captures the way that collectives such as professional associations or unions mediate how work is accomplished and shared among subjects directly involved in activities. Similarly, rules such as codes of conduct and management policies, whether explicit or not involving subjects and community, are conceived of as sociohistorical constructs that mediate the conduct of situated activity.

Considering the mediations identified by Engeström in his model, work settings can be framed as arenas where multiple strands of sociohistorical context manifest themselves in situated practices. Pertaining specifically to tools, Engeström (1990) states:

'(multivoicedness) becomes an objective challenge for a researcher who wants to make sense of *tools in use*, not just tools as ideally designed' (p. 174, italics in original).

We think that exploring the multivoicedness of *tools in use* offers an interesting opportunity to study the sociomaterial dynamics pertaining to the creation and use of design tools. Activity theory provides us with analytical tools to pursue research avenues we have identified as attracting scant attention in the design work literature. For instance, through tool mediation we can integrate the study of traditions linked to the materialisation of ideas as well as those pertaining to how workers come together to interact with design tools. Accordingly, our research investigates the particular dynamic through which a variety of historical constructs, regarding the material and social dimensions of tools, are actualised in context. The study of this dynamic process combining a variety of different traditions that are enacted, questioned or challenged in situated contexts allows us to offer a different reading of sociomateriality.

Investigating an horticultural project

Our research is guided by two questions: how are multiple sociohistorical constructs enacted, questioned, and challenged in the conduct of collective activity? How can dynamics around these constructs help us understand sociomaterial practices?

Our fieldwork captured a horticultural project from concept development to the moment the garden was in full bloom, in a North-American botanical garden. Recognised for its innovative style, with more than 22,000 plants covering 75 hectares, it is one of the top botanical gardens in the world. Its mission highlights values, such as education, preservation, and research.

The design project we studied centred on the garden situated at the entrance of the main building, which was constructed in the 1930s. Considered as the showcase of the organisation, it is configured as a French garden with a central alley along which a series of rectangular areas are symmetrically displayed. The Botanical Garden has been the subject of a historical and patrimonial study which noted, among the distinguishing features of its Beaux Arts style, the symmetric alignment of its French formal gardens in front of the imposing Art Deco building.

Every year a new horticultural project is designed for the entrance garden. During our study, the concept 'Islands in the City' was developed by Louise, the horticultural project leader, to replicate the landscape of a group of islands on the east coast of North America that consists of wild flower meadows on rolling hills dotted with colourful houses. Accordingly, she proposed a design that looked like a field of wild flowers and grasses with mounds of different elevations and the front part of a house made of cedar shingles.

Our research is based on a case study approach that uses multiples sources of evidence to investigate a complex phenomenon (Yin, 2008). We integrated data from observations (Groleau, 2003) and interviews (Demers, 2003) to constitute our case study.

Through observations, which constitute the bulk of our data, we documented the different phases of the project including its development, its approval, its preparation, and its execution over a period of 9 months. During the project development phase, we shared the project leader's office work environment 2–3 days a week during a 4-month period. As the project progressed, observations took place at other times in other locations. For instance, an important meeting in which the design for the entrance garden was discussed and approved was held in a meeting room in the presence of managers, horticulturists, and the foreman. Subsequently, we also observed Louise as she prepared the documents necessary for the execution of her design. Finally, we concluded our observations with the project leader and her team of gardeners as they executed the design in the entrance garden.

During our fieldwork, we captured Louise's interactions with Allan, her foreman, with other horticulturists, as well as with numerous passers-by such as clerks and gardeners. Observations were captured through field notes that constituted the most important part of our empirical data (Burgess, 2006). We used a video camera to record some of the interactions Louise had with her colleagues. We also interviewed the project leader at different times during the project. These interviews were audio recorded and fully transcribed. Finally, we documented historical garden styles and design work conventions with various specialised publications.

We analysed our data following the process suggested by Morse (2004). First, we organised our data chronologically to fully comprehend the evolution of the project. We then synthesised the data, grouping it according to the use of design tools during the preparation and execution of the design. Afterwards, we linked situated practices with broader sociohistorical constructs. Our analysis focused on interactions around these tools to see how they instantiated sociohistorical traditions. This type of analysis linking situated and sociohistorical practices is commonly found in research conducted by activity theorists. Before presenting the analysis, we will give a brief overview of the sociohistorical traditions that are particularly relevant in this case study. First, we will look at the occupation of horticultural design, focusing on work methodologies and tools. Then, we will present major gardening styles focusing on two particular traditions within landscape architecture.

The institutional context of horticultural design

Horticultural work, particularly garden design, is part of landscape architecture. While the term 'landscape architecture' is fairly recent, this occupation has a long history. In some countries in Europe, landscape architecture has a professional status similar to that of architecture. Formalised work methods involve extensive use of different kinds of drawing, which is the most popular tool, even if other tools, such as models or photographs, are also used. For designers, drawings are the medium through which a new reality emerges (Corner, 1992, p. 245). While some designers use computers to create their drawings, hand-drawn visuals remain very popular (Olin, 2008, p. 152). Moreover, there are different stylistic traditions that are part of the cultural roots of this occupation. We will now describe further the context of horticultural design.

The design process in landscape architecture

The horticultural design literature presents different work methodologies (Austin, 2002; Robinson, 2011). These methodologies frame horticultural design as a professional service catering to clients. Interactions around drawings with clients and technical workers implementing the horticultural design play an important role in these methodologies.

Labels to describe different phases of the design project vary. For instance, Austin (2002) identifies three phases: preplanning considerations, developing a preliminary plan, and developing the final planting plan. On the other hand, Robinson (2011) describes the process in four stages: inception, understanding, synthesis, and realisation. Regardless of these differences, these authors describe very similar processes. We will draw on Robinson's four-stage methodology in Table 1, using other authors to complement his description.

Robinson recognises this methodology as more linear than what actually happens in reality and that stages might be omitted in certain projects. He sees this process, not as a prescription, but rather as a guide for professional design work.

Garden styles in landscape architecture

There is a long stylistic tradition in garden design. An important literature documents the evolution of garden styles, in terms of architecture and aesthetics (Rogers, 2001; Thacker, 1979; Turner, 2005). In this field, there has been an on-going debate between two major garden styles: the French formal garden and the English informal garden. Each represents a different relationship with nature (Grant, 2013; Oudolf & Kingsbury, 2006). According to Oudolf and Kingsbury (2006, p. 25), the formal garden is characterised by control: the initial design must be maintained through constant upkeep; spacing of plants follows a formal pattern; there usually are a limited number of plants; and human intervention clearly dominates. In contrast, the informal, or naturalistic, garden is dynamic: plants grow without intervention; a large variety of species is used; and a spontaneous appearance is sought. A classical French style garden typically consists of artificially built symmetrical geometrical structures, in which plants are strictly laid out to form organised hierarchical patterns on a flat surface. An informal English garden seeks to represent an idealised conception of nature, 'including undulating land forms, rocks, moving water' (Grant, 2013, p. 15). It is usually an open space with irregularly placed trees and masses of mixed species with different elevations textures and colours.

When the Botanical Garden was built, the Beaux Arts style was very popular in North America. 'This style emulated European Renaissance and Baroque landscapes .... Linked together by formal geometry within an over-all landscape design, Beaux Arts garden "rooms" were defined by linear allées and hedges' (The Cultural Landscape Foundation, 2014).

In recent years, however, famous horticulturists in Europe and North America have popularised a new type of informal garden: the prairie style garden (Oudolf & Kingsbury, 2006). The prairie style garden is a 'wild' garden consisting mainly of perennials and indigenous plants. Here, it is the creation of a patchwork effect of colours, textures, and elevations that is sought through an informal mix of various plants. This style has been used to design new public gardens and parks, for instance at the Botanical Garden of Chicago.

As we will see, the design project we studied involved an innovative use of the informal prairie garden style.

DISCURSIVITY, RELATIONALITY AND MATERIALITY

Table 1. Stages and practices within the design process.

Stages of design process	Description of practices associated with stages of design process
Inception: aims at 'establishing the design brief and working relationships' (Robinson, 2011:160)	– designers initiate the contact with clients that are often organizations such as companies, public authorities or even community groups – clients transmit their instructions that may vary from vague notions to specific requirements
Understanding: refers to the research and analysis done by designers to capture characteristics of the site	– designers collect survey data pertaining to the physical, biological and cultural specificities of the site
Synthesis: ideas are generated and organized by designers	To do so, designers rely on various drawings and interactions: – conceptual plan: it captures first thoughts. It is a small and quickly drawn visual giving form to the concept prepared by the designer (Treib, 2008; Sullivan, 2014) – measured drawing: '(it) indicates layout, dimensions, elements, and in some cases material and details of construction' (Olin, 2008:144) Measured drawings most often adopt an aerial point of view to reduce distortion usually found in perspective drawings: – master plan[a]: often juxtaposed on measured drawings to respect exact dimensions (Sullivan, 2014), master plan provides a more detailed view of the design to better see how it will look in the actual setting. It indicates geometry of spaces, zones of planting, but also characteristics such as colours and patterns, giving a more precise image of the design. The amount of detail remains limited in this drawing. Robinson sees the master plan as 'an authoritative design document. It should always be discussed and agreed with the client and design team … by doing this we gain agreement for the extent and location of at least the major planting areas' (Robinson, 2011:170) – production or working drawings: 'This name (production drawings), of course, derives from the simple fact that the drawings are provided to the people who give physical form to our projects. Our work, these drawings – the products of our hands, eyes and imaginations – are really only the instructions upon which others base their work, which is the product of their hands, their eyes and their understanding'. p. 141. They provide 'all essential information for the physical setting out and the planting on site' (Robinson, 2011:186). These drawings are technical and are destined to gardeners who will execute the designs. The way planting is made visible on working drawings depends on the type of planting necessary to execute the design, particularly in function of the style of garden. Three traditions co-exist (Robinson, 2011): – exact location: working drawings indicate to scale, the exact location of each one of plants. Each plant has its visual code – areas: working drawing delineates particular areas which will be filled with only one type of plant – mixes: working drawings delineates a particular area to be filled by a combination of plants. The number and types of plants, their spacing, as well as a method of distribution, are given to gardeners to guide their work. This last type of planting based on 'mixes' is often used for informal gardens, such as prairie gardens
Realization: the proposed design becomes a reality.	Gardeners using working drawings realize the design. Designers might be present to overlook operations or to solve unforeseen problems. The actual planting is followed by an 'aftercare' step, in which the necessary attention is given to plants in order to insure their full bloom and to avoid weed and pest problems

[a]Within the horticultural design literature, the number and names of these drawings may vary. For instance, Andersson (2008) names them site plans.

DISCURSIVITY, RELATIONALITY AND MATERIALITY

In this section, we have mostly described the stylistic tradition in garden design, but within botanical gardens we find garden designs inspired by a variety of other sources. For example, gardens might depict the vegetation of particular geographic areas such as alpine or tropical environments. Designs might also be associated with particular cultures, such as Chinese and Japanese gardens, integrating man-made elements to recall the specificity of these national cultures. These are only a few of commonly used sources from which horticulturists draw to develop their design.

Making sense of tools in design work using modes

Our study aimed at understanding how historically constructed tools instantiate socio-material practices of design. As stated earlier, we view tools, in this case drawings, as mediators of means and methods by referring to constructs, such as work methodologies presented earlier in the section devoted to institutional context of horticultural design. To conduct our analysis, we also integrated organisational constructs regarding how work is traditionally conducted (work methods, routines, ..., etc.) at the studied botanical garden as we gathered all data presenting situated practices through which all these constructs are instantiated.

Our analysis pushes the characterisation of tools, beyond concepts presented in the literature review, by taking into consideration the end that these mediated means and methods serve in the conduct of activity. We use the term mode to refer to roles attributed to tools in relationship to action they serve. As such, modes will draw on historical constructs of different realms to see how they are instantiated in sociomaterial situated practices. Our analysis identifies three modes: the projective, the authoritative and the instructional modes. The projective mode through which the materialisation of a design idea gives form to something that is not yet realised. The authoritative mode is that through which the materialisation of a formal proposition gains ascendancy over upcoming actions. Finally, the instructional mode is that through which guidelines are formalised to orient actions. We will present and illustrate these modes by emphasising their distinct contributions to action as well as the multiple historical constructs that are enacted in each one of them.

The projective mode of the model-drawing

In this section, we will examine the projective mode through which an ideational project to be realised is formalised in a particular artefact, in this case, a design tool sharing the characteristics of a model and a drawing. Before we further explore this mode, we will describe the practices leading to the creation of the model-drawing.

The production of the model-drawing was preceded by the preparation of the conceptual drawing and the measured drawing. The conceptual drawing is a sketch that captures first thoughts while the measured drawing (28 in. × 36 in.) is a scaled replica of the planting areas of the entrance garden.

Different material artefacts are juxtaposed on the measured drawing to further develop the design first captured in the conceptual drawing. Following one of her colleague's suggestion, Louise prepared scaled clay balls materialising mounds that

Figure 2. The model-drawing.

were part of her concept. She said: 'Mary gave me this great idea ... so it will look more like a field, a prairie ... I wanted to give volume to flowerbeds'. These clay balls rest on cardboard, allowing them to be moved around on the measured drawing. She also added a cardboard mock-up house at the location she plans to install the front of her shingle house. On the measured drawing with mounds, she subsequently juxtaposed scaled pieces of tracing paper, respecting the size of planting beds on which she drew green, pink, and burgundy patches, to indicate the configuration of grasses and flowers according to their leading colour. The efforts to concretise her concept led to the production of this artefact, which we have labelled the model-drawing (Figure 2).

Once the design had taken concrete form in the model-drawing, Louise continued to explore it, often asking advice from other horticulturists as well as her foreman. This type of consultation is common. As she explained: 'We consult one another a lot. It is fun. Sometimes, we ask our colleagues, does it work? Is it going well? Then, I work on it, and I show it to them later on ...'. The team of horticulturists and its foreman have adopted a collaborative method that is coherent with the participative culture of the organisation. During fieldwork, we witnessed numerous interactions around the model-drawing, such as when Louise and Mary discuss mound position:

Louise: a small (mound), a big, a big a medium mound ... a big here, a small one here, and there, I have placed them like this (*she points to the mounds on the model-drawing as she is talking*)
Mary: Hum ...
L: Is there something bothering you?
M: This one (*she points to one of the mounds on the model-drawing*) ... if the big one is in front of it, will we be able to see the small one?
L: It doesn't matter.

DISCURSIVITY, RELATIONALITY AND MATERIALITY

M: OK., we can see it from this point of view.

L: Yes, yes, ... Because you know in a field it is not always the big mound on the side and the little ones in the back

The evolution of the design rested on this type of interaction as well as Louise's own assessment and modification of the model-drawing.

Inspired by Corner (1992), we conceptualise the model-drawing as a tool operating within a projective mode. Like him, we see drawings as materialising an ideational project, giving form to something that is not yet realised. It is this understanding of projection that we find to be the characteristic of various tools, such as drawings and models that we investigate further with our data.

First, the creation of the tool itself is of particular interest. The artefact materialising the concept is a hybrid combining characteristics associated with two different tools used in the horticultural occupation – drawings and models. While drawings and models have their distinctive codes and visual grammar, their combination does not really create a problem. Regarding the materialisation of garden design, the model-drawing combines socio-historical constructs taken from the occupation realm. In the choice of material and in the creation of this tool, Louise relied a lot on Mary for advice and guidance, instantiating an organisational tradition pertaining to collective work.

Second, the creation of the material artefact makes the designer's concept accessible to herself as well as to others, allowing them to further develop it through iterations between seeing and thinking. The proprioceptive cues picked up by Louise and her colleagues as they interact with the model-drawing made it possible to further develop and refine the design. As exemplified in the conversation between Mary and Louise regarding mounds, the design progressed often proceeded through trial and error by physically moving elements such as clay balls and coloured pieces of tracing paper. Again, this way of working with tools to individually or collectively think over, change, discuss and negotiate designs is found in occupations such as horticulture, architecture, and engineering. In this particular organisation characterised by a participative culture, these interactions were numerous and collegial.

Third, we observed a very different type of mediation with respect to the nature of the ideational project. Beyond the formal characteristics of the tool, which we have discussed earlier, that link occupational traditions pertaining to drawings and models in our study, tools within the projective mode carry with them a vision which can itself be attached to diverse traditions regarding the concept it conveys. Even if the form and content of tools come into being simultaneously, we want to analytically distinguish them because they can be rooted in various sociohistorical traditions. For instance, the traditions through which ideas are materialised, as we saw earlier, are found in conventions regarding the production and use of drawings and models. On the other hand, the nature of ideas or design concepts are rooted in particular traditions pertaining to the vision of the world they convey. As discussed at the end of the garden style section, ideas inspiring designers in the creation of horticultural designs may find their origin in various sources, among them geographical, cultural, or stylistic traditions. These sources are based on sociohistorical constructs that are distinct from historically

DISCURSIVITY, RELATIONALITY AND MATERIALITY

Table 2. Sociohistorical constructs instantiated as the tool is used in the projective mode.

	Projective mode: materialisation of an ideational project giving form to something that is not yet realized
Occupational sociohistorical constructs	Formal characteristics of the tool: Combination of techniques associated with two different artefacts: drawing and model Interactions with the tool: individual and collective interactions with the tool to further develop the concept
Ideational sociohistorical construct	Ideational project conveyed by the tool: Inspiration from the vegetation and architectural feature of a geographical region. The ideational project has a geographical referent
Organisational sociohistorical constructs	Collaborative work
Situated interaction	The project leader materialises and develops her 'Islands in the City' concept with the support of her colleagues

developed occupational practices through which drawings and models take form in keeping with particular codes and conventions.

In our case study, the ideational project found its source in the architecture and vegetation of a particular geographical area. The inspiration for Louise's design surfaced in the title she gave to her project 'Islands in the City'. Accordingly, she chose plants and design options to recreate the particular landscape of that area.

As Table 2 shows, the projective mode rests on historical constructs instantiating through the different means by which the ideas were materialised. They deal with physical features of the tool, the collective process of tool creation and the nature of the ideational project materialised through the tool.

The authoritative mode of the model-drawing

In this section, we will address how designs are approved introducing the authoritative mode attributed to the model-drawing. During an interview, Louise explained that she receives very few guidelines regarding design: 'we have a lot of leeway (in initiating design work). The constraints I have are not important …. Actually, I have to make sure that flowerbeds look good during three seasons'. Once the materialised design is developed to the satisfaction of the project leader, a meeting was planned to present it to managers in order to get their approval. That meeting brought together Louise, the project leader, Allan, the foreman, Mary, a colleague, and two managers named Richard and Sandra. Louise came to the meeting with the model-drawing to help participants visualise and evaluate the proposed concept.

The 'Islands in the City' design differed from past entrance garden designs in a number of ways. The design did not follow the symmetrical arrangement suggested by the material configuration of flowerbeds that had guided past designs. Accordingly, Louise stated:

> Usually the entrance garden has always been worked respecting the mirror effect. This year, it won't be like this, because in a field nothing is even. You will have a mound here, a hole there, a patch here and another one …. I do not want to have any clear relationship among elements, nothing to understand.

DISCURSIVITY, RELATIONALITY AND MATERIALITY

Furthermore, the integration of grasses changed the usual practice of planting flowers in the entrance garden. While relying on the model-drawing, she formulated comments like this one:

> The way I was seeing it, at the start, it was a field of flowers that I was seeing but there was too much grass that made it look too much like a field. So I integrated color patches with flowers that looked like wild flowers ….

Also, mounds had never been created in the entrance garden. Regarding the presence of mounds, again Louise relied on the model-drawing:

> we will have elevations in different areas of the entrance garden …. Exactly where you can see little pieces of play dough.

To complete the presentation of the projected design, Louise added: 'and I wanted to integrate the front of a cedar shingle house' as she pointed to the cardboard house on the model-drawing.

During her presentation, Louise often referred to the geographical area that had inspired her concept. Richard interpreted her design in a very different frame, expressing himself in stylistic terms. He made the following comments:

Richard: Look, it is a very structured garden. Ok, you come up with a new approach. I think we have to try mounds. It is very innovative.

…

Richard: What you have actually done is worked on a very informal approach that is very different from what is already there. I think it is work trying it.
Richard: we will have something very punchy and very innovative.

Richard saw in Louise's proposition an innovative stylistic contribution: a temporary prairie garden planted in a French garden configuration surrounded by art deco architecture. For him, the clash with the administrative building as well as the presence of grasses in an asymmetric garden with mounds created a unique statement in terms of garden style in which the shingle house did not fit. While for Louise, the house was an essential element to depict the geographical area she wanted to replicate, for Richard it was a piece of decor clashing with the environment and offering no particular stylistic interest. About its presence in the entrance garden, participants at the meeting said:

Richard: … to have a structure, a simulated house in the entrance garden. It is something that bothers me. I am not able to …. I can well imagine the evocation of a field, the flowers here. I can feel it. Is it necessary to put a house?

…

Sandra: You come in, you have the administrative building and you will see a little house in front of it. I am not sure.
Richard: There is something anachronistic in the presence of the house …

…

DISCURSIVITY, RELATIONALITY AND MATERIALITY

Richard: That's it. It is because the structure of the administrative building is so strong, that something beside it, it cannot be done.

Richard wanted all participants to express themselves but he remained firm regarding the elimination of the cedar shingle house from the proposed design. He eventually asked Louise to remove the cardboard house from the model-drawing. It marked the end of the discussion of the house as envisioned by Louise. From that moment on, they initiated a new discussion on plant alternatives that could evoke the shape of a house.

In the circumstances we have just described, the model-drawing became an authoritative tool. It materialised an idea on which individuals would take a decision. Through this artefact the main characteristics of the idea were set and made visible so that participants could debate about it and come to a conclusion that would have ascendancy on upcoming actions. The physical attributes of artefacts played an important role in that process. As such, as soon as the cardboard house was removed from the model-drawing, it vanished from the conversation, which moved on to explore other alternatives. This situation illustrates how a reality disappears both as a material artefact and as a topic to be addressed through social interactions.

The model-drawing can be equated with the master plan found in the occupational realm. As its name implies, it is a design document that is authoritative. It has enough details to give form to the design to bring clients and other partners to agree upon it. As discussed in the occupational literature presented in the section devoted to the design process in landscape architecture, the level of detail may vary according to the expertise of decision-makers. Once the drawing is agreed upon, it will be used for subsequent steps such as the production of working drawings that will operationalise the design.

The work methodology described in horticultural mostly refers to projects designed for clients, providing initial instructions and approving the concept from the master plan. Because our case study takes place in a botanical garden, we observed particular organisational traditions such as the leeway horticulturists possess in the choice of the design at the beginning of the process but the reduced latitude as they interact with managers to finalise the decision regarding the actual design.

The description of interactions during the decision-making process also illustrates another dynamic pertaining to ideational projects integrated into tools with a projective mode. In our case study, we saw two referents of different realms attributed to the ideational project. Louise described her concept adopting a referent of a geographical nature by simulating the landscape of a particular area which contrasted with Richard's reading of her project. To him, the design possessed the elements of a prairie style garden. As such, the model-drawing was understood as the vehicle through which this particular style of garden took form. This led Richard to discuss the validity of the proposed project in stylistic terms, finding the clash between various styles such as the art deco architecture of the main building, the French garden configuration and prairie garden plant design 'innovative' and 'punchy'. In doing so, he ignored the geographical referent presented by Louise. Instead, he substituted his own preoccupation with form and various art movements, using a stylistic referent.

Given the opposition between these referents from two different realms, it is not surprising that in the end the adoption of the design as a prairie style garden required

Table 3. Sociohistorical constructs instantiated as the tool is used in the authoritative mode.

	Authoritative mode: materialisation of a formal proposition having ascendancy over upcoming practices
Occupational sociohistorical constructs	Formal characteristics of the tool: Production of an artefact along the traditions of a master plan Interactions with the tool: Clients decide with the help of the materialised design
Ideational sociohistorical construct	Confrontation of the geographical and stylistic referent associated with the garden design
Organisational sociohistorical constructs	Decision-making process once the design is fully developed Decisions not taken with outside clients as suggested in the occupational realm but with managers Managers have the final word on the decision to be taken
Situated interaction	The project leader and managers discuss the project and approve its execution

Louise to remove her mock-up house that clashed with Richard's stylistic reading of the project.

Table 3 presents historically grounded constructs of various realms coming together in the authoritative mode. It highlights how the formal characteristics of tools as well as collective practices regarding decision-making processes rested on referents of a different nature.

The instructional mode of working drawings

Now, we will discuss the instructional mode of drawings through which an ideational project becomes operational. Drawings at this stage of the process are prepared accordingly to the planting technique that will be used to execute the design.

As Louise explained to us during an interview, working drawings at the Botanical Garden usually follow the logic of providing gardeners with the exact location for a plant: 'When I greet the teams of workers who will do the planting, I always show them, here is what we will be doing, planting this over there. All is very detailed'. This tradition at the Botanical Garden is exemplified by the following drawing (Figure 3).

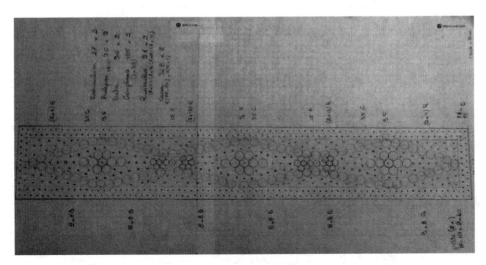

Figure 3. Working drawings produced by another horticulturist at the Botanical Garden.

In our case study, Louise combines two different traditions to prepare her working drawings. First, her working drawings depict the location of specific plants in the first rectangles she drew. Louise started by, cutting rectangles of tracing paper to reproduce the different areas of entrance garden and delineated the different colour patches drawn on the model-drawing. Afterwards, Louise pencilled in plants visually testing their location and distribution on the first sections of her working drawings. However, the drawings became less and less precise over time. We see the following examples of working drawings with varying degrees of precision regarding plant locations (Figure 4).

Second, most of her working drawings only indicate the delineation of different colour patches to be filled with a combination of selected plants, an approach within the horticultural design tradition based on mixes of plants. She was aware that the use of mixes instead of exact location would cause problems with gardeners on planting day. She said: 'As I am drawing this, I anticipate the planting and I tell myself they (the gardeners) will want to cut my head off …. But things always work out'. Thus, two traditions requiring different planting techniques coexist in the set of working drawings produced for the entrance garden.

On planting day, Louise explained to gardeners her concept, using her model-drawing. She provided no clear instruction regarding plant distribution within flower-beds. Gardeners looked for working drawings but they were incomplete. To most gardeners, the design was unclear. Some of them complained: 'We have to visualise what's in her imagination' or 'I have never been to those islands'.

After this presentation, Louise followed a few gardeners in a flowerbed to provide some instructions. But even those were difficult to grasp:

Louise:	For the burgundy patches, what I want, I want to spread the hibiscus, but, in some places, they have to be bunched up … It's really like, how can I say this …
Another woman gardener:	a natural feel.
A man gardener:	It's a bit like a natural look.
Louise:	That's it. Look, pretend you're in the middle of a field …

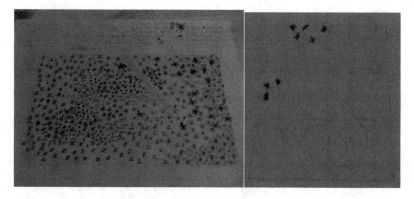

Figure 4. Different working drawings prepared for Louise's design.

A few gardeners fully integrated Louise's concept while others did not understand the design and were subsequently given tasks other than planting. As planting progressed, Louise made her distribution principles verbally more explicit, standing in flowerbeds and showing gardeners where plants should be located. Principles pertaining to plant concentration had not, until then, been accessible to gardeners.

The working drawing through its perceptual cues and visual grammar provided the necessary guidelines to execute planting. As such it was an instructional tool. In the preparation of her working drawings, Louise combined two occupational sociohistorical constructs reflecting two different planting techniques; exact locations and mixes. These techniques are incompatible. Furthermore, the organisational tradition of using exact location drawings makes it more difficult for most gardeners to adopt a different planting technique.

Beyond planting techniques, the problem lies in a particular division of labour in which the project leader plans the designs and gardeners execute it. By moving away from this strict role attribution to one in which gardeners are asked to determine plant configuration, Louise is going against the established tradition at the Botanical Garden. For most gardeners, the division of labour associated with working drawings relying on mixes is difficult to adopt. Our data reveals the traditional division of labour that is recreated as Louise, standing in flowerbeds, verbally orients the work of gardeners as they attempt to execute her design.

Table 4 presents the instantiation of sociohistorical constructs regarding formal characteristics of working drawings as well as work methods pertaining to the operationalisation of the design project.

In the following section, we will pursue our exploration of modes by looking at the relationship among them.

Discussion: grasping sociomaterial dynamics from tool creation to its use

We will now examine the modes we have explored in relationship to one another to highlight how historical constructs regarding material and collective dimensions of practice come together to support the whole design process and account for the entanglement of social, material, and relational dimensions of design project activity.

Table 4. Sociohistorical constructs instantiated as the tool is used in the instructional mode.

	Instructional mode: formalisation of guidelines to orient action
Occupational sociohistorical constructs	Formal characteristics of the tool: Artefact combining guidelines pertaining to two different planting techniques: • location • mixes Combination of different planting techniques Interactions with the tool: Designers prepare working drawings, gardeners execute the design
Organisational sociohistorical constructs	Working drawings done using exact location for plants
Situated interaction	Working drawings are misunderstood by gardeners – gardeners find it difficult to execute the design using the working drawings

DISCURSIVITY, RELATIONALITY AND MATERIALITY

From the projective to the authoritative mode

In our data, we observed how one tool, the model-drawing, changed status as it moved from the projective to the authoritative mode. Earlier, we defined the projective mode as the one through which projected ideas are concretised and the authoritative mode as one through which a proposition is legitimised to orient future actions. The authoritative mode distinguishes itself from the projective one because of the closure it entails and the change in status it brings to the model-drawing as a tool. Even if these modes were focused on the same physical artefact, they were characterised by particular interactional patterns among organisational members that allowed us to differentiate them.

We also noted that particular social dynamics characterised each one of these modes. Organisational members occupied different roles in various social configurations shifting from a collaborative atmosphere in the projective mode to one grouping individuals with differentiated status and influence in the authoritative mode. These social configurations result from the nature of the modes as well as from the combination of occupational and organisational traditions that are instantiated in these modes. For instance, signs of the participative culture of the organisation surfaces during design selection and development while the more dominant position taken by managers seems to replicate the designer–client relationship from the occupational realm even if the client comes from the same organisation as the designers, as was the case in botanical gardens.

By capturing the evolution from ideational project to formal proposition, modes account for the different status of design tools as well as their distinct social practices. Modes allowed us to refine the understanding of tools within an activity theory perspective. The distinction between projective and authoritative modes also adds to our understanding of thinking tools, as discussed by Henderson (1999, 1995). We observed that the iteration between thinking and seeing she associated mostly with concept development, also occurred during the decision-making process. For instance, managers iteratively saw and thought as they passed judgment during the meeting in which the design was approved. Consequently, our study highlights that the thinking process induced by design tools occurred beyond concept development, in what we have labelled the authoritative mode.

Apart from the relationship between these two modes, we feel our conceptualisation of the projective mode provides an understanding of social dynamics beyond interactional patterns among individuals manipulating tools. Building on Corner's study of drawings (1992), we framed the ideational project they carry as sociohistorical constructs. More specifically, our analysis reveals the different realms from which referents used to make sense of the design concepts originate.

In this section, we saw how humans were engaged in sociomaterial practices leading to the creation and stabilisation of a tool, its material and functional characteristics as well as the ideational project it carries. Accordingly, the authoritative mode marked a turning point in the whole process and extended to the instructional mode – one in which there was a shift from development to execution. We will explore further this process, which started with our analysis of how tools emerged from action to focus in the following section on how tools guide action.

From the authoritative to the instructional mode

The authoritative mode marked a turning point because the model-drawing gained a new status from the moment the projected design resting on it was approved. The model-drawing became a delegated agent. Following Kaptelinin and Nardi (2006, p. 248), we define delegated agency as intentions delegated by individuals that can be realised by other things or living beings. The legitimation process involving managers, according to organisational traditions, infused the model-drawing with the necessary power to guide workers in the final steps of the process. Within the instructional mode working drawings, as extensions of the model-drawing, operationalised the approved design and also became delegated agents. Working drawings were meant to give the necessary resources to guide gardeners in the execution of the design. As such, working drawings as well as the project leader, gardeners, and two foremen formed the sociomaterial configuration through which the design was executed in the instructional mode.

Our analysis reveals an interesting dynamic pertaining to the delegated agency of working drawings. It is not so much the legitimacy of the design or the legitimation process that created problems, but the way in which the design was operationalised in working drawings. We observed conflicting traditions surfacing in the preparation and implementation of working drawings. As discussed earlier, these drawings rest on two different planting techniques within the occupational realm (exact location and mixes), one of which was predominant (mixes) but contrary to planting techniques traditionally used in the organisation (exact location). This conflict reduced the delegated agency of the working drawings and led the project leader to adopt a very directive role in the situated practice of planting.

Our data also reveals the difficulty of reconciling various traditions pertaining to tools. As we saw with planting techniques, numerous competing traditions coexist within occupations making their selection and combination sometimes hazardous.

More generally, traditions from different realms might be more or less compatible or overshadow one another. For example, in architecture the occupational and organisational realms are subordinated to the regulatory context in which laws, in most country, determine the involvement of architects in various drawings and their legal responsibility in regards to these drawings (Groleau et al., 2012). Accordingly, we argue that diverging appreciations of design tools can be attributed to their distinct codes or physical characteristics but also to the authority attributed to them that can be recognised, ignored, or questioned in situated practice.

Conclusion

To conclude, by considering the three modes we were able to conceptualise a process extending from tool creation to tool manipulation that is rarely investigated within one single study. In this context, we saw how modes are tied to one another providing a unique outlook on a process, the scope of which is difficult to cover empirically with tools requiring longer development periods.

We feel that modes as concepts have a variety of implications for communication scholars. Modes offer an alternative to concepts such as affordances and scripts within the sociomaterial literature that have been criticised for being too deterministic and lacking the potential to fully integrate the social and material dimensions of human practices (Jarzabkowski & Pinch, 2013; Putnam, 2015).

Furthermore, our study of modes with design tools have integrated power issues, which often remain overlooked in studies of sociomaterial practices. Within the studied modes we saw tensions between different sources, most of which were not tied to the legitimation process itself but rather to the use of divergent constructs to make sense of shared situations. This was the case during the meeting when the referents of Louise and Richard conflicted because these referents came from different realms. We also witnessed a similar incident when two conflicting constructs regarding planting techniques were used by the project leader and gardeners to execute the design on planting day. This was made visible by analysing social dynamics beyond the actual interactions among organisational members who were manipulating tools in context. Doing so allowed practices of much broader scope to be integrated. As such, we illustrated how simple situated interactions with tools rest on constructs from a variety of realms that come together in various ways, some of which induce tension.

Regarding materiality, we have chosen tools that distinguish themselves by their physicality, but other studies regarding, for instance, digital tools could be undertaken with modes employed in our study. We feel modes could provide interesting analytical tools for communication scholars interested in these technological tools.

Together but also separately, modes are concepts that can enrich our understanding of tools and open up future research avenues. For instance, the projective mode can account for the materialisation of ideational projects integrating a variety of artefacts such as technologies or even written documents like policy and the text of law. As a turning point of the process, the authoritative mode could also be studied to see how closure is attained in settings with various power configurations. Finally, the delegated agency associated with instructional mode also opens up questions pertaining to the authority materialised by tools, its effective power and potential tensions they might create in the conduct of everyday actions.

Acknowledgements

The authors thank Colleen Mills as well as the anonymous reviewers for their helpful comments. They are also thankful to Bonnie Nardi for her suggestions and comments on a previous version of this paper.

Disclosure statement

No potential conflict of interest was reported by the authors.

Funding

This work was supported by HEC Montreal and by the Social Sciences; Humanities Research Council of Canada: [CRSH 410-2011-0375].

References

Andersson, T. (2008). From paper to park. In M. Treib (Ed.), *Representing landscape architecture* (pp. 74–95). New York, NY: Taylor & Francis.

Arnaud, N., Mills, C., Legrand, C., & Maton, E. (2016). Materializing strategy in mundane tools: The key to coupling global strategy and local strategy practice?. *British Journal of Management*, *27*, 38–57. doi:10.1111/bjom.2016.27.issue-1

Austin, R. L. (2002). *Elements of planting design*. New York, NY: John Wiley & Sons.

Barad, K. (2007). *Meeting the universe halfway*. Durham, SC: Duke University Press.

Bechky, B. (2003). Sharing meaning across occupational communities: The transformation of understanding on a production floor. *Organization Science*, *14*(3), 312–330. doi:10.1287/orsc.14.3.312.15162

Burgess, R. G. (2006). *In the field*. London: George Allen & Unwin.

Corner, J. (1992). Representation and landscape: Drawing and making in the landscape medium. *Word & Image*, *8*(3), 243–275. doi:10.1080/02666286.1992.10435840

Demers, C. (2003). L'entretien. In Y. Giordano (Ed.), *Conduire un projet de recherche; une perspective qualitative* (pp. 173–210). Paris: L'Harmattan.

Engeström, Y. (1987). *Learning by expanding: An activity-theoretical approach to developmental research*. Helsinki: Orienta-Konsultit Oy.

Engeström, Y. (1990). *Learning working and imagining: Twelve studies in activity theory*. Helsinki: Orienta-Konsultit Oy.

Ewenstein, B., & Whyte, J. (2007). Beyond words: Aesthetic knowledge and knowing in organizations. *Organization Studies*, *28*(5), 689–708. doi:10.1177/0170840607078080

Faraj, S., & Azad, B. (2012). The materiality of technology: An affordance perspective. In P. M. Leonardi, B. A. Nardi, & J. Kallinikos (Eds.), *Materiality and organizing: Social interaction in a technological world* (pp. 237–258). Oxford: Oxford University Press.

Faulkner, P., & Rund, J. (2012). On sociomateriality. In P. M. Leonardi, B. A. Nardi, & J. Kallinikos (Eds.), *Materiality and organizing: Social interaction in a technological world* (pp. 49–66). Oxford: Oxford University Press.

Gibson, J. J. (1986). *The ecological approach to visual perception*. Hillsdale, NJ: Laurence Erlbaum.

Giddens, A. (1984). *The constitution of society*. Cambridge, MA: The Polity Press.

Grant, S. W. (2013). *Gardens are a physical manifestation of culture: Postmodern public parks of the twenty-first century will be built on the infrastructure of the industrial age.* (Master of Liberal Studies Theses). Paper 37. Retrieved from http://scholarship.rollins.edu/mls/37

Groleau, C. (2003). L'Observation. In Y. Giordano (Ed.), *Conduire un projet de recherche; une perspective qualitative* (pp. 211–244). Paris: L'Harmattan.

Groleau, C., & Demers, C. (2012). Pencil, legos and guns: A study of artifacts used in architecture. In P. M. Leonardi, B. A. Nardi, & J. Kallinikos (Eds.), *Materiality and organizing: Social interaction in a technological world* (pp. 259–284). Oxford: Oxford University Press.

Groleau, C., Demers, C., Lalancette, M., & Barros, M. (2012). From hand drawings to computer visuals: Confronting situated and institutionalized practices in an architecture firm. *Organization Science*, *23*(3), 651–671. doi:10.1287/orsc.1110.0667

Henderson, K. (1995). The visual culture of engineers. In S. L. Star (Ed.), *The cultures of computing* (pp. 196–218). Oxford: Blackwell Publishers.

Henderson, K. (1999). *On line and on paper: Visual representations, visual culture and computer graphics in design engineering*. Cambridge, MA: MIT Press.

Jarzabkowski, P., & Pinch, T. (2013). Sociomateriality is 'the new black': Accomplishing repurposing, reinscripting and repairing in context. *M@n@gement*, *16*(5), 579–592. doi:10.3917/mana.165.0579

Jones, M. (2014). A matter of life and death: Exploring conceptualizations of sociomateriality in the context of critical care. *MIS Quarterly*, *38*(3), 895–925.

Kaptelinin, V., & Nardi, B. A. (2006). *Acting with technology: Activity theory and interaction design*. Cambridge, MA: MIT Press.

DISCURSIVITY, RELATIONALITY AND MATERIALITY

Kaptelinin, V., & Nardi, B. A. (2012). *Activity theory in HCI: Fundamentals and reflections*. San Rafael, CA: Morgan & Claypool Publishers.

Latour, B. (1986). Visualization and cognition: Thinking with eyes and hands. *Knowledge and Society: Studies in the Sociology of Culture Past and Present, 6*, 1–40.

Leonardi, P. M. (2012a). Materiality, sociomateriality, and socio-technical systems: What do these terms mean? How are they different? Do we need them?. In P. M. Leonardi, B. A. Nardi, & J. Kallinikos (Eds.), *Materiality and organizing: Social interaction in a technological world* (pp. 25–48). Oxford: Oxford University Press.

Leonardi, P. M. (2012b). *Car crashes without cars: Lessons about simulation technology and organizational change from automotive design*. Cambridge, MA: MIT Press.

Leonardi, P. M. (2013). Theoretical foundations for the study of sociomateriality. *Information and Organization, 23*(2), 59–76. doi:10.1016/j.infoandorg.2013.02.002

Leontiev, A. N. (1976). *Le développement du psychisme*. Paris: Éditions sociales.

Morse, J. (2004). Constructing qualitatively derived theory: Concept construction and concept typologies. *Qualitative Health Research, 14*(10), 1387–1395. doi:10.1177/1049732304269676

Olin, L. (2008). Drawings at work: Working drawings, construction documents. In M. Treib (Ed.), *Representing landscape architecture* (pp. 140–159). New York, NY: Taylor & Francis.

Orlikowski, W. J. (2007). Sociomaterial practices: Exploring technology at work. *Organization Studies, 28*(9), 1435–1448. doi:10.1177/0170840607081138

Orlikowski, W. J. (2010). The sociomateriality of organisational life: Considering technology in management research. *Cambridge Journal of Economics, 34*, 125–141. doi:10.1093/cje/bep058

Orlikowski, W. J., & Scott, S. V. (2008). Sociomateriality: Challenging the separation of technology, work and organization. *The Academy of Management Annals, 2*(1), 433–474. doi:10.1080/19416520802211644

Oudolf, P., & Kingsbury, N. (2006). *Jardins d'avenir: Les plantations dans le temps et dans l'espace*. Rodez France: Éditions du Rouergue.

Putnam, L. L. (2015). Unpacking the dialectic: Altenative views on the discourse-materiality relationship. *Journal Of Management Studies, 52*(5), 706–716. doi:10.1111/joms.2015.52.issue-5

Robinson, N. (2011). *The planting design handbook*. Surrey: Ashgate.

Rogers, E. B. (2001). *Landscape design: A cultural and architectural history*. New York, NY: Abrams.

Sullivan, C. (2014). *Drawing the landscape: The art of hand drawing and digital representation* (4th ed.). Hoboken, NJ: Wiley.

Thacker, C. (1979). *The history of gardens*. Berkeley, CA: University of California Press.

The Cultural Landscape Foundation. (2014). Designed landscape style. Retrieved from http://tclf.org/landscapes/glossary

Treib, M. (2008). Paper or plastic? Five thoughts on the subject of drawing. In M. Treib (Ed.), *Drawing/thinking: Confronting an electronic age*. New York, NY: Taylor & Francis.

Turner, T. (2005). *Garden history: Philosophy and design 2000 BC–2000AD*. London: Spon Press.

Vygotsky, L. S. (1978). *Mind in society: The development of higher psychological processes*. Cambridge, MA: Harvard University Press.

Yin, R. K. (2008). *Case study research: Design and methods*. Newbury Park: Sage.

The materiality of discourse: relational positioning in a fresh water controversy

Theresa Castor ⓘ

ABSTRACT

This project adds to current theorising in organisational communication on the interconnection between discourse and materiality through the refinement of a relational ontology perspective. The central proposition of this project is that in a relational ontology perspective, associations are *performed* such that relationships and thereby ontologies are communicatively negotiated. To illustrate the arguments of the project, a fresh water management controversy is examined by using public hearing and field research data. The case study illustrates how the materiality of discourse functions to position freshwater, communities, and organisational texts in various and shifting ways to each other.

What is the relationship between materiality and organising? That is the central question that organisational communication scholars have addressed as discussions of the communicative constitution of organisations (CCO) have turned to issues of agency and materiality (Aakhus et al., 2011; Ashcraft, Kuhn, & Cooren, 2009). A key move in this discussion has been to reject the separation of the social and material in favour of a 'relational ontology' to account for how humans and nonhumans (a.k.a. the material) interact to co-construct the world (see Barad, 2014; Cooren, 2015; Latour, 2008; Pickering, 1993). Within organisational communication studies, scholars from the Montreal school in particular have provided communication-based descriptions of organisational constitution in relation to materiality (e.g. Taylor & Van Every, 1999). This project builds on that work to examine how a relational ontology is enacted in communication. The central proposition that is advanced in this work is that in a relational ontology perspective, associations are *performed* such that relationships and thereby ontologies are communicatively negotiated. This project is intended to illustrate this dynamic by analysing a freshwater management controversy that demonstrates how the materiality of discourse functions to position and reposition freshwater, communities, and organisational texts in various ways. In order to demonstrate these relational processes, a case study is described that addresses an environmental controversy related to freshwater resource management and the Great Lakes of North America.

DISCURSIVITY, RELATIONALITY AND MATERIALITY

There are several analytic benefits to this focus. First, the Great Lakes and freshwater have a physical materiality that is undeniable. However, the materiality of nature can be made to matter in different ways as the analysis in this paper will demonstrate. Second, these (Lake Michigan, fresh water) are 'natural' rather than 'technological' entities; prior discussions of organisation and materiality have tended to focus on technology or texts (e.g. Aakhus et al., 2011; Ashcraft, Kuhn, & Cooren, 2009; Cooren, 2005; Leonardi, Nardi, & Kallinikos, 2012) which are in many ways extensions of human agency.[1] Third, as Crutzen (2006) explained, the planet is now in the age of the 'Anthropocene' where human actions are not just subject to nature and environmental conditions, but instead, human actions can shape and permanently alter the environment. As such, this provides an imperative for understanding communicative actions in relation to nature.

In the following sections, an overview of relevant background literature is provided by describing key ideas of a relational ontology. Then, background information for the case study is described, and finally, an analysis is presented to empirically demonstrate the central claims of the project. The analysis will show how organisational relationships with particular forms of materiality can be made to shift during and across communication events. Thus, different 'things' are made to matter in the environmental dispute of interest. By analysing the processes involved with how things are made to matter in interactions, this project addresses the question posed by Cooren, Fairhurst, and Huet (2012), 'material to whom or what?' In doing so, the analysis illustrates governance processes at work through water resource management. In the water resource dispute analysed, there are various accountings that are provided of city processes and reasoning, of state agency actions, as well as explanations from representatives of organisations who are attempting to stop the actions of a city in its attempts to obtain a new water resource. The central proposition of this project is that in a relational ontology perspective, associations are *performed* such that relationships and thereby ontologies are communicatively negotiated.

Literature review

Discussions on the relationship between discourse and materiality in organisations have been significant in advancing theorising on the CCO (e.g. Aakhus et al., 2011; Ashcraft, Kuhn, & Cooren, 2009). There are currently many excellent reviews and summaries available on this topic (e.g. Ashcraft, Kuhn, & Cooren, 2009; Leonardi et al., 2012). This review focuses on key issues in the relationship between discourse, materiality, and the CCO perspective as these relate to the points advanced in this work. Ashcraft, Kuhn, and Cooren (2009) identified two 'strands' of theorising and research in organisational communication that explicitly address how organisations are communicatively constituted: a structurational approach, as influenced by Giddens (1984), and a text/conversation approach as advanced by scholars of the 'Montreal School' (Taylor & Van Every, 1999) and as influenced by Latour's (2005) actor–network theory. While drawing from a variety of sources, this project is closely aligned to the latter CCO approach of text-conversation in focusing on language-use in social interactions or what Fairhurst and Putnam (2004) referred to as a 'grounded-in-action' approach where organisations are formed through discourse and associations between humans and nonhumans. This review begins with an overview of key ideas related to the bifurcation of nature, 'matter', and materiality, and a relational ontology in order to situate this project.

Materiality and matter

Central to understanding a relational ontology is Alfred Whitehead's (1920) discussion of the bifurcation of nature. Whitehead defined nature as 'that which we observe in perception through the senses' (Chapter 1, para. 6). The Merriam-Webster dictionary simply defines nature as 'the physical world and everything in it (such as plants, animals, mountains, oceans, stars, etc.) that is not made by people' (online). Dryzek (2013) noted that 'nature' has a connotative meaning as that which is untouched by human activity – a stance that is increasingly difficult to maintain in light of the 'Anthropocene' era.[2] The concept of 'nature' is problematic to define, which is what Whitehead emphasised in his discussion of the 'bifurcation of nature'.

Whitehead described certain perspectives of nature as subscribing to a 'two worlds' view: the world of nature or matter and the world of human beliefs about the world (also see Latour, 2008). Whitehead, however, was opposed to such a view as it presumes that there is only a spurious relationship between the natural and subjective worlds. Whitehead instead argued that the subjective world does not arise out of nothing but is connected to what is called the natural world. In other words, the natural world is constituted through human sensemaking. As such, it is a false separation to assume that the natural and social worlds are separated. Rather, they are inter-connected.

Latour (2004) differentiated between the concepts of 'matters of concern' and 'matters of fact' by drawing on the distinction between different meanings of the word 'thing': 'A thing is, in one sense, an object out there and, in another sense, an *issue* very much *in* there, at any rate, a *gathering*' (p. 233). Key here is the notion of 'gathering', which in the etymological origins of 'thing' refers to a social, specifically, quasi-judiciary situation (Latour, 2004). It is through social gatherings that 'objects' become 'things' or where 'matters of fact' become 'matters of concern'. In focusing on how 'matters of concern' are based on social 'gatherings', Latour emphasised that matters of concern are constructed in the realm of the social.

Cooren (2015), like Latour, also took an etymological tact by examining the root of the word 'matter':

> 'the substance from which something is made' or the 'origin, source, mother' (etymonline. com) .... In other words, we want to know what substantiates-that is, what literally stands under-what is taking place. (Cooren et al., 2012, p. 4)

For Cooren, matter and materiality are part of a relational dynamic in which what is material to a situation is based on what is made to matter. Rather than view materiality and discourse as existing in 'two-worlds' [a 'bifurcated world' view as described by Whitehead; also see Stewart (1995)], Cooren (2006) argued that the world consists of a 'plenum' of agencies of which some are human and some are not (also see Murphy, 2004). This view of matter, materiality, and the world shifts attention away from equating the material to objects to considering materiality as action performed in relationship: in other words, a relational ontology based on performance (Pentland & Singh, 2012).

What is a relational ontology?

In a relational ontology perspective, humans and nonhumans, discourse and materiality, participate in interactively constituting the world (e.g. Barad, 2007, 2014; Cooren,

DISCURSIVITY, RELATIONALITY AND MATERIALITY

2015; Latour, 2008; Robichaud, 2006). Cooren (2015) built directly on Whitehead's writings against the bifurcation of the natural and the social in his proposal of a relational ontology. Cooren (2015) applied Whitehead's ideas to materiality and organising by stating that to separate out materiality from communicative processes of organising is also a false bifurcation in that ontologically speaking, they are not separate. Cooren (2015) proposed a relational ontology based on 'addition' and 'subtraction', in which things could gain or lose their 'materiality' in a given situation. In Cooren's use of the term, materiality can be considered a proxy for the idea of relevance where things are made to matter more or less based on discursive practices and based on features of the things. As an example, Cooren (2015) examined an art exhibit that featured a statue of two monkeys in an odd position with odd expressions on their faces, and a painting positioned nearby in which a nicely dressed woman's head was positioned such that it was turned away from the monkeys. As the tour guide led the group into the room where these art exhibits were posed, she made reference to the positions, expressions, and positioning of the exhibits, thus 'materialising' them. However, this materialisation could not have happened in just anyway but rather was dependent on physical properties of the exhibit.

Cooren proposed a relational ontology where things are made to matter more or less in communicating and organising processes. In this proposition, various types of entities are participants in organising processes. While they are made 'to speak' through the discursive practices of humans (see Cooren, 2010), the properties of the material objects (e.g. placement in a room, expressions on statues, attire of a painted figure, etc.) *are also communicative* and as such, 'speak' on their own. As Cooren (2015) explained on the connection between matter and materiality:

> The materiality of something or someone – whatever it, he, or she is – always has something to do with its, his, or her state of being material (i.e. what materiality means) and being material means that this being is itself made of matter... (p. 5)

In other words, when people make interpretations, they do so in a way that is attuned to specific material features such that those features are made relevant or make a difference in how meaning is developed. These points are not meant to imply that the material determines interpretation but rather, that one must be socially accountable and rhetorically responsive to the given circumstances (see Shotter, 1984, 1993). A relational ontology entails being rhetorically responsive with materiality.

Drawing generally from a pragmatic perspective in conceptualising materiality, Pentland and Singh (2012) argued for a focus on 'action' rather than actants. Their reasoning is that it is not the inherent properties of materials that make them matter in a given situation, but rather, how those are involved in action. As an example, Pentland and Singh discuss a passcode or passkey. On its own, it may or may not matter (be material in a given circumstance), but if it is stolen and used, the passkey is made to matter. Thus, Pentland and Singh reversed figure and ground in how materiality is conceptualised by focusing on actions and consequences rather than on inherent properties of material items. Cooren (2010), drawing from Pomerantz and Fehr (1997), argued that actions are central. Similarly, Sidnell and Enfield (2014) defined 'action' as an 'emergent product' (p. 424).

DISCURSIVITY, RELATIONALITY AND MATERIALITY

Czarniawska's (2013) distinction between net and network is instructive here:

> Why a net rather than a network? The difference between action net and network lies not in space but in time. Network assumes the existence of actors, who forge connections. Action net reverts this assumption, suggesting that connections between and among actions, when stabilized, are used to construct the identities of actors. One becomes a publisher when one starts to publish books or journals, which means that connections have already been made with such actions as writing and printing. (p. 14)

A relational ontology proposes that the nature of an entity cannot be known separate from its relationships with others, with relationships being enacted through performance and actions (Barad, 2007; also see; Marsen, 2014). In making connections between entities, Latour's (2005) actor-network theory uses the terminology of 'associations' and 'translations'. However, *how* connections or relationships are made and performed vary and are related to the *materiality of discursive practices*.

A relational ontology emphasises the nature of entities (both human and material) as intertwined with how these various beings interact. However, relationships are not equivalent in how they are performed and what they mean. If we are to take 'performance' seriously as a description of action, relational enactment, or the formation of action nets, then we must take the materiality of discourse seriously by examining how particular discursive practices shape those relationships. To illustrate this point, a case study of a dispute regarding freshwater resource management will be analysed. The details of the case are presented in the following section before the specific research questions of the project are described.

Context: the Great Lakes of North America and the Compact

The Great Lakes of North America are the largest body of surface freshwater in the world, consisting of five lakes or inland freshwater seas that are surrounded by eight states of the United States and two Canadian provinces. In addition to their function as a natural resource that provides freshwater to the millions of residents that surround the Great Lakes, the Great Lakes are an economic driver for the region by facilitating commerce, transportation, tourism, and fishing as sport and food source.

As recent droughts have highlighted, freshwater is an important resource. However, only 1% of the waters of the Great Lakes waters are renewed each year through rainfall. As Annin (2009) has pointed out in his discussion of the Aral sea and its depletion through water diversions, diligent care must be taken in managing freshwater systems to ensure their sustainability into the future. The Great Lakes are managed through international agreements between Canada and the United States and through the International Joint Commission. Within the United States, the diversion or removal of water from the Great Lakes is addressed in federal law through the interstate agreement called the Great Lakes-St. Lawrence River Basin Water Resources Compact, also known as the Great Lakes Compact or Compact, which was approved in 2008 by the US Congress and President.

The Compact prohibits the diversion of water from the Great Lakes. However, there is an exemption clause for 'straddling communities' or communities in counties which are at the boundary of the Great Lakes basin. In 2011, the City of Waukesha, located in

DISCURSIVITY, RELATIONALITY AND MATERIALITY

Southeast Wisconsin, initiated the process of submitting an application to divert water from Lake Michigan under the terms of the Compact. The expressed rationale for their application is that their current water sources (underground aquifers) are contaminated with radium and the radium levels have reached such a high that Waukesha is under federal court order to reduce the radium-levels in its water to residents. Waukesha's solution is to divert and use water from Lake Michigan.

The City of Waukesha is located 15 mi from Lake Michigan; the city lies completely outside of the Great Lakes basin but is in the county of Waukesha which is partly within the basin. As such, Waukesha is considered a straddling community and therefore eligible to request an exception to the Compact's ban on Great Lakes water diversion. Under the terms of the Compact, there are nine conditions that must be met for Waukesha's application to be approved:

(1) 'the water is used solely for public water supply purposes';
(2) there is currently not 'an adequate supply of potable water';
(3) the request meets the 'exception standard' outlined in Wisconsin States Statutes;
(4) 'the proposal maximizes the amount of water that originated in the basin that is returned to the basin and minimizes the amount of water that originated outside of the basin that is returned to the basin';
(5) 'there is no reasonable water supply alternative ...' for the community;
(6) the diversion will not 'endanger the integrity of the Great Lakes basin ecosystem';
(7) 'the proposal is consistent with an approved water supply service area plan under section 281.348 of the Wisconsin Statutes that covers the public water supply system';
(8) 'the proposal is reviewed by the *regional body* [emphasis in original] (the Governors of the eight Great Lakes States and the premiers of Ontario and Quebec, Canada)'; and
(9) 'the proposal is approved by the Great Lakes-St. Lawrence River Basin Water Resources Council (consisting of the eight Great Lakes States) with no disapproving votes' ('Background', Wisconsin Department of Natural Resources, 2016).

Waukesha's application calls for purchasing water from the lake shore city of Oak Creek, then transporting it through a 15-mi pipe to a water treatment plant in Waukesha for distribution and use in the 'water supply service area' of Waukesha, treated in a water treatment plant, shipped back through a pipeline, and then discharged into the Root River to be returned to Lake Michigan south of Oak Creek, through the city of Racine.

Waukesha's request is controversial for several reasons with a key concern that being the precedent it could set for future water diversion requests. As such, the application and its process of review have been closely monitored by various environmental special interest groups. Moreover, because Lake Michigan is part of the Great Lakes basin, Waukesha's application has been undergoing regional and international scrutiny (including public hearings, letters to the editor, and editorials) in the seven other Great Lakes states and two Canadian provinces within the Great Lakes Basin.

DISCURSIVITY, RELATIONALITY AND MATERIALITY

Waukesha's water diversion request will be analysed as a case study for this project. In connecting this case to organisational communication, Cooren's (2001) analysis of the Great Whale River controversy is of relevance here. Cooren analysed the Great Whale River controversy by focusing on the development of coalitions among different organisations through the formation and association of interests. A key concept in these developments is that of 'translation' or of how various concerns are analytically translated to connect the interests of different parties on specific interests. It is in this process that a coalition among organisations is formed. There are several organisational parties involved in this water governance issue that includes the city of Waukesha, the state of Wisconsin (WI) and specifically, the WI Department of Natural Resources, several environmental special interest groups, the other Great Lakes US state governments and Canadian provinces, and the US federal government. However, rather than focus on associations between coalitions, this project examines how materiality is foregrounded in several ways that include Lake Michigan, water basin boundary lines, rivers, aquifers, and radium contamination. In doing so, I examine the role of the materiality of discourse in constituting matters of concern.

Analysis

Data gathering

Data for this project consist of field research from attending public hearings related to the Waukesha diversion request in August 2015 and February 2016, and documents and texts made available through the government agency websites[3] created to provide the public with information about the diversion application. Materials made available on the website include transcripts of the public meetings, written public comments, the environmental impact statement, a technical report, and other background documents on the diversion request including city memos and letters. In August 2015, there were three public hearings held on the diversion request in three cities located in southeast Wisconsin (Milwaukee, Racine, Waukesha) that the researcher attended. In February 2015, in Waukesha, there was another public briefing on the application, site tour, meeting of the regional decision-making body for the application, and another public hearing that the researcher attended. The data for the project include discursive data in the form of hearing transcripts, public comments, and organisational texts, in addition to field research data from the author's observations of public briefings, public hearings, and the site tour.

The primary focus of this analysis is on the 3 August 2015, public hearings. The hearings occurred over a 2-day period with the first occurring in Waukesha on a Tuesday evening, the second on the following day in the afternoon in the city of Milwaukee (located in between Waukesha and Lake Michigan and on the shore of Lake Michigan), and the third occurred later on the second day in the evening in the city of Racine (located on the shore of Lake Michigan and where the river where the treated wastewater would be discharged and returned to Lake Michigan). Each public hearing began with a 20–30-min briefing from a Wisconsin Department of Natural Resources representative on the Waukesha application followed by an audience question period. Each public hearing lasted between 2 and 3 h, had approximately 100–200 people in attendance for each, and consisted of approximately 40–60 presenters per hearing. Each presenter had 2–3 min to express their views.

The hearing transcripts are an ideal data source to get these issues as the public hearings also feature conflicting positions as representatives of different groups and individuals express contradictory opinions in favour of or against the diversion request. The public hearings provided several examples of divergent ways for constructing relationships between different entities. In this process, some entities, relationships, and conditions are made to matter more or less.

Method of analysis

The data were analysed using discourse analytic procedures guided by a discursive constructionist approach (Buttny, 2004).[4] This approach was selected as it is attuned to the details of language-use in social interactions. Moreover, a discursive constructionist approach highlights how individuals discursively 'position' themselves within the narrative of events. Buttny outlined the following steps of analysis as a way of developing analytic claims from discursive data:

(1) Describe the identifying characteristics or qualities of the data.
(2) Examine the data as part of an interactional sequence.
(3) Identify what the phenomenon makes relevant.
(4) Identify how participants orient to the phenomenon of study.
(5) Analyse how the 'phenomenon is conjointly produced by participants' (p. 11).
(6) Identify how the phenomenon may fit within a larger discursive structure.
(7) 'Consider the rhetorical aspects of participants' versions of what happened' (p. 12).
(8) 'Examine how participants position themselves, or are positioned by others, in the course of talk-in-interaction' (p. 12).

In this analysis, I do not explicitly apply all of the above steps which presume an inductive start to the data analysis. Step one was addressed in the preceding section in describing the data. Because this analysis began with the explicit purpose of identifying the materiality of nature in the water dispute, steps two and three are not emphasised. Steps four, five, seven, and eight are addressed in the following analysis. Step six regarding the larger discursive structuring of the communication events as public hearing meetings is not a focus of this project. In addition to my individual reading of the transcripts, I utilised AntConc, a software program for corpus text analysis and concordancing (Anthony, 2014).[5] AntConc was used as a way to check broader trends in the data regarding term usage and to enable identification of the contextual usages of terms across several instances.

Given the purpose of this project on explicating how aspects of the natural environment are made to matter in the public hearing, I identified references to Lake Michigan and water in the discussions by manually reading through the transcripts and by using AntConc to systematically identify those instances. This step also involved developing interpretive inferences on the different meanings for speakers of Lake Michigan and freshwater. Researcher interpretations were developed by examining the utterance-

DISCURSIVITY, RELATIONALITY AND MATERIALITY

context of their uses in the public hearing transcripts. By utterance-context, I refer to an individual's speaking turn of approximately 2–3 min. This context provided insight into how participants oriented to Lake Michigan and water and positioned themselves as well as Lake Michigan and fresh water within the dispute. Given the interpretive focus of the analysis, excerpts from the transcripts are displayed to provide the reader with context for understanding researcher interpretations.

The analysis that follows describes the dispute in three sections focusing first on freshwater and its associations as both problem and solution, section two addresses Lake Michigan as a 'matter of concern' that is acted upon, and section three describes the role of an organisational text, the Great Lakes Compact, as a mediator. These themes were identified because of their relevance in displaying different ways that speakers oriented to the lake and their repetition across speakers.

The materiality of freshwater and radium

Based on the Waukesha diversion application narrative, there are several key figures in this situation that centre on freshwater in various forms and settings:

> The application asserts that Waukesha needs a new source of water to address water quantity and quality concerns. Waukesha currently obtains its public water supply primarily from groundwater wells in the deep aquifer. Water levels in the deep aquifer are hundreds of feet lower than they were predevelopment. Groundwater pumped from the deep aquifer contains high levels of radium, a carcinogen. The public supply is supplemented by water from the shallow aquifer. Waukesha seeks an exception from the prohibition of diversions under the Great Lakes-St. Lawrence River Basin Water Resources Compact. (Wisconsin Department of Natural Resources)

Waukesha's water problem, and thus the exigency claimed to stimulate the diversion request, is the level of radium in its water (radium was mentioned 45 times across the public hearings). The radium has reached a level such that, by federal standards, it has been deemed unsafe and Waukesha is under a federal court order to provide radium-free water to its residents by 2018.[6]

According to Waukesha representatives, radium is made to matter, as are the federal standards and the federal court order. In other words, radium *in conjunction with* the federal court order can be said to be a hybrid agent that is compelling action on the part of Waukesha to request to divert water from Lake Michigan. Based on this narrative, the primary cause for Waukesha's action is the high radium level of their current water supply, prompting the need for safe drinking water. However, there are several contributors to the problem that are emphasised in the application overview as well as on the websites of the city of Waukesha and the Wisconsin Department of Natural Resources regarding the Waukesha water problem. Specifically, Waukesha's current water supply is based on groundwater from deep and shallow aquifers. The deep water aquifer is formed by a thick layer of shale rock and it is this property of the aquifer that is contributing to the developing radium problem (Waukesha Water Utility, n.d.).

To use the language of actor-network theory, radium can be said to be a non-human agent or actant that is part of a hybrid or collective of associations (see Callon & Law, 1995). The physical materiality of radium as a human carcinogen is made to matter. However, it operates in association as part of a chain of agencies that include shale

DISCURSIVITY, RELATIONALITY AND MATERIALITY

rocks, a deep aquifer, scientific analyses, and federal standards through a social gathering in which radium has become a 'matter of concern'. In the water diversion application narrative, radium, by virtue of being a chemical agent, is cast more generally as an agent. Meaning, radium has transformed Waukesha's water source into an unsafe one and therefore, Waukesha needs a new water source. Waukesha has designated that that new source should be water from Lake Michigan. However, in order for Waukesha to obtain water from Lake Michigan, another organisational text is involved – the Great Lakes Compact – which delineates the conditions and processes that Waukesha must follow to legitimately obtain Lake Michigan water.

However, while no speakers disagreed with the claims of the presence of radium or the need for safe water, *how* this was related to particular follow-up actions was disputed by various speakers. The two excerpts below illustrate the contrasting views on radium and *how* radium to be made relevant for Waukesha's water problems and proposed solutions:

Excerpt 1:
Lake Michigan water is the only viable option for a safe, long-term water supply that will address the radium issue and the needs of the Waukesha Water Service area now and for generations to come.

Excerpt 2:
...they treat, they treat the water for radium. It's a simple concept that was actually a conversation before the Compact was even negotiated.

Both excerpts take the presence of radium and its danger to human safety as given. Where they diverge is in the appropriate way to address the radium problem with the first excerpt emphasising Lake Michigan water as the only viable solution and the second excerpt emphasising the alternative of treating the current water supply to remove the radium. In other words, how radium is *positioned* varied across speakers. In some instances, Waukesha was positioned as the active or potentially active agent that *could* have and could still address the radium problem. However, some speakers blamed Waukesha for not taking action sooner when the federal court and agencies were pointing out the radium problem. Other speakers blamed Waukesha for inadequate actions in investigating *solutions* to their problem and honing in on the Lake Michigan solution without adequate investigation of alternatives.

The involvement of radium in this case is not just an issue of its presence, but of how it is related in the 'activity net' (Czarniawska, 2013) of this controversy. Those who support Waukesha's water diversion application frame radium as the causal agent that is prompting Waukesha's actions to obtain a safe water supply. Those who are against the water diversion accept the presence of radium but reference it as something to be acted upon and emphasise the agency of Waukesha as a city and its leaders in choosing how to respond.

DISCURSIVITY, RELATIONALITY AND MATERIALITY

Lake Michigan as a matter of concern

Lake Michigan is a central figure in this discussion as Waukesha is proposing to withdraw water from Lake Michigan. In some ways, Lake Michigan follows Latour's definition of agent as something which makes a difference. From the perspective of the Waukesha application narrative, Lake Michigan makes or can make a difference as a source of fresh water. However, in terms of how it is positioned in the dispute, it is something to be acted upon by groups who favour *and* by groups who are against the diversion application.

Across the three public hearings, 'lake' was referenced 169 times (66 times in Waukesha, 59 times in Milwaukee, and 44 times in Racine). A majority of the time when Lake Michigan is mentioned, it is as something that is acted upon by having something that can be taken *from* Lake Michigan or done *to* Lake Michigan:

> Excerpt 3:
> I'm supportive of the current plan. It makes sense to me. I'm just Joe Blow citizen, but it makes sense. Take water **from** Lake Michigan, use it, clean it, and return it **to** Lake Michigan. It makes sense and I ask you to continue to support this process. (Waukesha Public Hearing)

> Excerpt 4:
> And I think that the, you know, the return of the water **to** Lake Michigan is, you know, if it's good enough to go down the Fox River, it's good enough to go down the other river, too. (Waukesha Public Hearing)

> Excerpt 5:
> We cannot allow Waukesha **to take** water out of Lake Michigan. (Milwaukee Public Hearing)

> Excerpt 6:
> I think it's important to note that the Department of Natural Resources and the compact requires us to return the water **to** Lake Michigan…. (Racine Public Hearing)

The materiality of Lake Michigan is significant as a freshwater resource that can make a difference in the water needs of Waukesha. However, there are different types of associations or 'relationships' with Lake Michigan that have been discursively built up by different parties during the public hearings. For the City of Waukesha, Lake Michigan is a potential source of freshwater. However, it is a resource whose relationship with Waukesha is mediated by the Great Lakes Compact and its criteria for water withdrawals. It is *also* a relationship that is mediated by physical distance (15 mi of land between Waukesha and Lake Michigan), and moreover, a relationship that is mediated by a water basin line that separates the city of Waukesha literally from Great Lakes water. The proposed pipeline is an attempt by Waukesha to develop a material association with Great Lakes water.

In addition to being a resource to be obtained, Lake Michigan or Great Lakes fresh water is a 'matter of concern' to be protected. The discourse of protection and sustainability however is utilised by individuals who support the diversion *and* by individuals who oppose the diversion. As stated by the Mayor of Waukesha in support of the water diversion application:

Excerpt 7:

In summary, the DNR's extensive analysis got it right, Lake Michigan is the only reasonable water supply for Waukesha. Let's move forward so Waukesha can have a sustainable and healthy water supply, and let's prove that the Compact does and will protect the Great Lakes.

In the Mayor's comments, he positions Lake Michigan water as a resource to be used by Waukesha (as 'water supply' and 'sustainable and healthy water supply'). The Mayor also associates Waukesha's water diversion application as a means of *protecting* the Great Lakes. This is done through a chain of associations that can be summarised as follows: Waukesha's application meets the criteria of the Compact; this association of meeting criteria has been confirmed through the DNR analysis; the Compact protects the Great Lakes; therefore, Waukesha's application protects the Great Lakes.

The compact as mediator and matter of concern

A key figure in this controversy is Lake Michigan as freshwater resource and as member of the Great Lakes Basin. In order for Waukesha to 'associate' with Lake Michigan, it must do so through the terms of the Compact. As explained by the attorney functioning as the public hearing officer:

Excerpt 8:

As it has been mentioned already tonight, under the Great Lakes/St. Lawrence River Basin Water Resources Compact, the City of Waukesha is a community within a straddling county, which means that the City's boundaries are in a county that lies partly within the Great Lakes Basin and partly outside the basin. Therefore, the City of Waukesha must apply to the Department of Natural Resources in order to divert Lake Michigan water to the city.

Waukesha's next action, to obtain water from Lake Michigan, is mediated through the Compact. The attempt to obtain water from Lake Michigan is mediated by the Compact in which the Compact provides criteria such that if Waukesha successfully addresses all of the criteria, it may withdraw Lake Michigan water. The Compact is both blocker and helper (see Marsen, 2014).

Opponents opposed the diversion by speaking on behalf of the Great Lakes to protect the Great Lakes *and* on behalf of the Compact to protect the Compact which also protects the Great Lakes. For example, as one resident explained during the Waukesha Public hearing:

Excerpt 9:
The Great Lakes is Pandora's Box. If we don't protect the Great Lakes from everybody's need, from Kenosha, to going 30 miles from Chicago to Des Plaines, to doing a diversion from Fond du Lac to Green Bay, it's all over.

The above comments implicitly highlight one of the concerns of opponents relating to the precedent-setting potential of Waukesha's diversion application. As described by a resident of the city of Racine:

Excerpt 10:
In allowing an outlying community to draw upon Lake Michigan's water, it sets an extremely dangerous precedent for all other communities who want to follow suit.

The precedent however is not solely about the action of withdrawing water from Lake Michigan. It is also about the Great Lakes Compact and how such applications are to be handled by the Compact. As one speaker who was a member of a non-profit special interest group explained during the Waukesha public hearing:

Excerpt 11:
The outcome of this diversion application will set a precedent for future diversion applicants and basically determine the threshold for conditions that warrant a Great Lakes diversion.

Thus, the matter of concern in this water dispute is not just about Lake Michigan, the Great Lakes, and freshwater, it is also about the Compact as protector of the aforementioned entities with protection of the Compact standing for protection of the Great Lakes.

Discussion

Latour's (2008) points on the 'builtup' nature of matter are illustrated through the data and analysis for this project. The case study demonstrated how things such as radium, fresh water, and a Great Lake are not 'natural' per se but rather are mediated through institutions and, as such, are 'matters of concern' in which their materiality is ontologically tied to social and political 'gatherings'. Within the water dispute case study examined here, there are several key figures that include radium, water from a Great Lake, a city, and federal and state legislation. The controversy illustrates how the roles of the figures were matters of dispute as one central problem (e.g. radium contamination) receded to the background with other problems (e.g. water diversions) moving to the foreground. In focusing on fresh water from the Great Lakes, the analysis illustrated how relationships in an action net are performed as Lake Michigan shifted from potential agent as a water supply for Waukesha to something that is acted upon by other agents to be preserved and protected. These agents included both human spokespeople, speaking on behalf of their organisations and specific interest groups to the

Great Lakes, and organisational texts such as the Great Lakes Compact and state statutes and other documents produced by state and city 'agencies.'

The role of the Compact is especially significant as the Compact became a significant mediator in the conflict in regulating how Waukesha could associate with Lake Michigan and in 'protecting' Lake Michigan and the Great Lakes. However, the Compact also assumed a role in which it needed to be 'protected' itself. In other words, the controversy consisted of a 'plenum of agencies' (Cooren, 2006) or 'action net' (Czarniawska, 2013) with shifting relationships and thus, shifting ontologies. Of relevance here is Barad's (2007) philosophical analysis of quantum physics. In describing a relativist perspective of physics (stemming from the work of physicist Niels Bohr), Barad emphasised that for Bohr, the key issue in a relativist perspective is one of ontologies rather than epistemology. In other words, when examining relationship, we are not examining how independent, autonomous objects connect to each other (an epistemological approach), but rather, the nature of the object is interdependent with how it is positioned in relation to others (an ontological approach). While Lake Michigan and its fresh water have a particular materiality, *how* that materiality is made to matter is a matter of discursive performance.

Conclusion

The purpose of this project was to contribute to the understanding of a relational ontology by illustrating how relationships are performed in discursive actions. In a relational ontology, the nature of various entities such as persons, groups, organisational texts, environmental resources, etc. exists in relation to each other. How these relationships are formed is based on the materiality of discourse in which discursive practices position and relate various entities to each other. This key idea was illustrated through the analysis of discursive and field research data related to a water dispute. Within this dispute, the meaning of water and its role as 'agent' was discursively negotiated during the dispute such that fresh water became an object to be acted upon. The proposed actions to Lake Michigan were mediated through organisational texts that included the federally approved Compact, state agencies, scientific reports, and state legislation.

Barad (2014) argued that the primary semantic units are not 'words' but material discursive practices through which boundaries are constituted. This dynamism is agency. Agency is not an attribute but the ongoing reconfigurings of the world (p. 818).

This project emphasised the 'dynamics' of how various agencies in organisational actions shift and are 'reconfigured'.

This special issue has highlighted relational approaches to organising and materiality. The purpose of this work was to contribute to the understanding of a relational ontology in how inter-organisational actions and an environmental dispute are negotiated. This project illustrated how 'reconfigurings', as described by Barad (2014), occur in performance as the ontologies of various entities were intertwined with their relationships to each other in a dynamic where discourse and materiality are not separated but rather are co-constituting.

This analysis addressed several key issues in the development of constitutive perspectives of organising and materiality by building on the ideas of a relational ontology.

DISCURSIVITY, RELATIONALITY AND MATERIALITY

First, the key state of a 'material' object (e.g. radium, freshwater, a lake) is not just about whether it is present or not. Rather, the nature of its materiality is dependent on its role in particular actions, whether that is as a causal agent or passive actor to be acted upon. Second, these actions are 'built up' in discourse as speakers may discuss doing something *to* something or describe material objects that leave 'no other choice' for human actors. The water controversy surrounding the Lake Michigan diversion was used as the case study for this project illustrated these dynamics. On 21 June 2016, at a meeting that took place in Chicago, the Compact Council voted to approve Waukesha's diversion request. The analysis in this project involved examining a controversy as it was occurring. Now that an official decision has been made, future research issues to explore examine looking back to assess which relational framings seemed to make a difference in the organisational decision-making process.

Notes

1. There are some exceptions such as Vásquez and Cooren's (2013) work on space-time in the Chilean space programme and Cooren's (2001) study of a Canadian river controversy.
2. Dryzek also noted that the environment as a concept did not exist until the 1960s.
3. See http://www.waukeshadiversion.org/ and http://dnr.wi.gov/topic/wateruse/waukeshadi versionapp.html.
4. There are many different social constructionist approaches, some of which are and some are not compatible with a recognition of how the materiality of the world participates in the social construction of the world (see Burr, 1998).
5. As a corpus linguistic analysis tool, AntConc is able to do frequency counts of specific words that occur with a given text or texts and to display these in the 'context' by showing the half dozen or so words that precede or follow as well as link back to the specific area of the text where specific terms occurred. AntConc is able to do additional forms of linguistic analysis, but for this project, its usage was limited to frequency and word context identification.
6. Currently, the water that the Waukesha Water Utility provides to its customers is safe (Waukesha Water Utility, 2014). However, there is still radium in the water and a key issue in the dispute involves the anticipation of and attempt to prevent a potential, future problem.

Disclosure statement

No potential conflict of interest was reported by the author.

ORCID

Theresa Castor http://orcid.org/0000-0002-8951-3974

References

Aakhus, M., Ballard, D., Flanagin, A. J., Kuhn, T., Leonardi, P., & Mease, J. (2011). Communication and materiality: A conversation from the CM cafe. *Communication Monographs, 78*(4), 557–569. doi:10.1080/03637751.2011.618358

Anthony, L. (2014). *AntConc (Version 3.4.3) [Computer Software]*. Tokyo, Japan: Waseda University. Retrieved from http://www.laurenceanthony.net/

Annin, P. (2009). *The Great Lakes water wars*. Washington, DC: Island Press.

Ashcraft, K. L., Kuhn, T. R., & Cooren, F. (2009). Constitutional amendments: "Materializing" organizational communication. *The Academy of Management Annals, 3*(1), 1–64. doi:10.1080/19416520903047186

Barad, K. (2007). *Meeting the Universe Halfway: Quantum physics and the entanglement of matter and meaning*. Durham, NC: Duke University.

Barad, K. (2014). Posthumanist performativity: Toward an understanding of how matter comes to matter. *Signs: Journal of Women in Culture and Society, 28*(3), 801–831. doi:10.1086/345321

Burr, V. (1998). Overview: Realism, relativism, social constructionism and discourse. In I. Parker (Ed.), *Social constructionism, discourse and realism* (pp. 13–25). London: Sage.

Buttny, R. (2004). *Talking problems: Studies of discursive construction*. Albany, NY: State University of New York.

Callon, M., & Law, J. (1995). Agency and the hybrid collectif. *South Atlantic Quarterly, 94*(2), 481–507.

Cooren, F. (2001). Translation and articulation in the organization of coalitions: The Great Whale river case. *Communication Theory, 11*(2), 178–200. doi:10.1111/j.1468-2885.2001.tb00238.x

Cooren, F. (2005). Arguments for a plurified view of the social world: Spacing and timing as hybrid achievements. *Time & Society, 14*(2–3), 265–282. doi:10.1177/0961463X05055138

Cooren, F. (2006). The organizational world as a plenum of agencies. In F. Cooren, J. R. Taylor, & E. J. Van Every (Eds.), *Communication as organizing: Empirical and theoretical explorations in the dynamic of text and conversation* (pp. 81–100). Mahwah, N.J.: Lawrence Erlbaum Associates.

Cooren, F. (2010). *Action and agency in dialogue: Passion, incarnation and ventriloquism*. Amsterdam: John Benjamins.

Cooren, F. (2015). In medias res: Communication, existence, and materiality. *Communication Research and Practice, 1*(4), 1–15. doi:10.1080/22041451.2015.1110075

Cooren, F., Fairhurst, G. T., & Huet, R. (2012). Why matter always matters in (organizational) communication. In P. M. Leonardi, B. A. Nardi, & J. Kallinikos (Eds.), *Materiality and organizing: Social interaction in a technological world* (pp. 296–314). Oxford: Oxford University Press.

Crutzen, P. J. (2006). The "anthropocene". In E. Ehlers & T. Krafft (Eds.), *Earth system science in the anthropocene* (pp. 13–18). Berlin: Springer.

Czarniawska, B. (2013). Organizations as obstacles to organizing. In D. Robichaud & F. Cooren (Eds.), *Organization and organizing: Materiality, agency, and discourse* (pp. 3–22). New York: Routledge.

Dryzek, J. S. (2013). *The politics of the earth: Environmental discourses*. Oxford: Oxford University Press.

Fairhurst, G. T., & Putnam, L. L. (2004). Organizations as discursive constructions. *Communication Theory, 14*(1), 5–26. doi:10.1111/j.1468-2885.2004.tb00301.x

Giddens, A. (1984). *The constitution of society: Outline of the theory of structuration*. Berkeley: University of California.

Latour, B. (2004). Why has critique run out of steam? From matters of fact to matters of concern. *Critical Inquiry, 30*(2), 225–248. doi:10.1086/421123

Latour, B. (2005). *Reassembling the social: An introduction to actor-network-theory*. Oxford: Oxford University Press.

Latour, B. (2008). *What is the style of matters of concern?: Two lectures in empirical philosophy*. Assen: Koninklijke Van Gorcum.

Leonardi, P. M., Nardi, B. A., & Kallinikos, J. (Eds.). (2012). *Materiality and organizing: Social interaction in a technological world*. Oxford: Oxford University Press.

Marsen, S. (2014). "Lock the doors": Toward a narrative–semiotic approach to organizational crisis. *Journal of Business & Technical Communication, 28*(3), 301–326. doi:10.1177/1050651914524781

Murphy, R. (2004). Disaster or sustainability: The dance of human agents with nature's actants. *Canadian Review of Sociology & Anthropology, 41*(3), 249–266. doi:10.1111/j.1755-618X.2004.tb00778.x

Pentland, B. T., & Singh, H. (2012). Materiality: What are the consequences? In P. M. Leonardi, B. A. Nardi, & J. Kallinikos (Eds.), *Materiality and organizing: Social interaction in a technological world* (pp. 287–295). Oxford: Oxford University Press.

Pickering, A. (1993). The mangle of practice: Agency and emergence in the sociology of science. *American Journal of Sociology, 99*(3), 559–589. doi:10.1086/230316

Pomerantz, A., & Fehr, B. J. (1997). Conversation analysis: An approach to the study of social action as sense making practices. In T. A. Van Dijk (Ed.), *Discourse as social interaction* (Vol. 2). (pp. 64–91). London: Sage.

Robichaud, D. (2006). Steps toward a relational view of agency. In F. Cooren, J. R. Taylor, & E. J. Van Every (Eds.), *Communication as organizing: Practical approaches to research into the dynamic of text and conversation* (pp. 101–114). Mahwah, NJ: Lawrence Erlbaum.

Shotter, J. (1984). *Social accountability and selfhood*. Oxford: Basil Blackwell.

Shotter, J. (1993). *Conversational realities: Constructing life through language*. London: Sage.

Sidnell, J., & Enfield, N. J. (2014). The ontology of action, in interaction. In N. J. Enfield, P. Kockelman, & J. Sidnell (Eds.), *The Cambridge handbook of linguistic anthropology* (pp. 423–446). Cambridge: Cambridge University Press.

Stewart, J. (1995). *Language as articulate contact: Toward a post-semiotic philosophy of communication*. Albany, NY: State University of New York.

Taylor, J. R., & Van Every, E. J. (1999). *The emergent organization: Communication as its site and surface*. Mahwah, NJ: Routledge.

Vásquez, C., & Cooren, F. (2013). Spacing practices: The communicative configuration of organizing through space-time. *Communication Theory, 23*(1), 25–47. doi:10.1111/comt.12003

Waukesha Water Utility. (2014). Radium public notice. Retrieved March.25, 2016, from http://www.waukesha-water.com/downloads/PublicRadiumNotice2014.pdf

Waukesha Water Utility. (n.d.). Frequently asked questions: Waukesha's water supply is unsustainable and does not meet drinking water standards. Retrieved March 25, 2016, from http://www.waukesha-water.com/faqH4.html

Whitehead, A. N. (1920). *The concept of nature: Tarner lectures delivered in Trinity College, November, 1919*. Cambridge: Cambridge University Press.

Wisconsin Department of Natural Resources. (2016). Background. Retrieved March 16, 2016, from http://dnr.wi.gov/topic/WaterUse/waukesha/background.html

A spatial grammar of organising: studying the communicative constitution of organisational spaces

Consuelo Vásquez (iD)

ABSTRACT

This article contributes to the growing body of literature on organisational spaces by taking a communication-centred approach to organising that stresses a performative view of communication as constitutive of organisation. Based on this constitutive premise, I propose to study the 'spatial grammar of organising', which implies (a) describing the spatial imaginary of an organisation: the spatial images that are voiced and embodied, and their effects on the production of organisational spaces; and (b) attending to the processes through which these organisational spaces are performed and to their implications. Applying these analytical steps in the study of an outreach organisation's development strategy, the article shows that the constitution of organisational spaces is a communicative process of boundary setting in which actors of various ontologies are related. Hence, the spatial imaginary of an organisation is not abstract and neutral: it has concrete organisational and political effects in defining the organisation's space of action.

'Cover the whole country', 'Spread nation-wide', 'Create a multiplication effect', 'Go farther and farther', 'Be in every corner of the country', 'Conquer Chile in the name of science and technology'; these are some of the expressions commonly used by ConCiencia,[1] a Chilean outreach organisation whose mission is to promote science and technology 'all over the country'. These expressions convey a spatial definition of what this organisation does (or should do) and consequently of what it is (or should be). They are part of what I propose to call a *spatial imaginary*, which emerges through the collective experience of space and the way people make sense of it when engaging in processes of organising. However – and this will be a main point in my argument – a spatial imaginary is not an abstract and neutral sensemaking device for organising (see Weick, 1995). To fully account for it, one needs to study its different embodiments/ materialisations (artefacts, discourses, buildings, decision, locations, and images), the relation between them, and, more importantly, the concrete effects of these relations; what Amin, Massey, and Thrift (2003) call a 'grammar of relations'.

Responding to the call to bring space back into organisation studies (see Hernes, 2004; Kornberger & Clegg, 2004), this article contributes to the growing body of literature on organisational spaces (e.g. Taylor & Spicer, 2007; Van Marrewijk & Yanow, 2010) by taking a communication-centred approach to organising that stresses a performative/material view of communication as constitutive of organisation. In doing so, it avoids falling into the traps of the representational reasoning that has dominated current studies on organisational spaces (Beyes & Steyaert, 2012), which are (a) the blackboxing and masking of the processes through which organisational spaces are produced, (b) the disregard for other forms of agency (not only human) in the production of those spaces, and (c) the separation between the physical/material dimension of organisational spaces and their experience and understanding.

The communication-centred approach adopted in this study puts forth a relational ontology that draws attention to how the heterogeneous agencies through which organisational spaces are communicatively constituted/embodied/materialised operate. It does so by proposing a performative/material definition of communication as 'the means by which organizations are established, composed, designed, and sustained' (Cooren, Kuhn, Cornelissen, & Clark, 2011, p. 1150). Following this constitutive premise, the questions that drive this article are as follows: What kinds of organisational spaces are constituted/materialised/embodied through communication? What are the processes through which communication constitutes/materialises/embodies (these) organisational spaces, and what are their implications?

In order to answer these questions, this article proposes to study the 'spatial grammar of organising', which entails two analytical steps: First, describing the spatial imaginary of an organisation: the different spatial images that are voiced and embodied, and their effects on the production of organisational spaces. Second, attending to the processes through which these organisational spaces are performed and to their implications in constituting an organisation's space of action. As Bannerman et al. (2005; see also Vásquez & Cooren, 2013) have noted, the way we mobilise the notion of space – perhaps in ways we do not intend – has social, material, and political implications. Investigating the spatial grammar of organising adds significance to the study of organisational spaces because it unveils the links between how we talk about space and experience it, and how this experience shapes our meanings and actions.

The communication-centred approach to organisational spaces proposed in this article is grounded in ethnographic fieldwork I carried out at ConCiencia, which was mainly based on shadowing a science and technology outreach project. From the analysis of the empirical material constructed during this fieldwork, three dominant spatial images emerged: network, region, and trajectories. Each of these images presents a particular sociomaterial configuration that shows that the constitution/materialisation/embodiment of organisational spaces is a communicative process of boundary setting in which actors of various ontologies are related. The analysis also reveals that these configurations are not neutral; they have concrete organisational and political effects in defining ConCiencia's 'space of action'.

This article offers two main contributions to the literature on organisational spaces. First, as mentioned, the communication-centred approach developed herein avoids falling into the traps of representational reasoning that has influenced this literature. It does so by accounting for the interpretative, material, and political dimensions associated with the constitution of organisational spaces. The integration of these dimensions is made possible by the focus on the performative/material effects of a spatial imaginary, which is operationalised in the proposition to study the spatial grammar of organising. The article also pays attention to how the politics of geography are embedded in an organisation's spatial imaginary by showing that different images materialise different ways of 'occupying' a territory.

The second contribution is methodological. It shows the heuristic force of taking communication events as units of analysis for this kind of study. This focus brings forward an analytical coherence in the inquiry, which implies starting from and remaining within communication (Cooren, Taylor, & Van Every, 2006). It also allows the analysis to be grounded in the historical context of the event while seeing how it unfolds through time and space.

In the remainder of the paper, I will further elaborate on the proposition to study a spatial grammar of organising by further developing the shortcomings of the literature on organisational spaces. I will also present the key premises of the communication-centred approach on which this article relies, focusing primarily on the argument that communication constitutes/materialises/embodies organisational spaces. This leads to a presentation of the proposition for studying a spatial grammar of organising. The research context and methodology will then be presented, followed by a description and discussion of ConCiencia's spatial imaginary. I will conclude with the implications of thinking about space from a communication-centred approach for the study of organisation.

Bringing space back in

In the last decade, there has been an increasing interest in organisation studies in taking space as an analytical and/or empirical construct. While works related to organisational spaces have a long tradition (see e.g. Becker, Blanche, Everett, & Strauss, 1961; Mayo, 1933), they now figure more explicitly in current analyses of organisations and organisational practices (Van Marrewijk & Yanow, 2010). In their effort to systematise the fragmented contributions to this literature, Taylor and Spicer (2007) identified three different conceptions of space: space as distance, space as materialised power relations, and space as lived experience. While the first conception of space – usually associated with (post-)positivist research – has traditionally received more attention, it is mainly the two latter ones that have inspired academic development (Kornberger & Clegg, 2004).

These two conceptions of organisational space, associated respectively with the critical and phenomenological traditions, have addressed different topics, ranging from the aesthetics of space and building design (Gagliardi, 1990; Van Marrewijk, 2009), to the material elements of workspaces and physical settings (Becker, 1982; Hatch, 1990; Mills, 2002) to cultural and symbolic dimensions of space (Bauman, 1987; Doxater, 1990; Yanow, 1993). Other works have focused on spaces of control (Dale, 2005; Dale & Burrell, 2008; Hancock, 2006; Hernes, 2004) and resistance to organisational spaces (Baldry, 1999; Fleming & Spicer, 2004), as well as on spatial transformation (Dobers & Strannegard, 2004) and spatial scales (Spicer, 2006; Taylor & Spicer, 2007). These examples show the variety of studies that give explicit attention to organisational spaces, proving that the call made for bringing space back into organisation studies (see Kornberger & Clegg, 2004) has been heard.

However, as mentioned by Beyes and Steyaert (2012, p. 49), this growing body of literature has tended to favour a representational mode of theorising that results in a reification of space that 'turn[s] spatial becoming into representations of the beings of organizational spaces, prioritize[s] the spatial products over the processes of their productions'. This tendency can be explained by the great influence of Lefebvre's (1974/1991) groundbreaking work *The Production of Space*. Beyes and Steyaert (2012) showed that Lefebvre's work does not imply the reification of space per se (as the emphasis on the production of space connotes), but the ways it has been used to define organisational spaces – especially the three-part notion of space as 'conceived', 'perceived', and 'lived' – have shifted the emphasis from the processes of production to their results, neglecting the performative character of space (for some exceptions, see Dale, 2005; Knox, O'Doherty, Vurdubakis, & Westrup, 2008; Van Marrewijk, 2009; Tyler & Cohen, 2010).

Two other consequences of the representational logic that underlines the appropriation of Lefebvre's framework and, more broadly, the definition of organisational spaces in organisation studies can be depicted. First, there is an overemphasis on the *social*, that is, *human*, production of space. Even though Lefebvre acknowledged that a natural world exists prior to the intervention of human beings, he insisted that this world is only revealed (and concealed) in the process of its inhabitation (Lutterbie, 2001). Hence, Lefebvre's heuristic is essentially human centred: 'organizational spaces then easily come to be seen as either planned (conceived), or routinely practised (perceived), or embodied or "othered" (lived)' (Beyes & Steyaert, 2012, p. 49) by humans. And yet, space is certainly much more than the result of human action. In its most common conception, space refers to a concrete and physical space: a room, territory, ground, or land (Online Etymology Dictionary, http://www.etymonline.com). A more processual and performative definition of space highlights the relations and movements between a set of actors (not only humans) with various ontologies (Massey, 2005). Reducing space to human action masks the agency of the many other actors that also take part in the production of space (Ingold, 2011).

A third consequence of the representational logic underpinning studies of organisational spaces is the analytical separation between an abstract and a concrete space (Dale & Burrell, 2008). This dichotomy, which can also be found in the qualifications of Lefebvre's conceived, perceived (abstract) spaces and lived (concrete) spaces, echoes an ongoing debate in human geography about space and place. In a nutshell, this debate questions the distinction between space (considered as an abstract and general category) and place (the concrete and physical context where spatial experiences are lived; Tuan, 1979). Whereas space is associated with a more general mode of representation, place is related to the familiar, lived, and actual experience in the world. In this dichotomy we find a clear manifestation of what Whitehead (1920) denounced as the bifurcation of nature, clearly summarised by Latour (2005, pp. 225–226) in the following way:

> Bifurcation is what happens whenever we think the world is divided into two sets of things: one which is composed of the fundamental constituents of the universe – invisible to the eyes, known to science, yet real and valueless – and the other which is constituted of what the mind has to add to the basic building blocks of the world in order to make sense of them.

The problem with such bifurcation, according to Whitehead (and Latour), is that it creates an artificial and incorrect separation of primary qualities (the physical part of the world) from secondary qualities (its experience and understanding by human beings), when in fact these two qualities constitute the same world (Cooren, 2010). This problem is represented, for example, in the separation between studies that focus on the symbolic production of organisational spaces (Bauman, 1987; Doxater, 1990; Yanow, 1993) and those that attend to physical organisational settings (Becker, 1982; Hatch, 1990).

To sum up, while organisational scholars have increasingly responded to the call to bring space back into the study of organisation, the dominant representational reasoning that has been mobilised to do so has reduced the heuristic force of this 'spatial turn'. Three main limitations can be seen in this literature: (a) the blackboxing and masking of the processes through which organisational spaces are produced, (b) the disregard for other forms of agency (not only human) in the production of those spaces, and (c) the separation between the physical dimension of organisational spaces and their experience and understanding. In this paper, I address these shortcomings by proposing a communication-centred approach to organisational spaces. As I will develop in the following pages, this approach avoids falling into the traps of a representational view by adopting a performative/material definition of communication as constitutive of organisation and, more specifically, of organisational spaces.

A communication-centred approach to organisational spaces

Communication-centred approaches to organisations have gained considerable momentum in recent years (for a recent overview, see Brummans, Cooren, Robichaud, & Taylor, 2014). Emphasising the fundamental and constitutive role of communication in the constitution of organisational phenomena (what has come to be called the Communicative Constitution of Organisation (CCO) approach), the supporters of this perspective claim that communication is the process by which organisations 'are established, composed, designed, and sustained' (Cooren et al., 2011, p. 1150). It follows that communication does not merely serve representational purposes but creates, constitutes, materialises, and shapes instances of reality, including phenomena such as organisations.

Herein lies the main contribution of the CCO approach to the study of organisational spaces: in highlighting the performative (or constitutive) dimension of communication, it fosters renewed reflections for understanding organisational spaces as being collective, situated, and hybrid accomplishments. This argument, which is at the heart of the CCO approach, is based on the three following premises (adapted from Cooren et al., 2011; see also Schoeneborn & Vásquez, in press). First, *CCO scholarship studies communication events*. This premise highlights the eventful nature of communication and invites scholars to study the occurrence of organisational communication events on the level of practices.

A communication event, according to Cooren et al. (2011, p. 1151), is 'a segment of an ongoing and situated stream of socio-discursive practices'. These practices are embedded not only in language, discourse, and texts but also in objects, architecture, bodies, and so on. Moreover, as an event, communication not only has a temporal dimension (i.e. events are marked by a beginning and an end) but also a spatial dimension (i.e. events occur in and through certain locations and corporeal elements such as architectural configurations, etc.). As argued by Vásquez Schoeneborn, and Sergi (2016), the notion of a communication event acknowledges the contingent nature of communication and grounds the analysis in situated local practices. At the same time, it highlights its processual, material, and historical dimensions. Methodologically speaking, communication events are considered to be the primary unit of analysis.

The second premise is that *CCO scholarship should be as inclusive as possible in its definition of (organisational) communication.* Although communication scholarship traditionally focuses on studying the use of language and its symbolic manifestations, this premise calls for a broadening of the definition of communication to include bodies, clothes, architecture, objects, and infrastructure. In a similar vein, Cooren (2000) and Cooren, Bencherki, Chaput, and Vásquez (2015) proposed defining communication as the 'establishment of a link, connection or relationship through something'. Taking this definition, one can say, for instance, 'Paul communicated this contract to Mary', 'This official announcement is communicating important information to the employees', or 'The way this office is set up communicates coldness and rigidity'. In all of these sentences, something materialises the connection between entities: Between Paul and Mary, the connection/materialisation is a contract; between the official announcement and the employees, it is pieces of information; between the office and us, it is coldness and rigidity.

The third premise, which is related to the second, is that *CCO scholarship holds that who or what is acting is an open question.* This premise deals explicitly with the question of agency and opens it up to non-human actors (e.g. texts, tools, technologies, or buildings). Importantly, this opening is related to the inquiry itself and so has methodological implications. CCO inquiry entails not deciding a priori who or what is acting: the answer will arise from studying and questioning the empirical phenomena at hand. According to Cooren et al. (2011), CCO scholars should therefore develop a sensibility to the various agents (human or non-human) that participate/materialise themselves in communication events.

Taken together, these premises invite scholars to study the communicative events through which the organisational world materialises. Emphasising the collective, situated, and hybrid character of (organisational) communication, the CCO approach opens a renewed reflection on organisational spaces that, as mentioned, avoids falling into the traps of representational reasoning. Similar to other non-representational theories (Anderson & Harrison, 2010; Cadman, 2009; Thrift, 2007), the CCO approach emphasises everyday practices, materiality, and emergence (Beyes & Steyaert, 2012). Now – and herein lies its specificity – it does so by starting from (rather than arriving at) communication as the reason for every inquiry (Cooren et al., 2006).

Applied to the study of organisational spaces, this communication-centred approach puts forth a relational ontology that draws attention to how heterogeneous agencies constitute/materialise/embody organisational spaces communicatively. Building on the premises of the CCO approach, I next propose to examine the spatial grammar of organising, which allows us to answer to the following questions: What kinds of organisational spaces materialise themselves through communication? What are the

DISCURSIVITY, RELATIONALITY AND MATERIALITY

processes through which communication constitutes/materialises/embodies (these) organisational spaces, and what are their implications?

A spatial grammar of organising

The concept of grammar has traditionally been used in organisation studies as a metaphor to describe organisational processes (e.g. Bantz, 1989; Barley, 1986; Bengtsson, Mullern, Soderlhom, & Wahlin, 2007; Taylor & Van Every, 2000). Commonly associated with linguistics, the notion of grammar emphasises the structural patterns of organising and suggests that organisation, as language, has syntax (Pentland, 1995). One of the first (and undoubtedly the most influential) scholars to develop this idea was Weick (1979, p. 3), who defined organising as a 'consensually validated grammar for reducing equivocality by means of sensible interlocked behaviors'. Organising is like grammar, he argued, in the sense that it is 'a systematic account of some rules and conventions by which sets of interlocking behaviors are assembled to form social processes that are intelligible to actors' (p. 3). The grammar consists of recipes, he continued, for 'getting things done' and for 'interpreting what has been done' (p. 3), as it helps actors to collectively make sense of past and future actions. Hence, organising as grammar can be seen, following Weick (1995), as processes of making collective experience intelligible or sensible.

Weick's notion of organising stresses the need to go beyond a structuralist definition of grammar, which would reduce organising to structural (language) patterns. Proposing to focus on verbs (as the gerund in the word 'organis*ing*' suggests), he puts action at the centre of organisation: the interlocking of behaviours takes place in actions that connect actors (Bakken & Hernes, 2006). This shift from structure to action turns the analyst's attention away from the content of organisational activities to the implicit rules and patterns involved in the organising processes associated with these activities (Robichaud, 2002, p. 131). It also captures the key role of interpretation, as interlocked behaviours need to be intelligible to actors in order to make sense of present and future actions. Hence, the metaphor of organising *as* grammar allows us to acknowledge the constitutive character of communication as both action and interpretation (Hernes, 2008; for a similar argument see Taylor & Van Every, 2000). It fails, however, to account for the embodied and material dimensions of organising (Cornelissen, Mantere, & Vaara, 2014).

In order to include these dimensions, I turn here to Amin et al.'s (2003) geographical analysis of British politics. In this study, the notion of grammar is used in a different yet, to my mind, complementary way. In analysing an array of governmental strategies and policies related to the circulation of people and goods, the definition of city boundaries, the location of social institutions, and so forth, this study outlines the politics of geography that are at work in the 'spatial grammar' of the United Kingdom (see also Massey, 1994, 2004). In tracing both the material and discursive dimensions of these governmental strategies, Amin et al. (2003, p. 4) show how seemingly mundane expressions such as 'the regions' (meaning beyond London), 'the rest of the UK', or 'we have to be there', as well as buildings, streets, and physical boundaries, 'lie at the heart of the unequal distribution of power' in British democracy. Through this analysis, the authors highlight the importance of a spatial grammar for studying geography from a political and moral stance, advocating for a grammar of relations 'in which all kinds of unlike things can knock up against each other in all kinds of ways' (Amin et al., 2003, p. 4).

This notion of a grammar of relations echoes the three premises of the CCO approach previously presented. The emphasis on relationality can be linked to the broad definition of communication as relations given by this approach (Premise 2). Also, the acknowledgment of the heterogeneity of the things connected in this grammar of relations can be associated with the recognition of the many agencies that populate communication, which are related in multiple and various ways (Premise 3). While the idea of communicative events (Premise 1) is not directly expressed in Amin et al.'s (2003) study, there is a common thread within the CCO approach regarding the embedding of practices in an historical framework.

Moreover, Amin et al.'s (2003) study emphasises the political effects of a spatial imagery through its concrete manifestations/materialisations in the discourses, policies, buildings, locations, and strategies it informs (understood here literally as 'to give shape' or 'to form'). The notion of 'spatial grammar' shows the heterogeneity of agencies that constitute/materialise/embodies (organisational) spaces and thus goes beyond the socio-cognitive approach commonly associated with 'organising *as* grammar' (Weick, 1979), which tends to focus the analysis on processes of human action and interpretation. It also captures the political nature of these hybrid processes – another clear difference with Weick's (1979) more neutral definition of grammar.

Taking both Weick's and Amin et al.'s notions of grammar together, and in light of the CCO premises outlined in the previous section, I propose the expression *a spatial grammar of organising* to refer to the communicative processes involved in the constitution/materialisation/embodiment of organisational spaces. These processes, I argue, rely on a spatial imaginary that materialises itself in language, artefacts, devices, and practices. It is important to note that in order to describe the spatial grammar of organising, the analyst must pay attention to the relations through which a spatial imaginary is enacted and to how these relations take part in the constitution/materialisation of organisational spaces. These relations are made possible in communication, defined broadly as the 'establishment of a link, connection or relationship through something' (Cooren, 2000). Methodologically speaking, as developed next, we can study a spatial grammar of organising by focusing on communication events that are performed in distinct space-times.

Research context and methodology

Research context

The fieldwork took place in ConCiencia, a Chilean outreach organisation whose mandate is to create a national scientific culture – in other words, to disseminate scientific knowledge in 'every part of the country', as ConCiencia proudly announces on its website (my translation). More specifically, ConCiencia's activities are aimed at elementary and middle school-aged children with the goal of 'open[ing] their eyes, minds, and hearts to knowledge' (ConCiencia's website, my translation).

DISCURSIVITY, RELATIONALITY AND MATERIALITY

Before going further, it is important to explain the implications of ConCiencia's mission in light of the contextual specificity of the country in which it aims to 'spread widely'. ConCiencia's mission is intrinsically associated with assuring a national presence over the 6500 km (roughly 4000 miles) of the country. Chile's peculiar geography and administrative governance make this quite a challenge. With the Andes to the east and the Pacific Ocean to the west, Chile is squeezed into a long strip of territory. Its northern frontier becomes the Atacama Desert, while massive glaciers cover its southern extremity (see Taylor & Van Every, 2011). While most Chileans (around 60%) live in the centre of the country, there are those who defy the extreme conditions at the 'ends' and the centralised administration that concentrates many of the country's political, cultural, and economic activities in Chile's capital, Santiago.

Going national, in a Chilean context, is therefore a challenge, one that ConCiencia has taken seriously and that has become a key feature in defining this organisation. Although its head office is located in Santiago, the majority of its activities are organised in regional branches, which are typically located in regional universities. Supporting regional activities is one of ConCiencia's main goals; developing what is called a 'network of regional branches' ensures the organisation's presence in the 'whole country' and, to a certain extent, acknowledges Chile's regional diversity.

It is worth noting that the expression 'in every part of the country' implies not only a geographical notion of presence but also a democratic one. ConCiencia was created in 1995 as part of governmental initiatives aiming to democratise education. Mainly led by the centre-left coalition *Concertación de Partidos por la Democracia* (Coalition of Parties for Democracy), these initiatives reacted against the massive privatisation of education during Pinochet's dictatorship. They aimed in particular to reduce the gap between private and public education by enhancing the accessibility and quality of the latter. In this context, ConCiencia was seen as a complement to the formal educational system. Through the development of extracurricular activities related to science and technology, it was mainly intended to give opportunities to schools, teachers, and children who did not have access to them in the formal education system. Activities include the organisation of field trips, visits to laboratories, conversations with scientists, a regional conference where students present their projects, an exhibition, scientific camps, guided tours, and a news bulletin.

Methodology

Most of the research was conducted in a central region of the country located south of Santiago, in one of ConCiencia's regional branches that I call 'ConCiencia Sur'. Taking an organisational ethnographic approach (Ybema, Yanow, Wels, & Kamsteeg, 2009), I shadowed[2] the coordination of ConCiencia's showpiece event of the year: the National Science and Technology Week (hereafter, 'Science Week'). I video recorded different activities (several meetings, numerous telephone calls, and 'silent work') and events (a scientific congress for children, a technological exhibition, scientific conferences, and so forth). To complement this shadowing, I also collected work documents (emails, design materials, organisational charts, websites, and posters) and interviewed the members of the regional staff, as well as those from ConCiencia's head office. In total, the empirical material covered 170 h of audiovisual recordings, 12 semi-structured interviews, 1 focus group, and 25 documents. Ethical approval was also obtained. ConCiencia's head office was informed of this study and accepted its conditions, as did the research participants.

My role in this research was that of a non-participant observer. However, it should be noted that I had previously worked for ConCiencia during my pre-graduate studies as a communications intern and, consequently, personally knew part of the staff. My professional (and personal) involvement with ConCiencia was particularly useful for understanding the framework of the staff used for making sense of their work. Having myself been in a similar position was key to acknowledging the meaningfulness of action through 'the way we experience and feel reality' (Gagliardi, 1990, p. 13). I could also relate to work practices and staff concerns and expectations. Yet, this shared experience and understanding created some expectations for staff members who would, for example, ask for my opinion during a meeting. Adding this to the peculiar *liaison* that shadowing creates between the shadower and shadowee (Czarniawska, 2007), the efforts to maintain a non-participatory role during observation were not always successful. This is why it was important to keep a researcher's diary in order to enhance reflexivity.

This study was conducted for my PhD dissertation, which aimed to understand the constitutive role of communication in an organisation's continuity through space and time. In this article, I focus more specifically on the performative role of communication in constituting organisational spaces by asking what kinds of organisational spaces are constituted through communication? What are the processes through which communication constitutes (these) organisational spaces, and what are their implications? The analytical strategy to answer these questions entailed two steps: (a) describing ConCiencia's spatial imaginary, that is the spatial images that were voiced and embodied, and their effects on the production of organisational spaces; and (b) attending to the processes through which these organisational spaces were performed and to their implications. These steps were grounded in an abductive reasoning that involves a 'back-and-forth movement between a body of knowledge and an observed phenomenon' (Vásquez et al., 2016, p. 636), which allowed accounting for the relations between ConCiencia's organisational spaces (step 1) and the communicative processes and organisational implications (step 2).

Why focus on a spatial imaginary? One of the first things that struck me while conducting this ethnographic fieldwork was the recurrent use of spatial images by ConCiencia's staff to talk about their organisation, work, mission, and challenges in promoting science and technology. From the use of spatial metaphors to explicit references to Chile's peculiar geography (more specifically that of the region in question) or to development and enrolment strategies, everything seemed to be oriented towards occupying Chile's territory – or, to put it differently, 'to conquer Chile in the name of science and technology'. This led me to question ConCiencia's spatial imaginary and to try to figure out what meanings, materials, and actions were associated with it.

Yanow (2010) refers to a 'spatial sensibility': 'an hermeneutic-phenomenological orientation towards a spatial dimension of the material world in which we act and through which we move...' (p. 415). This sensibility, she argues, 'extends also towards researchers' (p. 415). Following this 'spatial sensibility' and being inspired by Amin et al.'s (2003) study, the analysis aimed to track down the 'grammar of relations' that

DISCURSIVITY, RELATIONALITY AND MATERIALITY

characterises ConCiencia's spatial imaginary. To do so, I first wrote a composite narrative of ConCiencia's history based on an analysis of the interviews and documents. This led me to identify the main development strategy through which ConCiencia expands its presence across Chile, strategy that is mainly linked to the development of networks (local, regional, and national). Second, starting from the revision of the audiovisual recording, I selected 10 representative communicational events in which this development strategy was at work. These events were transcribed according to the convention system developed by Jefferson (1984). After watching the video recordings while reading the transcripts, I identified three dominant spatial images – network, region, and trajectories – through a semantic sorting process. Third, and keeping with a relational logic (Hennion, 1993), I traced the ways in which these images circulated through material, languages, and actions in order to outline the grammar of relations. Finally, I chose four communication events to illustrate ConCiencia's spatial imaginary. However, when discussing these events, as we will see next, I also bring up other empirical material to position the event in its historical background.

In the following section, I will present and discuss the three images that characterise ConCiencia's spatial imaginary. This presentation focuses on the description of the kinds of organisational spaces that are performed by each spatial image and the communicative processes through which these spaces are constituted (i.e. the grammar of relations). The narrative style I have adopted to present the results of this research is consistent with the ethnographic approach underlining this study. It also reveals my epistemological positioning, which can be associated with a critical line of CCO thinking that recognises the need for critical reflexivity (Cunliffe & Jun, 2005) vis-à-vis the object or subject of study.

ConCiencia's spatial grammar of organising: networks, regions, and trajectories

Space as network: ConCiencia is like a virus ... and there is no antidote

One of the images that Alejandra, ConCiencia Sur's regional coordinator, often used when talking about this organisation is that of a virus. Each time she presented it, she would mockingly say:

> You know, ConCiencia is a very contagious virus and we spread it everywhere. The thing is there is no antidote. Once you catch it, or it catches you, you cannot get rid of it! (Field notes)

And usually, at that moment, she would laugh and kindly but firmly touch the shoulder of the next 'victim' as if her finger were a stinger.

This image is interesting in many ways. It associates what ConCiencia is, a virus, with what it does, spreading (like a virus), or catching (a virus)! These actions, especially when referring to spreading, connote a spatial dimension of ConCiencia's way of being. The main characteristic of a virus is that it is contagious, a contagion that materialises a specific space that the virus manages or not to colonise. Thus, keeping with this image, for the virus to spread, ConCiencia's staff members need to infect as

DISCURSIVITY, RELATIONALITY AND MATERIALITY

many people, institutions, and local authorities as possible. Concretely, they do this through enrolment.

The two following excerpts demonstrate this enrolment strategy at work in the coordination of one of the Science Week's main activities: *1000 Scientists, 1000 Classrooms*. In this activity, the idea is to marshal visits by practicing scientists to at least 1000 schoolrooms. It is worth noting that all of the scientists involved participate on a voluntary basis. Yet *1000 Scientists, 1000 Classrooms* is a mandatory activity for ConCiencia's regional branches requested by the central committee. The two chosen excerpts refer to the door-to-door strategy that was implemented in order to increase the number of participants, which at that time was 70% above the projected goal. The first excerpt corresponds to ConCiencia Sur's weekly meeting and focuses more specifically on the moment when Patricia (the coordinator of the *1000 Scientists, 1000 Classrooms* activity) presents the door-to-door strategy to the others member of the staff. Alejandra, the regional coordinator, is chairing the meeting.[3]

Excerpt 1:

Alejandra:	OK. This closes our discussion about 'Science Day at my School' ((another activity programmed for the National Science and Technology Week))? OK. Now we turn to '1,000 Scientists, 1,000 Classrooms' ((She points to Patricia who is sitting on her right. Patricia clears her throat)). **OK. Tell them.**
Patricia:	**I had problems ((she says this with an ironic tone. She laughs.)).** What happens is that those that I sent, in fact those who participated last year … at least 25 of those who participated last year will not participate this year.
Alejandra:	They said no?
Patricia:	They said no. ((She nods.))
Alejandra:	Why? ((She seems surprised and preoccupied.))
Patricia:	Because some are sick, some left the country, and others do not have the time.
Alejandra:	OK.
Patricia:	So, hmm, it's complicated. **But we already have 25.**
Alejandra:	OK. [Luckily
Patricia:	**[hopefully today=**
Alejandra:	**=with the door-to-door**
Patricia:	**Yes, I'll go now** ((she points toward Andrés who is sitting next to her)) to Chemistry, Biology Faculty, and Physical Sciences.
Alejandra:	Great.
Patricia:	Tomorrow, I will=
Alejandra:	**=are you taking the consent form?**
Patricia:	Yes.
Alejandra:	Great. And you're going to bring **a lot of forms**.
Patricia:	Jenny is printing them for me ((She nods)).
Alejandra:	**They fill it out, they fill it out, and you bring them back to me. Perfect. And the virus spreads.**

This first excerpt shows the rationale behind the implementation of the door-to-door strategy: there is a problem (in Patricia's words, *her* problem: only 25 enrolled scientists), and thus a need for a more persuasive enrolment strategy. In a previous meeting between Alejandra and Patricia, when the idea of a door-to-door strategy was first discussed, Alejandra said: 'It's much easier to have that commitment, it's much more difficult for people to say no when you are looking them in the eye. (…) A direct action is much more effective'. The door-

96

DISCURSIVITY, RELATIONALITY AND MATERIALITY

to-door strategy relies on this physical and direct presence for the virus to spread. This does not only mean Patricia's presence, but also the presence of the consent forms.

As we can see in the excerpt, Alejandra double-checks that Patricia is bringing 'a lot of forms' with her. In this case, the form acts as a contract between the scientist and ConCiencia, which they 'fill out, fill out', and that Patricia brings back to Alejandra: that's how the deal is closed or materialised, so to speak. In this sense, the form is a materialisation of the scientist's commitment: with it, Patricia can add a number to the list and get closer to reaching ConCiencia's objective. One commitment at a time, the virus thus creates the space of its colonisation.

The second excerpt, which comes after the staff's weekly meeting, shows Patricia (with the consent form) enrolling one of the scientists.

Excerpt 2:

Patricia:	**We're from ConCiencia.** I don't know if you have heard of it?
Scientist:	Yes.
Patricia:	**And the activity '1,000 Scientists, 1,000 Classrooms?'**
Scientist:	Yes. I once=
Patricia:	=Yes=
Scientist:	=I participated a few years ago. The first version.
Patricia:	OK, and this year would you like to participate?
Scientist:	No, I'm busy [with other project] this year.
Patricia:	Yes?
Scientist:	**I'm starting a project, actually.**
Patricia:	**And you do not have much time.**
Scientist:	**I do not have much time. The problem is time.**
Patricia:	OK.
Scientist:	I'm still interested; I think it's a good motivational tool for anyone, for any professor to participate in this program.
Patricia:	OK.
Scientist:	I attended the first year, the first version, let's say. Several years ago. **Now I have a problem: time. That's the problem.**
Patricia:	**Because, like the previous version, this will be only one day. It's October 3 it's a Tuesday and if you want, to go to a closer place, a town nearby, we can manage that. In fact if it is a matter of=**
Scientist:	What? ((He looks at his calendar.)) What is the basic idea? ((He turns to look at Patricia.))
Patricia:	The idea is that you develop one, one, one conference, the topic you want and you go to a school or college that is motivated. We're going to offer them the topics that each professor proposes.
Scientist:	OK. OK.
Patricia:	And it will be only the school that is really interested in this subject that will welcome you and hear your conference. Then=
Scientist:	=and this, when do you want to do it?
Patricia:	**October 3. ((The professor takes the calendar on his desk.)) Only that day. And this will be no other day. It's an activity that will be done at the national level.**
Scientist:	Yes, yes, I participated.
Patricia:	So, that day in every=
Scientist:	=October 3?
Patricia:	Exactly
Scientist:	The [Tuesday]
Patricia:	[Tuesday]

DISCURSIVITY, RELATIONALITY AND MATERIALITY

> ((The scientist agrees to participate. He asks Patricia to call him back the next day to confirm his topic and the school to which he will be going. She hands him a consent form and writes down his phone number in a small notebook.))

This second excerpt shows the door-to-door strategy at work. It should be mentioned that before this encounter, Patricia had already tried to enroll five other scientists, without much success. She was thus more comfortable in the interaction and had already crafted her arguments to convince a potentially reluctant scientist. Overall, with this scientist, the outcome was positive. She did not have to push too much to obtain consent. One explanation of this is the fact that the scientist had already participated in this activity, which he mentioned at the beginning of the interaction. To some extent, and keeping with the image of the virus, we could say that he had already been 'stung' by the virus; it was 'dormant' in his system and just needed to be 'awakened'.

Patricia quickly felt that the scientist's previous experience was positive and that he was much more open to her invitation than other scientists she had already encountered. Unlike in her previous interactions, upon entering his office, this scientist had invited us to take a seat, brought his chair closer to us, and engaged with me in a conversation about my PhD – all signs materialising the presence of a welcoming person. Moreover, his reaction after Patricia's introduction, 'We're from ConCiencia', was also positive: he didn't question Patricia's legitimacy as a spokesperson and did not argue about the real goals behind ConCiencia's mission (which were some of the responses she received from other scientists during the door-to-door strategy).

In this case, the scientist gave a very pragmatic and reasonable response: no time. This said, Patricia is the one who names the scientist's problem as 'having no time'. In doing so, she is empathising with him and, at the same time, anticipating her following argument. As we can see in the excerpt, she quickly presents the solution to this problem: 'like in the previous version, this will be only one day', 'if you want to go to a closer place, a town nearby, we can manage that'. She further adds that this activity is 'national', an argument that confirms what the professor already knew. Her arguments work: she closes the deal by leaving the form, which acts as a reminder of her presence in the scientist's office, a presence of which she will also remind him the next day when she will call to confirm some further information.

Taken together, the two excerpts illustrate how the image of the virus is embodied in a particular strategy. Based on the ethnographic study that I conducted, this mode of operating can also be extended to a broader strategy of development, that of creating networks. Alejandra often described ConCiencia's work as 'connecting worlds through communication'. For her, ConCiencia is an outreach organisation whose main goal is to constitute a network for the diffusion and valorisation of science and technology. Following an enrolment strategy quite similar to the one we saw in the previous excerpts, two networks materialised themselves in this specific regional branch: the 'institutional network', composed of local educational and cultural institutions that were prominently invested in the organisation of the Science Week, and the 'regional network', composed of elementary or high school science teachers acting as ConCiencia's local coordinators in 39 cities in the region. In addition to coordinating the activities of the Science Week in their cities, these teachers are also in charge of developing local activities for promoting science and technology during the school year. It should also be noted that the creation of networks was also transferred to ConCiencia's other regional branches and, even today, still constitutes a successful modus operandi at a regional and national level.

Following Murdoch and Marsden (1995), we could say that ConCiencia has put forward a successful network strategy for 'spreading like a virus'. Drawing on Latour's (1986) power of association, these authors argued that the success of a network lies in the definition and use of the resources mobilised to establish links: 'to be successful an actor must colonize the world of others' (p. 372). The organisational space that results from the network is one delineated by the 'links and dots' that constitute/materialise it. Its success is measured in terms of the density of the network and its expanding capacities. The notion of space as network, as we can see in the previous examples, also conveys what Massey (2005) refers to as a 'colonial space'. The conquest of Chile 'in the name of science and technology' through a network imaginary has very concrete effects: forms, stories, enrolment, and metaphors all take part in creating/performing/materialising ConCiencia's space of action to colonise Chile's territory. In the next section, I will focus on the region: a common way of referring to space, and particularly to organisational sites. While more static than the network, the region also conveys the image of a colonised space; the difference being that in the region, space is 'out there' waiting to be conquered.

Space as region: delineating maps and boundaries

I will begin by showing the figure that ConCiencia Sur proudly displays on its website (see Figure 1). It is the map of the region where Conciencia Sur operates, which I call 'Region Sur'. But more interestingly, as its title indicates, the map portrays ConCiencia's presence in this region by the use of small red dots. When clicking on a red dot, a new window opens with the name of the city, as well as a picture of and contact information for ConCiencia's local representative from that city, which, as mentioned, is a science teacher of a local elementary or high school.

The geographical imaginary that arises from this figure can be associated with an imaginary of space as a region: an entity with established boundaries, which is occupied by ConCiencia. The map materialises ConCiencia's presence in a geographical space and thus implies the occupation of a pre-existing space, one that has been divided and territorialised even before ConCiencia's 'occupation'. The spatial grammar associated with regions is very common. A region, like a state or a province, refers to a Euclidean space: one in which objects in three dimensions exist and can be transported, measured, and stacked. On this map, the region is depicted as space literally stripped of its relationship with the 'outside world', suggesting a certain autonomy and independence. As Massey noted (2007, p. 20) in reference to the region, 'it is an imaginary that has been fundamental to modernity and to the commonsense, as well as politically useful' (Massey, 2007, p. 20). ConCiencia Sur is proud to show this map filled with red dots because it materialises its success in conquering Region Sur 'in the name of science and technology'.

The following excerpt shows how the image of the region is mobilised by Alejandra, ConCiencia Sur's coordinator, in a meeting with the local representatives (science teachers) that was held a month before the launch of the Science Week. Let me recall that these

Figure 1. ConCiencia's presence in Region Sur.
Retrieved from ConCiencia Sur's website.

teachers, as part of ConCiencia Sur's 'regional network', are in charge of coordinating the Science Week activities in their cities. This meeting is the last one they have before 'D Day'. The stakes are high because ConCiencia Sur has historically been the most successful regional branch at the national level, meaning that it has had the highest number of students, teachers, scientists, cities, and local institutions participating in its activities. Alejandra and her staff want to maintain these high scores. But, more importantly, as they discussed when preparing for this meeting, they need to collect the information to support these scores.

As Alejandra explained to her team during that discussion, 'So, the concept we want to highlight is the importance of collecting data, of collecting information. Because they [the science teachers] do many activities and everything, but what is difficult for us [the staff] is to collect this information.' As we will see next, the staff came up with two symbols to put this idea forwards: the map of the region (see Figure 1) and a calculator.

Excerpt 3:

> The meeting ended with a short activity in which each teacher was handed a paper flag of ConCiencia's logo and was invited to stick it on the map of the region (a printed copy of the map had been put up on one of the walls of the meeting room). Alejandra called each of the 39 cities that make up the 'regional network'. Responding to her call, each teacher said his or her name and placed his or her flag on the map. At the end of the activity, the result showed that some flags were missing: the region was not completely covered. Alejandra takes the floor and talks to the teachers.

DISCURSIVITY, RELATIONALITY AND MATERIALITY

Alejandra: I want you to remember the first meeting we had this year in March. What was the objective we said we would work on this year? ((Mumbling in the room))

Alejandra: Yes, **strengthen the Network** ((referring here to the regional network)). But, in addition to strengthening it, how were we going to be able to demonstrate that we have strengthened it? We would demonstrate it by **being rigorous** in what? In counting the number of attendees, in reporting the activities we do. Do you remember or not? ((Mumbling in the room))

Alejandra: Well, then, one of the things we wanted was to put **in a concrete place, with a punchy visual**, how we are seeking to demonstrate specific information and goals outside the Network. **This ((pointing to the map)). We are not covering the whole territory, that's the first point. There are supposed to be – 39 cities are integrated into the Network and there are not 39 cities here ((pointing to the map again))**. These are things we have to attend to and we do not solve them alone. Because in March we had already talked about the problems related to the existence of the Network. This not only a problem for the people who run ConCiencia. **It's an important matter for all of us ((she makes a movement with her arms embracing the assembly))**. The beneficiaries of ConCiencia are children, teachers, schools, etc. The existence of this Network is beneficial to all of us who work in the diffusion of science and technology. **So, we have to start thinking about our neighbors**. What is happening in [names one of the cities]? It was a city where everybody was involved, but now there is the case of [**names a city**] **that is not there ((shows the map))** because the coordinator is sick. Will someone be willing to support this city now that the coordinator is sick? Or here everybody scratches themselves with their own nails ((Chilean expression)) and doesn't gives a damn about what happens in the rest of the world? (0.2) These are all reflections that matter. **My goal when we talk about strengthening the network is the contact between you ((shows the dots in the map))**. (…)

Alejandra: Now because the goal was to actually **show what we really are, we had made the decision to record all the activities** that we were doing on a piece of paper and write down, the participants, the participation. Remember? Well, then, to mark this year's Science Week, one of the most important things is that **we know how to count**. We do not have to enlarge or shrink the numbers. This needs to be as real as possible. Like each year ((with a smile on her face)) we have a symbolic gift for you ((she takes a small box wrapped in blue paper with ConCiencia's logo on top)), that implies a concrete and corresponding action. ((The staff members start distributing the gifts to the teachers)). We have a little present for you this year. A matchbox with matchsticks? No! ((She teases.)) Open it! An eraser to erase with your elbow what you wrote with your hand? No! ((The teachers laugh. They open their gifts: it's a calculator.))

Alejandra: Good. All right. It's small, it fits in a backpack, a purse … but it's big enough for your fingers. I have such big fingers that I usually press four keys at the same time. All right. They all work? Did you check them? Perfect. OK, so this is the strength and impulse we are waiting for you to put into our activities.

((Alejandra ends the meeting with logistic information about the Science Week.))

DISCURSIVITY, RELATIONALITY AND MATERIALITY

Two ideas are worth noting about this excerpt. First is the connection that Alejandra establishes between the region and the network, a connection that puts forth the evaluation or measurement of ConCiencia's success. For her, a strong network is what materialises ConCiencia's presence in the region. Materialising this presence on the map is a way of showing ConCiencia's impact in the region, and this impact is measured in terms of the number of cities that participate in the regional network (each city can also be measured in terms of schools, students, teachers, local institutions, etc.). More numbers means more coverage of the region, thus more success for the network. Conversely, fewer numbers or less coverage means less success. The region is seen here as a territory to conquer, and the numbers (cities, schools, and students) are not only the way of measuring this conquest but are actually seen as an objective and 'real' materialisation of what ConCiencia Sur is. The following sentence by Alejandra is most revealing: 'Now because the goal was to actually show what we really are, we had made the decision to record all the activities that we were doing on a piece of paper and write down, the participants, the participation.'

Alejandra is referring to 'the quantification sheet', a form her staff created to facilitate the counting of the public who participated in the activities organised by ConCiencia. This form (see Appendix) presents a table with blank spaces to be completed with information concerning the activity. The emphasis is put on the number of participants, divided into two categories: persons and institutions. It is worth noting that this document was created from the proposal form for the Science Week, the goal being to facilitate the transfer and collection of information when writing the report of the event. Counting is required for ConCiencia Sur to be accountable for the activities organised during the Science Week vis-à-vis the central committee. This requirement for measurement explains the symbolism of the gift that Alejandra and her team gave to the teachers: a calculator.

The second aspect I want to emphasise about this excerpt is Alejandra's use of the map to question the responsibility of the regional network. After mentioning that 'we are not covering the whole territory', she says that 'this is not only a problem for the people who run ConCiencia. It's an important matter for all of us'; and she later adds, 'we have to start thinking about our neighbors'. Using the example of a city that is not represented on the map because the coordinator is sick, she highlights the collective responsibility for the regional network and its success. We can see another kind of accountability that does not only rest on counting and measurement but on being responsible for 'our neighbors'. The absent flag on the map representing the region materialises this lack of collective responsibility.

The association that we find in the previous excerpts between region and network is not a surprise. As Law (2002, p. 97) argued, 'networks make regions make networks'. He explained this sentence through two arguments: 'Part of the argument is relatively straightforward. It is that volumes (for instance vessels), regions (for instance countries) and measurements of distance (for instance from Lisbon to Calicut) get made by network means'. The second part of the argument ('regions make networks') is less intuitive: Law (2002) suggested that the subsistence of a network depends on the

DISCURSIVITY, RELATIONALITY AND MATERIALITY

homeomorphism of the Euclidean space (i.e. the region). He takes the example of a Portuguese vessel to illustrate his argument:

> But [the vessels] are also objects within Euclidean space. Give or take, a vessel is only an unbroken network shape if it is also an unbroken Euclidean shape. And here is the rub. To generate network homeomorphism it is also necessary to work in Euclidean space and make an object, a vessel-shape, whose relative Euclidean co-ordinates are constant.

Applied to ConCiencia, the strategy of materialising a network is what also materialises the region that ConCiencia wants to conquer. Yet, for this network to exist, it needs a set of constant coordinates. It needs a relatively static space in order to plan and control its conquest.

Space as coexistent trajectories: 'stories-so-far' of inclusion and exclusion

One last spatial configuration that can be found in the analysis of ConCiencia's spatial imaginary is associated with space as a coexistence of trajectories, where trajectories are defined as 'stories-so-far'. This definition, which I borrow from Massey (2005, 2007), highlights the heterogeneity of (organisational) spaces. Heterogeneity is in this sense understood as the coexistence of multiplicities. In this case, there is not a single entity, nor a single trajectory or single vision of the organisation. Space as we experience it is '...a field of multiple actors, trajectories, stories, with their own energies – which may mingle in harmony, collide, even annihilate each other' (Massey, 2007, p. 22).

In ConCiencia's spatial grammar, several stories mingle in apparent coherence. Network and regional imaginaries, with their respective forms of occupation, follow a logic which is based on assembling what is fragmented, singular, and diverse. However, there is another way of relating what difference is. It results in an organisational space as 'a meeting-place of jostling, potentially conflicting, trajectories' (Massey, 2007, p. 89).

Consider the following excerpt taken from an ethnographic interview I conducted with Alejandra, ConCiencia Sur's regional coordinator. At that moment, we were discussing ConCiencia's mission:

Excerpt 4:

> Is it important for the ConCiencia program to actually achieve geographical coverage? Because, for example, Maria said: 'No, because I do not think... It doesn't make sense to send a traveling exhibition to Easter Island. There are 1,600 people and it costs the same amount to bring five exhibitions to the Gran Valparaíso region'. Then, she said: 'It seems to me that it is an effort that does not make sense'. On the other hand, I said: 'OK, but then these are populations that will always be marginalized from these activities?' (Alejandra, interview)

Alejandra is talking about one of ConCiencia's activities: traveling exhibitions. For ConCiencia's members, these are significant and concrete ways of reaching every corner of the country and, more particularly, as Alejandra argued, marginalised populations (in rural and geographically distant cities). By traveling around the country, these exhibitions are able to bring science and technology to those populations, giving them access to scientific knowledge. For Alejandra, this raises important issues regarding ConCiencia's occupation of Chile's territory, which can be summarised in two interrelated questions: 'Where to go?' and 'Where to be?'

DISCURSIVITY, RELATIONALITY AND MATERIALITY

As the excerpt shows, these questions do not have a simple answer. Alejandra presents two different points of view – her own and that of Maria, the regional coordinator of the Grand Valparaíso region. But she also voices the perspective of the Easter Islanders, who we could possibly say are 'marginalised populations'. By explicitly contesting Easter Island's exclusion from ConCiencia's activity, she is allowing for other trajectories to be part of the organisation's space and also, incidentally, part of the country. Here, we are dealing with a different type of geography, a geography of multiple trajectories or stories-so-far, that highlights the discussion about these 'other regions' by recognising them through their own stories and the ever-changing relationships in which they are made. Organisational space takes on a new significance here; it becomes the result of (potential) relations (Amin et al., 2003).

We see in the previous excerpt that the question of the inclusion or exclusion of Easter Island from ConCiencia's organisational space can be tackled in different ways. Economically speaking (Maria's argument), the question follows cost–benefit logic to determine what part of the national territory is 'worth' being occupied. Politically speaking, one could also highlight that ConCiencia is an organisation that depends on a governmental programme and infrastructure. In the interview with Alejandra, she addresses this question by referring to the lack of a governmental policy about what is national and what is not. This lack of policy allows for different interpretations of ConCiencia's mission. Hence, the question of the inclusion or exclusion of 'marginalised' populations depends on local (the regional branches') and, even more so, personal (the regional coordinator's) criteria. ConCiencia Sur has established, for example, the principle of 'positive discrimination' for their decision making. Based on ConCiencia's democratic values (access and quality of education), positive discrimination means always choosing those who have no (or less) access and/or quality in education; in other words, prioritising marginalised populations.

An example of the positive discrimination can be traced in the 'quantification sheet' mentioned in the previous section (see Appendix). In the list, corresponding to 'estimated attendance', we can see an item that reads as such: 'others (girls or boys who are not in the educational system)'. This item is not present in the project proposal of the Science Week or the correspondent report requested by the central committee. Moreover, it is rare that the activities organised by ConCiencia aim towards this type of audience, as teachers working in the formal education system organise them. The addition of this item by ConCiencia Sur's staff, at the request of Alejandra, is a materialisation of the inclusion, even if potential, of a trajectory that could be part of these initiatives. The fact that it is present in this quantification sheet acknowledges that it exists: there are children in Chile who are not part of the formal education system and, consequently, are difficult for ConCiencia to reach out. As for Easter Island, the inclusion of this coexistent story opens up possibilities for the participation of a marginalised population, one that would otherwise be excluded.

The coexistence of other trajectories (i.e. different from ConCiencia's official trajectory) was also depicted in other occasions during the ethnographic study. For example, in one of the cities, part of ConCiencia Sur's regional network, the science teachers were discussing about including or not a rural community in one of the activities they were organising for the Science Week. Most of them expressed that it was a good opportunity to invite this far-away school that rarely could participate in the activities organised by the city. Inviting the rural school would also be a way, as they mentioned, for the students of urban school to meet students who live a different school and family reality. Yet, the fact that the science teacher of this rural school was not well regarded by her colleagues made them at the end discard this invitation. Other arguments such as the expenses related to bringing the students to the city were also voiced. In this example, the trajectory of rural schools was recognised as 'being out there', but there were no efforts to include it.

As we can see, the image of space as trajectories leads to ethical and political issues associated with what could be called boundary setting: *who* participates in the organisation and *who* is in the territory, *who* is included and *who* is not. Now the question of boundary setting is quite different than in the previous images. A space understood in terms of trajectories does not convey the image of a flat surface (a region or a network). Instead, we can see how different trajectories are materialised by different actors and institutions, giving them a voice or silence them.

In the region, boundaries are set and mostly static. They can be more dynamic in the network, but in the end, they also need constant fixed coordinates to function. In a space as coexistence of trajectories, these boundaries shift and become fluid. Hence, what could be the politics of such a fluid space? Law (2002, p. 99) outlined some considerations: (a) first, no particular structure of relations is privileged and change is necessary; (b) relations need to change progressively rather than all at once; (c) no particular boundary around an object is privileged; and (d) mobile boundaries are needed for objects to exist in fluid space. From this reading, the politics of a space as coexistence of trajectories can be said to be based on the capacities of this spatial image to materialise distinct stories by shifting boundaries and keeping them mobile. Unlike regions or networks, the politics of space as trajectories do not associate space with functionality, centrality, or efficacy in a way that forbids and deletes alternatives. On the contrary, they embrace them through the respect of differences (Derrida, 1997). This is what Massey (2007) calls 'the responsibility of place' that comes with the recognition of distinct and multiple trajectories.

Concluding thoughts

This paper has taken a communication-centred approach to study organisational spaces that avoids falling into the traps of the dominant representational reasoning that has influenced most of the literature on this topic in organisation studies. These shortcomings, as mentioned, refer to the (a) blackboxing of the processes that produce organisational spaces, (b) the non-recognition of other agencies (apart from human agency) that take part in this production, and (c) the divide between physical (concrete) organisational spaces and their experience and understanding (abstract space). By proposing a communication-centred approach to the study of organisational spaces that stands on the premises of a performative/material view of communication, this article contributes to the growing body of literature on organisational spaces by emphasising the situated, embodied, and performative character of space, defined as a communicative and political process.

Two contributions can be highlighted. First, by combining Weick's (1979) and Amin et al.'s (2003) notions of grammar in this study of a spatial grammar of organising, this article allows for the integration of the interpretative, material, and political dimensions associated with the constitution of organisational spaces. The integration of these dimensions is made possible by the focus on the performative/material effects of a spatial imaginary. As we saw in the discussion of ConCiencia's spatial images, this imaginary is expressed/embodied/materialised through various forms: language, material, strategies, practices, and discourses. It conveys different (yet coexisting) ways to 'occupy' and 'colonise' the territory. In the analysis, three main spatial images appeared: network, region, and trajectories. Each had its own configuration and thus materialised distinct organisational spaces. While the first two put forward a 'conquering style' that resulted in a stable, coherent, and unique organisational space, the third presented a form of occupation based on the 'respect of difference' (Derrida, 1997) and resulted in a more fragmented, fluid, and changing space.

The analysis also shows that politics of geography are embedded in an organisation's spatial imaginary (Amin et al., 2003). This was mostly manifested in the discussion around boundaries and boundary setting. As argued by Ashcraft, Kuhn, and Cooren (2009), a communication-centred approach to organisational spaces suggests that boundaries are reconfigured in interaction. In studying ConCiencia's spatial grammar, the *boundedness* of organising (what is included and excluded) is revealed as key to understanding ConCiencia's mode of occupation. We can then see, as Hernes (2004, p. 80) suggested, that organisation 'evolves through processes of boundary setting...[it] emerges through the process of drawing distinctions, and it persists through the reproduction of boundaries'.

Moreover, this process of boundary setting is not neutral: it responds to specific criteria, policies, standards, and strategies that manage to materialise themselves in specific situations. As Clegg and Kornberger (2006) have argued, the manifestation of boundaries is the most basic way of organising space. By studying the spatial grammar of an organisation, we pay attention not only to the heterogeneity of agencies that materialise organisational spaces, but also to the politics that can hide behind these spaces and the ways they are constituted (Massey, 2004).

The second contribution is methodological. It shows the heuristic force of taking communication events as units of analysis. However, focusing on communication events does not mean isolating them from the historical context. In this paper, I have paid specific attention to grounding the events not only in the history of the organisation that was studied, but also in the broader geographical, political, and social history of its country. This analytical strategy offers a richer description of the phenomena than that which can be found in other analyses, such as those inspired by ethnomethodology or conversation analysis, which focus on one or two communication events without accounting for their spatio-temporal grounding. Finally, focusing on communication events is also a way to start from, and remain in, communication (Cooren et al., 2006), and thus to escape the pull of representational reasoning.

Finally, in this paper, I have advocated for a grammar of relations as a means with which to engage with the ontological and political implications of thinking about space in the study of organisation. This meant paying attention to the many and various actors and relations between them through which ConCiencia's spatial imaginary was embodied/materialised/expressed. This focus allowed showing that space is actually made or performed through these relations; as such it is material and symbolic, concrete and abstract, thought, lived and experienced. Moreover, the article shows that the geography that is constituted through these different relations embraces ethical and moral stances, mostly because it is based on boundary setting.

In doing so, it reveals the politics behind the different ways an organisation can 'occupy', 'constitute', and 'materialise' its space of action, showing that the spatial imaginary of an organisation is neither abstract nor neutral: it has concrete organisational and political implications that define who/what takes part in the organisation and who/what does not.

Notes

1. I have used a pseudonym for the organisation and the participants of the study in order to preserve anonymity and confidentiality.
2. In general, shadowing is defined as a research technique that involves following a person as his or her shadow, walking in his or her footsteps, and taking field notes. Similar to participant observation, shadowing is used over a relatively long period of time, and the researcher's objective is to follow the person throughout his or her different activities over the course of a day (McDonald, 2005). Without engaging in the debate over the status of shadowing in organisation studies (see Meunier & Vásquez, 2008), I adopt a pragmatic approach (as suggested by Czarniawska, 2007) that defines shadowing as a (non-)participatory technique of direct observation (the other technique being stationary observation) mainly characterised by its mobility.
3. I have translated all the excerpts from Spanish to English and transcribed them following the conventions for conversation analysis. The passages in bold are considered key to the analysis.

Acknowledgements

I would like to thank Karen L. Ashcraft for her comments on previous versions of the article and her support, as well as Colleen Mills and François Cooren, editors of this special issue, for their guidance.

Disclosure statement

No potential conflict of interest was reported by the author.

Funding

This work was supported by a scholarship from the Social Sciences and Humanities Research Council of Canada (SSHRC).

ORCID

Consuelo Vásquez ⓘD http://orcid.org/0000-0002-3904-9878

References

Amin, A., Massey, D., & Thrift, N. (2003). *Decentering the nation: A radical approach to regional inequality.* London: Catalyst.

Anderson, B., & Harrison, P. (2010). *Taking-place: Non-representational theories and geography*. London: Ashgate.

Ashcraft, K. L., Kuhn, T. R., & Cooren, F. (2009). Constitutional amendments: "Materializing" organizational communication. In J. P. Walsh & A. P. Brief (Eds.), *The academy of management annals* (Vol. 3, pp. 1–64). London: Routledge.

Bakken, T., & Hernes, T. (2006). Organizing is both a verb and a noun: Weick meets Whitehead. *Organization Studies, 27*(11), 1599–1616. doi:10.1177/0170840606068335

Baldry, C. (1999). Space — The final frontier. *Sociology, 33*(3), 535–553.

Bannerman, C., Massey, D., Boddington, G., Layzell, R., Lee, R., & Miller, G. (2005). *Making space [seminar transcript]*. London: Royal Institute of British Architects.

Bantz, C. R. (1989). Organizing and the social psychology of organizing. *Communication Studies, 40*(4), 231–240. doi:10.1080/10510978909368276

Barley, S. R. (1986). Technology as an occasion for structuring: Evidence from observations of CT scanners and the social order of radiology departments. *Administrative Science Quarterly, 31*, 78–108. doi:10.2307/2392767

Bauman, Z. (1987). *Legislators and interpreters*. Cambridge: Polity Press.

Becker, H. S. (1982). *Art worlds*. Berkeley, CA: University of California Press.

Becker, H. S., Blanche, G., Everett, C. H., & Strauss, A. (1961). *Boys in white*. Chicago, IL: University of Chicago Press.

Bengtsson, M., Mullern, T., Soderlhom, A., & Wahlin, N. (2007). *A grammar of organizing*. Glos: Edward Elgar Publishing.

Beyes, T., & Steyaert, C. (2012). Spacing organization: Non-representational theory and performing organizational space. *Organization, 19*(1), 45–61. doi:10.1177/1350508411401946

Brummans, B., Cooren, F., Robichaud, D., & Taylor, J. R. (2014). Approaches in research on the communicative constitution of organizations. In L. L. Putnam & D. Mumby (Eds.), *Sage handbook of organizational communication* (3rd ed., pp. 173–194). Thousand Oaks, CA: Sage.

Cadman, L. (2009). Non-representational theory/non-representational geographies. In R. Kitchin & N. Thrift (Eds.), *International encyclopedia of human geography* (Vol. 7, pp. 456–463). London: Elsevier.

Clegg, S., & Kornberger, M. (2006). Organising space. In S. Clegg & M. Kornberger (Eds.), *Space, organizations and management theory* (pp. 143–162). Slovenian: Liber & Copenhagen Business School Press.

Cooren, F. (2000). *The organizing property of communication*. Amsterdam: John Benjamins Publishing.

Cooren, F. (2010). *Action and agency in dialogue: Passion, incarnation and ventriloquism*. Amsterdam: John Benjamins Publishing.

Cooren, F., Bencherki, N., Chaput, M., & Vásquez, C. (2015). A communicational approach to strategy- making: Exploring the constitution of matters of concerns in fleeting moments of strategy. In D. Golsorkhi, L. Rouleau, D. Seidl, & E. Vaara (Eds.), *Cambridge handbook of strategy as practice* (2nd ed., pp. 365–388). Cambridge: Cambridge University Press.

Cooren, F., Kuhn, T., Cornelissen, J. P., & Clark, T. (2011). Communication, organizing and organization: An overview and introduction to the special issue. *Organization Studies, 32*(9), 1149–1170. doi:10.1177/0170840611410836

Cooren, F., Taylor, J. R., & Van Every, E. J. (2006). *Communication as organizing: Empirical and theoretical explorations in the dynamic of text and conversation*. Mahwah, NJ: Lawrence Erlbaum.

Cornelissen, J. P., Mantere, S., & Vaara, E. (2014). The contraction of meaning: The combined effect of communication, emotions, and materiality on sensemaking in the Stockwell shooting. *Journal of Management Studies, 51*(5), 699–736. doi:10.1111/joms.2014.51.issue-5

Cunliffe, A. L., & Jun, J. S. (2005). The need for reflexivity in public administration. *Administration & Society, 37*(2), 225–242. doi:10.1177/0095399704273209

Czarniawska, B. (2007). *Shadowing and other techniques for doing fieldwork in modern societies*. Malmö: Liber.

Dale, K. (2005). Building a social materiality: Spatial and embodied politics in organizational control. *Organization, 12*(5), 649–678. doi:10.1177/1350508405055940

Dale, K., & Burrell, G. (2008). *The spaces of organisation and the organisation of space: Power, identity and materiality at work*. London: Palgrave.

Derrida, J. (1997). *Politics of friendship*. London: Verso.

Dobers, P., & Strannegard, L. (2004). The Cocoon - A travelling space. *Organization, 11*(6), 825–848. doi:10.1177/1350508404047253

Doxater, D. (1990). Meaning of the workplace: Using ideas of ritual space in design. In P. Gagliardi (Ed.), *Symbols and artifacts: Views of the corporate landscape* (pp. 107–128). Berlin: De Gruyter.

Fleming, P., & Spicer, A. (2004). You can checkout anytime, but you can never leave: Spatial boundaries in a high commitment organization. *Human Relations, 57*(1), 75–94. doi:10.1177/0018726704042715

Gagliardi, P. (1990). *Symbols and artifacts: Views of the corporate landscape*. Berlin: De Gruyter.

Hancock, P. (2006). The spatial and temporal mediation of social change. *Journal of Organizational Change Management, 19*(5), 619–639. doi:10.1108/09534810610686706

Hatch, M. J. (1990). The symbolics of office design: An empirical ConCienciation. In P. Gagliardi (Ed.), *Symbols and artifacts: Views of the corporate landscape* (pp. 129–146). Berlin: De Gruyter.

Hennion, A. (1993). *La passion musicale. Une sociologie de la médiation*. Paris: Métaillé.

Hernes, T. (2004). *The spatial construction of organization*. Amsterdam: John Benjamins.

Hernes, T. (2008). *Understanding organization as process. Theory for a tangled world*. London: Routledge.

Ingold, T. (2011). *Being alive: Essays on movement, knowledge and description*. London: Routledge.

Jefferson, G. (1984). On stepwise transition from talk about a trouble to inappropriately next-positioned matters. In J. M. Atkinson & J. Heritage (Eds.), *Structures of social action: Studies of conversation analysis* (pp. 191–222). Cambridge: Cambridge University Press.

Knox, H., O'Doherty, D., Vurdubakis, T., & Westrup, C. (2008). Enacting airports: Space, movement and modes of ordering. *Organization, 15*(6), 869–888. doi:10.1177/1350508408095818

Kornberger, M., & Clegg, S. (2004). Bringing space back in: Organizing the generative building. *Organization Studies, 25*(7), 1095–1114. doi:10.1177/0170840604046312

Latour, B. (2005). *Reassembling the social: An introduction to actor-network-theory*. Oxford: Oxford University Press.

Latour, B. (1986). The powers of associations. In J. Law (Ed.), *Power, action and belief: A new sociology of knowledge?* (pp. 264–280). London: Routledge.

Law, J. (2002). Objects and spaces. *Theory, Culture & Society, 19*(5–6), 91–105. doi:10.1177/026327602761899165

Lefebvre, H. (1974/1991). *The production of space*. (D. Nicholson-Smith, Trans.). Oxford: Blackwell.

Lutterbie, J. H. (2001). Phenomenology and the dramaturgy of space and place. *Journal of Dramatic Theory and Criticism, 1*, 123–132.

Massey, D. (1994). *Space, place, and gender*. Minneapolis, MN: University of Minnesota Press.

Massey, D. (2004). Geographies of responsibility. *Geografiska Annaler, Series B: Human Geography, 86*(1), 5–18. doi:10.1111/geob.2004.86.issue-1

Massey, D. (2005). *For space*. London: Sage.

Massey, D. (2007). *World city*. Cambridge: Polity Press.

Mayo, E. (1933). *The human problems of an industrial civilization*. New York, NY: MacMillan.

McDonald, S. (2005). Studying actions in context: A qualitative shadowing method for organizational research. *Qualitative Research, 5*(4), 455–473. doi:10.1177/1468794105056923

Meunier, D., & Vásquez, C. (2008). On shadowing the hybrid character of actions: A communicational approach. *Communication Methods and Measures, 2*(3), 167–192. doi:10.1080/19312450802310482

Mills, C. (2002). The hidden dimension of blue-collar sensemaking about workplace communication. *Journal of Business Communication, 39*(3), 288–313. doi:10.1177/002194360203900301

Murdoch, J., & Marsden, T. (1995). The spatialization of politics: Local and national actor-spaces in environmental conflict. *Transactions of the Institute of British Geographers, 20,* 368–380. doi:10.2307/622657

Pentland, B. T. (1995). Grammatical models of organizational processes. *Organization Science, 6*(5), 541–556. doi:10.1287/orsc.6.5.541

Robichaud, D. (2002). Greimas' semiotics and the analysis of organizational action. In P. B. Anderson, R. J. Clarke, K. Liu, & R. K. Stamper (Eds.), *Coordination and communication using signs: Studies in organizational semiotics* (pp. 129–149). Boston, MA: Kluwer Academic.

Schoeneborn, D., & Vásquez, C. (in press). The communicative constitution of organization (CCO). In C. Scott & L. Lewis (General Eds.), J. Barker, J. Keyton, T. Kuhn, & P. Turner (Associate Eds.), *The international encyclopedia of organizational communication.* Chichester: Wiley Blackwell.

Spicer, A. (2006). Beyond the convergence-divergence debate: The role of spatial scales in transforming organizational logic. *Organization Studies, 27*(10), 1467–1483. doi:10.1177/0170840606067515

Taylor, J. R., & Van Every, E. J. (2000). *The emergent organization. Communication as its site and surface.* Hillsdale, NJ: Lawrence Erlbaum Ass.

Taylor, J. R., & Van Every, E. J. (2011). *The situated organization. Case studies in the pragmatics of communication research.* New York, NY: Routledge.

Taylor, S., & Spicer, A. (2007). Time for space: A narrative review of research on organizational spaces. *International Journal of Management Reviews, 9*(4), 325–346. doi:10.1111/ijmr.2007.9.issue-4

Thrift, N. (2007). *Non-representational theory: Space, politics, affect.* London: Routledge.

Tuan, Y. F. (1979). Space and place: Humanistic perspective. In S. Gale & G. Olsson (Eds.), *Philosophy in geography* (pp. 387–427). Dorddrecht: Reidel Publishing.

Tyler, M., & Cohen, L. (2010). Spaces that matter: Gender performativity and organizational space. *Organization Studies, 31*(2), 175–198. doi:10.1177/0170840609357381

Van Marrewijk, A. (2009). Corporate headquarters as physical embodiments of organisational change. *Journal of Organizational Change Management, 22*(3), 290–306.

Van Marrewijk, A., & Yanow, D. (2010). *Organizational spaces. Rematerializing the workaday world.* Glos: Edward Elgar Publishing.

Vásquez, C., & Cooren, F. (2013). Spacing practices: The communicative configuration of organizing through space-times. *Communication Theory, 23*(1), 25–47. doi:10.1111/comt.2013.23.issue-1

Vásquez, C., Schoeneborn, D., & Sergi, V. (2016). Summoning the spirits: Organizational texts and the (dis)ordering properties of communication. *Human Relations, 69*(3), 629–659. doi:10.1177/0018726715589422

Weick, K. E. (1979). *The social psychology of organizing.* New York, NY: Random House.

Weick, K. E. (1995). *Sensemaking in organization.* Thousand Oaks, CA: Sage.

Whitehead, A. N. (1920, November). Theories of the bifurcation of nature. In *The concept of nature: The Tarner lectures delivered in Trinity College* (pp. 26–48). Cambridge: Cambridge University Press.

Yanow, D. (1993). Reading policy meanings in organization-scapes. *Journal of Architecture and Planning Research, 10,* 308–327.

Yanow, D. (2010). Giving voice to space: Academic practice and the material world. In M. Van Marrewijk & D. Yanow (Eds.), *Organizational spaces. Rematerializing the workaday world* (pp. 138–158). Glos: Edward Elgar Publishing.

Ybema, S., Yanow, D., Wels, H., & Kamsteeg, F. (2009). *Organizational ethnography.* London: Sage.

Appendix

	Name of the activity	
Science and technology field		
Description		
Begins:	Ends:	
Date, month, year, time	Date, month, year, time	
Place (street, city)		
Estimated attendance		**Total number of participants**
	Preschool	
	Elementary school	
	Junior high school	
	High school	
	Others (girls or boys who are not in the educational system)	
	Teachers	
	Scientists, scholars, or other professionals	
	University students	
	General public	
	Other	
Estimated number of institutions attending		
	Public schools	
	Semi-public schools	
	Private schools	
	Scientific institutions	
	Cultural institutions	
	Territorial organisations	
	Governmental organisations	
	International organisations	
	Public companies	
	Private companies	
	Medias	
	Others	
Expected results (in numbers)		

Making mundane work visible on social media: a CCO investigation of working out loud on Twitter

Viviane Sergi and Claudine Bonneau

ABSTRACT

This article examines an emergent communicative practice called *working out loud* (WOL), defined as a process of narrating work during the course of its realisation, by studying instances of WOL on Twitter. Anchored in a relational ontology, our inquiry aims to investigate what these tweets, defined as sociomaterial agents, accomplish. Our results show that as a practice, WOL adopts a variety of forms. We link the actions achieved by the tweets to their inherent characteristics, hence documenting their agency. We show that WOL tweets are performative in that they make visible things that otherwise tend to remain hidden, private, or difficult to reveal in an explicit way. More precisely, through our CCO inquiry, we suggest that given the characteristics associated with these tweets and, more broadly, with that which Twitter enables or constrains, WOL tweets have the potential to actively participate in the constitution of work and professional identity of workers engaging in working out loud.

Introduction

For most of the 20th century, 'work' meant working for someone, in an organisation. However, with the fast-paced development of information and communication technology in recent decades, we have seen the form of organisations – the places where work was traditionally done – transform and mutate. Post-bureaucracy was declared to have replaced an old, inefficient bureaucracy; then virtual (Boudreau, Loch, Robey, & Straud, 1998) and project-based organisations (Hobday, 2000) appeared. New forms of work and new work practices are still emerging, especially in the midst of the digitalisation of work and the rise of social media platforms. These platforms can be seen both as allowing new forms of work (such as the crowdsourcing of human intelligence tasks via Amazon.com's digital labor market, Mechanical Turk; see Aytes, 2013) and as new sites where work (conventional or not) can be done and where the experience of work is expressed. Increasingly, professionals use social media to narrate their work (Winer, 2009), allowing them to 'talk' about their work as it is happening. But what, precisely, are workers doing when they use social media in relation to their working situations?

DISCURSIVITY, RELATIONALITY AND MATERIALITY

In this study, we examine an emergent communicative practice referred to as 'working out loud' (or 'WOL'; Bonneau, 2013), which can be broadly described as a process of narrating one's work during the course of its realisation, highlighting its daily and mundane accomplishment. We begin with the premise that the 'working out loud' phenomenon is a communicative practice (see Nicolini, 2012) that blends talk and text in an interesting way, as it is a form of talk that incorporates elements commonly associated with text, as well as a form of text that may adopt particularities of talk and conversation. We can be practiced on various social media we have chosen to empirically focus on working out loud on Twitter. As we will present, WOL instances (in other words, tweets) can be investigated from both their discursive and material sides. After all, these microtexts are inscriptions afforded and constrained by Twitter as an online platform. Anchored in a relational ontology, our inquiry does not choose between what is too often constructed as separate worlds (Cooren, 2015) and suggests exploring WOL tweets as sociomaterial. Moreover, inspired by the communicative constitution of organizations (CCO) perspective, we propose conceptualising tweets as sociomaterial agents. Hence, in this article, we investigate what arises from the contributions of human and non-human actors in relation to the daily accomplishment of work. In doing so, we expand upon studies that have documented textual agency (e.g. Cooren, 2004; Sergi, 2013; Smith, 1984, 2001), by exposing the characteristics that are the basis of these tweets' textual agency.

This article is structured as follows: first, we describe what working out loud, understood as a communicative practice, is about. We then present the theoretical framing of our study, namely the CCO, and how it leads us to problematise working out loud on Twitter. After having discussed the methodology of our study, we describe the variety of forms the working out loud practice can adopt, which lead us to develop a repertoire of WOL tweets. We then discuss what these tweets accomplish for the workers who produce them in the course of their work. More precisely, we reveal how WOL make visible and materialise aspects of work that otherwise tend to remain unnoticed or hidden, which allows us to document their textual agency. As we show, WOL tweets participate in the constitution of work and professional identity of workers engaging in the practice of working out loud. This leads us to address in more broader terms the performativity of these tweets, and to show that WOL tweets exist between talk and text. We then conclude our article by reflecting back in a prospective manner on the relationships between communication, work and organisation.

Working out loud on social media

Working out loud presents a number of intriguing characteristics that suggest that it should be carefully studied: it is informal, adopts both a conversational and a written form, and is not limited to a specific audience. First, this practice is mostly informal and does not correspond to any form of organisational requirement. Workers talk about their daily tasks, what they are doing and experiencing in a way akin to casual 'water cooler conversations'. Second, contrary to these water cooler conversations, working out loud takes on a double form by being both conversational and textual. As communication technologies such as email, chat, instant messaging, and short message service (SMS) have become embedded in the work practices of many occupations, formal and informal interactions rely extensively on written communication, even when collaborations occur in co-located settings (Fayard & Metiu, 2014). Social media are another form of text-based communication technology increasingly used in work organisations. These technologies comprise 'Internet-based applications that build on the ideological and technological foundations of Web 2.0, and that allow the creation and exchange of User-generated content' (Kaplan & Haenlein, 2010, p. 62). The term 'social media' thus refers to different types of online platforms such as social networking sites (SNS), wikis, and blogging platforms.

Working out loud is also not limited to a predefined audience, a characteristic linked to social media's affordances. Treem and Leonardi (2013) identified four affordances of social media that distinguish them from other communication technologies commonly used in organisations: visibility, persistence, editability, and association. In their view, affordances are not exclusively properties of people or artefacts – they are constituted in relationships between human agency (people's goals) and the material agency of the things with which they come into contact (the things a technology's materiality allows or not) (Leonardi, 2011). Flyverbom, Leonardi, Stohl, and Stohl (2016) later recognised that the affordance of visibility supersedes the others. For the purposes of this article, we pursue their idea in order to show how social media affords visibility in particular ways. Contributions to social media (posts, status updates, comments, etc.) are visible to all who have access to the user's profile, as opposed to email, where the visibility of a message is limited to those to whom the message was addressed. This higher level of openness and the 'many-to-many' communication patterns inherent to these platforms bring us to the third characteristic of working out loud: its absence of *a priori* limits in terms of an audience, which results in a broader reach. Workers using social media to narrate their work can broadcast online texts to the world, in a public and communal fashion, rather than having to select *a priori* which audience to address (Majchrzak, Faraj, Kane, & Azad, 2013) and interact with.

When considering social media uses in organisational contexts, it is important to distinguish 'public social media' like Facebook, LinkedIn, and Twitter from 'enterprise social media' (ESM), which are corporate versions of these platforms, designed only for internal audiences (Leonardi, 2014; Leonardi, Huysman, & Steinfield, 2013; Oostervink, Agterberg, & Huysman, 2016). The private nature of ESM platforms limits their interorganisational reach, as they are intended for communication and social interaction within the enterprise. In our study, we investigate instances of working out loud that are not restricted to a specific corporate audience, but are made visible on public social media by workers who narrate their work to people inside or outside their organisation. Given the increased use of personal smartphones by employees (Archambault & Grudin, 2012) and the growing popularity of 'Bring Your Own Device' (BYOD) policies (Willis, 2013), employees can use their personal mobile devices to discreetly access public social media at the workplace, whether authorised or not by their employers.

Working out loud can be practiced on any social media platform, like on blogs. However, we chose to study it on the microblogging platform Twitter for several reasons. First, Twitter has been recognised as the most popular channel for disseminating work-related content and as an effective tool for dialogue in organisational communication (van Zoonen, Verhoeven, & Vliegenthart, 2016). Second, Twitter accounts are by default created as public, meaning that anyone can follow them without first asking for permission. Unless users configure their account to make it private, their publications and conversations are visible, which facilitates the discovery of users and messages through serendipity. This allows workers to use Twitter to make information visible to others outside their organisation.

Moreover, the asymmetrical attribute of connections – which can be unidirectional or bidirectional – distinguishes Twitter from other social media where 'friendship' is reciprocal. Twitter users can follow someone even if that person does not follow them in return. 'Following' a user means that their tweets are displayed on one's newsfeed. This broadcasting capability opens visibility and communication to non-targeted users since there is no need to specify an addressee (Zhang, Qu, Cody, & Wu, 2010). Tweets can be broadcast to the user's audience with the hope that they reach appropriate recipients, without having to know 'who knows what', 'who knows whom', or 'who knows who knows what' (Nardi, Whittaker, & Schwarz, 2000). The addition of the '#' sign in front of keywords (e.g. '#work') is another convention developed by users to categorise subjects. Such 'hashtags' also affect the visibility of tweets because users can access all tweets containing the same hashtag by clicking on it. They therefore facilitate the articulation of collective narrative activities on a specific topic, which can lead to open conversations between users sharing the same interests. While workers can share information about their work via other tools such as email or instant messaging, these tools cannot be used to reach people outside of their initial network. This is why working out loud is particularly present on Twitter. As stated by Winer (2009), 'Twitter is very much a Narrate Your Work environment', since it provides an easy way for employees to make their work behaviours, their expertise, the information they possess, and the activities they conduct visible to other users inside or outside their organisation, in a non-intrusive way.

Communication, organisation and work under a CCO perspective

To begin our investigation, we define and theorise this communicative practice from the stream of research called the CCO, whose central idea is that organisation is a process of becoming that stems from communication (Taylor, 2009), rather than being the location where communication happens. In other words, CCO starts from the organising properties of communication in order to address the fundamental question of the ontology of organisation, and suggests that organisation is constituted in communication (see, e.g. Ashcraft, Kuhn, & Cooren, 2009; Cooren, Kuhn, Cornelissen, & Clark, 2011; Taylor & Van Every, 2000). Generally speaking, CCO aims to '[...] unpack the black box or the idealized abstraction of an organization that is rarely questioned' (Putnam & Nicotera, 2009, p. 161). As Brummans, Cooren, Robichaud, and Taylor underlined, '[w]hat sets this research apart [...] are its novel ways of theorizing and analysing how organizations as discursive-material configurations are reproduced and coproduced through ongoing interactions' (2014, p. 173). CCO studies are grounded in a performative view of language, wherein the use of language is not simply understood as carrying meaning, but as doing things (Austin, 1962). Our study can also be identified with the Montreal School (see Schoeneborn et al., 2014, for an explicit comparison of the different schools making up CCO), which, as underlined by the quote from Brummans et al., suggests that organisational communication is at the same time material and discursive (see also Cooren, 2015; Cooren, Fairhurst, & Huët, 2012).

Moreover, the Montreal School is concerned with the question of the organisation's stabilisation. Cooren's work (see, e.g. Cooren, 2004, 2006, 2010, 2012; Cooren & Fairhurst, 2009; Cooren et al., 2012; Cooren & Matte, 2010) has suggested that it is through a hybrid understanding of agency – as extended to non-humans, such as tools, documents, settings, bodies, numbers, and even more 'abstract' elements such as emotions and values, what he calls 'figures' – that we can shed light on how organisation, through communication, achieves stabilisation. Borrowing from Latour (1994, 2005)), hybrid agency in CCO suggests that 'communicating' is not limited to human actors. In other words, constituting an organisation implies creating, assembling, and mobilising elements (especially in textual form) that can hold on and endure – elements that do so because of their capacity to stay the same over time. This property is highlighted by the contribution of texts (Cooren, 2004; Smith, 1984, 2001). However, in the Montreal School, as in CCO in general, the textual side of organisation cannot be separated from its conversational side (Taylor & Van Every, 2000): the organisation is always in movement (what the verb 'organising' refers to), but this emergence is always the result of a variety of human and non-human contributions in interactions (Cooren & Fairhurst, 2009; see also Cooren's idea of organisation as a plenum of agencies, 2006). Finally, it is through these recurrent interactions *in situ*, which involve human and non-human actors, that an organisation acquires a distinct entitative character, existing with an 'identity', possessing an authority, and 'doing' things through people speaking and acting on its behalf (in other words, being authored; see Taylor & Van Every, 2011). As Taylor and Van Every note, '[t]he mystery [of organization] is in the personification that occurs [...]' (2011, p. 2). Many of the studies conducted in this communication-centred perspective try to dissipate this mystery by exploring how, in detailed and empirical terms, the organisation is accomplished and achieved in mundane interactions – or, to use Brummans et al.'s formulation, '[to] explain how generality emerges from performativity' (2014, p. 187).

This broad overview of CCO serves as the backdrop to our own study, and allows us to problematise what is shared on Twitter and address what contributes to this phenomenon. Tweets, and conversations that take place via the exchange of tweets, are usually not problematised: they are taken for granted, considered *de facto* as talk and conversations, or, in other cases, as texts. Despite the fact that what happens on social media can be understood as communicative events (Cooren et al., 2011), social media have rarely been studied from a CCO perspective (for a notable exception, see Albu & Etter, 2016). However, informed by CCO and by work both on working out loud (Bonneau, 2013) and textual agency (Sergi, 2013), we believe that there is more than meets the eye with tweets. What are the tweets that give shape to the practice of working out loud and, more precisely, what do they *do*? Are the results they produce linked to the combination of talk and text that we see in tweets? Previous studies have revealed the organising effects of talk and conversation (e.g. Boden, 1994; Robichaud, Giroux, & Taylor, 2004) and of texts (e.g. Anderson, 2004; Callon, 2002). Do tweets more resemble talk, or text? More importantly, why should we have to choose between them? We therefore pursue two research questions in our study: what are people doing when they engage in working out loud, and what are tweets associated with this practice accomplishing and producing? We emphasise the idea that tweets are not a banal short form of text, but that, as is the case with any form of communication understood from a communication-centred perspective, it presents performative properties: it *does* things (Austin, 1962).

Our exploratory study also allows us to reflect on relationships between work, communication, and organisation in a more theoretical manner. Taylor and Van Every's ideas about the constitution of organisations revolve around this interplay between text and conversation, underlining that their separation is analytical. When we turn to empirical, situated investigations, both are in constant relation. This interplay – the transition from text to conversation and from conversation to text – creates, sustains, and transforms (or *constitutes*) the organisation. In their words, '[...] organization is generated in the cross-over translation process from the more durable constructions of language, or texts, into the fleeting processes of human interaction, or conversations, and vice versa' (Taylor & Van Every, 2011, p. 192). This is also the line of thinking that Cooren developed (2015) when he wrote, '[...] communication is constitutive of the mode of existence of *any being*, whether we are speaking of a human being, an organisation, an artwork, an idea, an emotion, a virus, or a technology. [...] Communication is the way by which all these beings manage to exist [...]' (p. 318; italics in the original). In the CCO perspective, an organisation, in its most basic form, involves at least two individuals (Taylor & Van Every, 2011) and some stabilisation regarding roles, responsibilities, hierarchy, and the like (Cooren & Fairhurst, 2009).

With this study, we acknowledge that WOL tweets are not fully part of what could be defined as an organisational context. Rather, we are looking at tweets and conversations related to, and about, work. Interestingly, work has not been among the primary conceptual focuses of most CCO scholars. Given the central ontological question that these scholars explore (that of the definition, existence, and continuation of organisation), this is not surprising. At the same time, work is quite present in CCO studies, as these tend to be illustrated with detailed examples that essentially showcase people at work. After all, these studies deal with *organisational* communication, and an organisation is broadly understood as a place where people work. But if CCO is about understanding organisations from a communication-centred perspective, it could be fruitful to 'bring work back in', to evoke Barley and Kunda's call (as stated in the title of their 2001 article). Although, the concept of work has gained preeminence in recent years (see Phillips & Lawrence, 2012, for an overview of the varieties of work that have been discussed in organization studies lately), much remains to be studied when it comes to work and social media, especially mundane work. Our study provides us with insights that could stimulate inquiries about work. These elements will be discussed in the final sections of our article.

Methodological approach

Twitter has become social science researchers' favourite site because they can take advantage of the mass of 'big data' generated by the platform to perform quantitative data analysis (Marwick, 2014). Key terms and phrases are identified for automatic extraction from tweets in order to create a large analytical corpus. However, these text-mining functionalities cannot be used to effectively collect tweets concerning such distributed and widespread phenomena as our present topic. Tweets concerning 'work being done' cannot be identified using specific semantic or narrative patterns, nor predefined keywords or hashtags, since the topics being addressed vary according to the type of professional activity being tweeted about. One key particularity of our research is that the forms of working out loud we are studying can emerge as employee-driven initiatives and be found in any organisation and professional field. Based on our ongoing observations, the practice of working out loud appears to be more informal than formal. It is only recently that some employees and consultants have begun referring to it and trying to make it into a more formalised work practice (as exemplified by the recent first 'WOL Week', see Hinchcliffe, 2015; and by books published on the topic [Bozarth, 2014; Stepper, 2015]). Working out loud is available to any worker, employee, or professional, in any field of activity, and evolves in all imaginable settings, from temporary self-employment to a permanent position in a transnational firm. The only condition necessary for working out loud, in the sense that we explore here, is to use Twitter to convey comments, observations, and material related to the daily experience and processes of work.

In this context, we cannot circumscribe our data collection to specific organisations that encourage or prescribe working out loud, nor can we limit *a priori* our investigation to one professional community in which working out loud would already be quite common. Such open-endedness raises methodological challenges, especially in organisation studies, as most studies in this field begin with organisations that already exist. From an ontological point of view, CCO studies challenge the definition of organisations as reified entities existing independently of situated and repeated interactions. Nevertheless, most research conducted in this line of inquiry still aims to explain how organisations that can be recognised (even those that can be deemed fluid, such as online communities [e.g. Faraj, Jarvenpaa, & Majchrzak, 2011], precarious, such as Anonymous [e.g. Dobusch & Schoeneborn, 2015], or nascent [e.g. Chaput, 2012]) persist over time (or not), and express or achieve different features, such as organisational identity. In the vast majority of cases, there is an organisation to explain. Our study clearly starts from a different point, *outside* any specific and formal organisation, which does not exclude the possibility that someone who has a formal and contractual relationship with an organisation via his or her work may still practice working out loud.

Because the boundaries of the 'WOL field' do not objectively exist prior to our inquiry, we needed to devise a flexible methodological approach that would allow us to find out what we could not precisely delineate in advance. Also, we needed to understand WOL tweets in the context of their production, with their technical and social dimensions. For these reasons, we chose a qualitative approach, based on the manual collection of a small corpus of data, to allow us to capture the specificities of the phenomenon under study. Such a 'small/thick data' approach 'encourages exploration and fosters greater familiarity with the traces in their 'native' format, as they are envisioned by social media users' (Latzko-Toth, Bonneau, & Millette, in press). Furthermore, it allowed us to provide 'thick description' (Geertz, 1973) of the tweets collected in order 'to illuminate specific patterns of use that would have been difficult, if not impossible, to ascertain with a more automated method' (Marwick, 2014, p. 118).

Our data collection strategy is inspired by digital ethnography (Hine, 2015). We immersed ourselves in WOL practice by observing publications and interactions of people tweeting about their work activities and by selecting tweets that corresponded to our definition of working out loud:

> Any tweet narrating the work as it is being done, spontaneously published by any worker or professional that can take the form of observation, description, questioning, reflection or exclamation. The tweet can be directed (or not) to other people and can include pictures, videos and/or links to external web pages or online documents.

This definition is the main element that guided us through the construction of a corpus of 200 naturally occurring public tweets in English and French between February 2014 and March 2016.[1] It is voluntarily inclusive so as to account for a wide spectrum of tweets related to the daily experience and processes of work, but, at the same time, excludes tweets consisting of content curation (e.g. selecting and sharing existing content, even if it is work related) and promotion of completed work. For instance, a tweet from a journalist describing an ongoing investigation would be included in our WOL corpus (see Figure 1), while a tweet presenting her latest published article would not (see Figure 2).

In this way, we can describe our selection process as a combination of a theoretical sampling (Eisenhardt, 1989) (based on our research objective and definition of working out loud) and a convenience sampling (based on the public accessibility of the tweets and the language in which they were published). Since our primary objective was to identify the various forms of working out loud and WOL tweets, we were also looking for atypical cases and thus selected tweets based on their 'potential for learning' (Stake, 2008) (i.e. tweets that could show us different ways of practicing working out loud). In sum, the

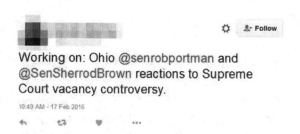

Figure 1. Example of a tweet included in the WOL corpus.

Figure 2. Example of a tweet not included in the WOL corpus.

'diversity criterion' was preferred over representativeness; our goal was to collect enough tweets to be able to provide an exhaustive representation of a new technology-enabled phenomenon, but not to produce generalisable results. Also, our intent was not to establish a portrait of the workers concerned by these practices, but rather to consider the tweets themselves as the object of inquiry. For these reasons, we did not compare user accounts, nor did we identify the impact of the different variables (e.g. professional domain, employment status, sociodemographic description, etc.) on their WOL practices.

On an operational level, we connected to Twitter via TweetDeck[2] with our own accounts, and therefore did not use other third-party applications (API) or Twitter data-mining tools. We began our collection process by observing Twitter users we were already following (mainly scholars, journalists, and knowledge workers). Using a snowball sampling approach, we were able to find new users through their discussions and retweeted publications. Along the way, we found that dedicated hashtags were adopted by some professionals (e.g. #showyourwork, #shareyourwork, #WOL, #WOLWeek) following the unexpected publication of books and articles related to the topic of working out loud. We then started to monitor those hashtags closely, while not limiting our selection to tweets found through those means. Previous studies have shown that the majority of Twitter users do not use hashtags (Boyd, Golder, & Lotan, 2010) and that using hashtags as a sole criterion can be problematic (Tufekci, 2014). Workers who are actually working out loud on Twitter do not necessarily know that those hashtags exist, nor are they conscious that what they are doing can be described as working out loud. In order to collect WOL tweets in other professional areas, we also performed queries on Twitter's internal search engine after asking ourselves, 'Who would share his or her work and what would he or she say about it?' For example, we searched for related verbs, like 'working on', or used domain-related keywords such as 'nurse'. This drew our attention to users in other professional domains, like healthcare, farming, the arts, and construction. Again, we used the search engine only for discovery purposes and not with the intent of finding all instances of WOL tweets for the given period.[3]

All 200 tweets collected were documented in a log, along with their date of publication, URL, and details about how we found them. The log also includes field notes where researchers' impressions were recorded along with provisional thoughts and ideas about what to look at next (Hine, 2015).

Qualitative textual analysis was used to proceed to a manual thematic coding of each tweet in an open and inductive manner (Miles, Huberman, & Saldana, 2013). The first step of our coding process included coding for descriptive features and for the presence of links, pictures, or hashtags. For example, a tweet was coded for 'material description' if it exposed the materiality of the work environment and tools. Then, we grouped tweets based on commonalities. These categories were then associated with their performative effects, which were operationalised based on concepts drawn from CCO, such as the related notions of textual agency and performativity. The validity of coding was ensured through reconciliation (Schreier, 2012). This categorisation allowed us to identify the various forms that working out loud can adopt, and to reveal what the WOL tweets created in relation to work.

Variety of the working out loud practice

As previously mentioned, working out loud is a communicative practice that combines both talk and textual elements.[4] This section aims to answer the two empirical questions driving our research efforts: (1) What different forms can working out loud take? (2) What results from or is produced by each of these forms? We first categorise the corpus of tweets we collected in order to show the variety of this practice, and then we ask what these tweets create. As presented in Table 1, our analysis led us to uncover six distinct forms that the WOL practice can adopt. Each form is described in the table and illustrated with examples of tweets. The last column presents the actions accomplished by the tweets associated with each of these forms of working out loud. In this sense, each form of the WOL practice is associated with a specific effect, which should be understood as what tweets belonging to each category do. It should be clear that we attribute these effects to the action of tweets. These actions arise from their capacity to act and are linked to their characteristics. Therefore, in this section, after presenting each form of working out loud, we will move on to discussing how these tweets can act.

1. Exposing. This form of working out loud groups tweets that generate tangible manifestations of work throughout its execution. External links to work-in-progress documents, pictures, or videos are often included in order to share concrete traces of the work at the moment it is done. In the example shown in Figure 3, a composer publishes a sketch of a music sheet written during the day and explains that it took him more than 2 hours to produce 15 seconds of music. This tweet demonstrates how the process unfolds and how the product evolves. Such tweets give visibility to backstage work (Star & Strauss, 1999) that is usually inaccessible to people who are not in the situation. Drawing on a work-in-progress culture, some workers no longer think that something has to be finished before they let strangers see it. Working in such an open manner can generate input on preliminary, incomplete, and imperfect iterations. Professionals can test drafts and prototypes and improve them based on the feedback received. Workers turn to Twitter to engage in such sharing. Tweets belonging to this category of working out loud are thus charged with the duty of materialising traces of the work.

2. Contextualising. The tweets belonging to this form of working out loud describe and/ or show the context and the place in which work unfolds and give details about its spatial and material setting. Figure 4 shows an example of a tweet posted by a dairy farmer performing his day-to-day tasks. Other workers provide information on their availability, schedule, and geographical location. We also found examples where expertise and credibility are demonstrated through the narration of actions. These tweets have the potential to establish and maintain a common ground, thus facilitating the interpretation of work practices by others. In this sense, tweets belonging to this category promote the work observability needed to maintain the 'ambient awareness' of workers' environment and activities (Ellison, Steinfield, & Lampe, 2011; Leonardi & Meyer, 2015). Ambient awareness is thus established and maintained through the publication of these tweets.

3. Documenting. Through these tweets, workers keep a record of milestones accomplished and decisions they have made. They describe their methods and ways of doing things. In the example shown in Figure 5, an ethnographer reports on the work completed (fieldwork and interviews) and announces his next step (writing). Others formulate intentions, project ideas, goals, and objectives, therefore articulating the planning and continuation of actions. The tweets belonging to this category mainly describe and follow patterns similar to those found in project team discussions (e.g. in

Table 1. Emerging repertoire of the various forms that the WOL practice can adopt.

Form of WOL	Description	Example	Action of tweets
1. Exposing			
1.1 Work in development	Post preliminary work, notes, and sketches	It took roughly two hours to realize this sketch into the piece today. It's about 15 seconds of music. *[photo of a music sheet]* #showyourwork	**Producing traces of work processes**
1.2 Difficulty	Describe problems and obstacles	Oh crap – Google spreadsheet I'm using to capture #SAA2014 tweets has just about reached its max number of records	
1.3 Interaction	Depict exchanges, give credit	I asked *@username* for feedback on my session I did at #DevLearn. She's honest and fair. I haven't even opened the email yet. #ShareYourWork	
2. Contextualising			
2.1 Environment and resources	Present work setting	I've probably used up like one thousand sticky notes in the last week. #work #twork *[photo of a wall covered with notes]*	**Creating and maintaining an ambient awareness**
2.2 Day-to-day tasks	Give access to 'behind-the-scenes' experiences	Spa day on the farm. All the cows get 'moonicures' before heading out to spring pastures #farm365 #dairyfarm *[photo of a farmer]*	
2.3 Expertise	Exhibit skills	Shared @AdobeConnect virtual session tips w/instructor from another dept. teaching online 4 1st time – he was pleasantly surprised	
3. Documenting			
3.1 Progression	Report completed actions	Gosh, 18 months of village fieldwork over. Ethnography plus we interviewed 370 individuals, now comes the writing.	**Planning the course of action**
3.2 Method	Communicate strategies and choices	Going for flesh coloured rectangles over the eyes as the 'cleanest' mode of anonymising the photos for the What They Post book.	
3.3 Goal	Formulate intentions	I think things are pretty much in place. Now I just have to fill the cracks and make it read better. #nanowrimo	
4. Teaching			
4.1 Ways of doing things	Show ongoing process	Streaming game engine development @url Watch the process! #GameDev #Gaming #Programming #Coding #Streaming *[Link to a video live stream]*	**Transforming the experience into reusable knowledge**
4.2 Lessons learned	Solve problems	I implemented the edge-sorting algorithm and tried it with real data. Lesson: separate connected components first.	
4.3 Best practices	Show samples of work	Everyone loves code! I wrote some more today – it's way complicated because.. JavaScript! Which is cool.;-) *[link to code]*	
5. Expressing			
5.1 Feelings	Express emotions	Lord help me, my other 90yo just got seriously delirious and had to call another Code White! Breaks my heart to have to strap them in	**Creating a cathartic space**
5.2 Mockery	Use sarcasm, humor	I'm beta-testing a new game today called 'How long will it take to get to the bottom of my inbox after a week-long vacation.' #amworking	
5.3 Complaints	Whine about work	When I say don't turn the patient and don't make ventilator changes don't f*ing do it. How hard is this?	
6. Thinking in a reflective manner			
6.1 Consideration	Evaluate and recognise	so creating a curriculum for a new undergraduate #UX program is not as easy as it seems. Prereqs & sequencing are killing me.	**Making judgments about what has happened**
6.2 Dilemmas	Describe inner struggle	Tough meeting *@username* in Maban. Refugees who had no role in killing aid workers are the 1st to suffer the impact of NGO withdrawals.	
6.3 Assessment	Consider the situation and make decision	Between doing my annual review and replying to a mentor about what I've been up to, I think I need some 'say no' counseling soon.	

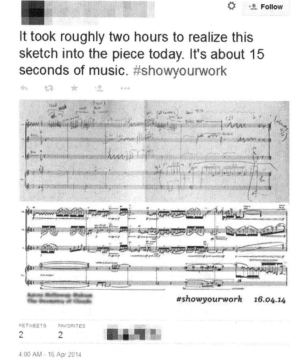

Figure 3. Example of WOL tweet exposing work in development.

Figure 4. Example of WOL tweet contextualising workers' day-to-day tasks.

Figure 5. Example of WOL tweet documenting progression of work.

project status meetings) and reports. However, their style is less formal. In announcing what has been done or what will be done, these tweets act as 'spokesobjects' (Vásquez & Cooren, 2011), talking for the workers who have written them.

4. Teaching. This category of WOL tweets displays features of work in ways that are designed to make them observable and somehow reproducible (see Figure 6 for an example). In Example 4.1 shown in Table 1, a software engineer provides a link to a live

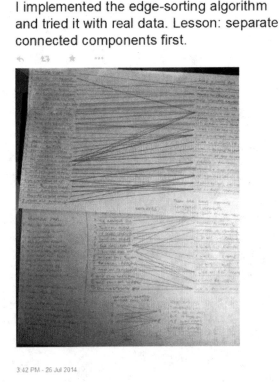

Figure 6. Example of WOL tweet teaching lessons learned.

streaming video showing his computer screen while he is programming a video game. Workers also expose details of their trials and errors, indicate how to solve a problem, and expose their best practices. For example, an information architect discusses the results of his experimentations with a data sorting algorithm and explicitly formulates the lessons learned ('separate connected components first'). These types of WOL tweets display work practices in ways that are designed to attract the attention of readers to the activity, or to certain features of it. By articulating their thoughts for themselves and others (Fayard & Metiu, 2014), and by exposing their ways of doing things, workers also share tacit knowledge with others. Workers re-materialise their experience into bits of textualised practices that can support 'indirect' forms of learning. However, it is the tweet, with its bits of knowledge, that can do the teaching, based on its capacity to remain the same (its durability), and to transcend time and space.

5. Expressing. The examples we have presented so far mainly talk about the work itself. But we also found a great number of tweets in which workers verbalise and exteriorise their emotions and feelings, whether positive (e.g. happy moments) or negative (e.g. frustration or regrets). This fifth form of WOL practice is more expressive than simply informative and may have a cathartic function, with Twitter providing an emotionally supportive environment where workers can 'blow off steam' and reduce stress and tension. In the example shown in Figure 7, a nurse expresses how she feels about having to place a patient in a restraint. Another user responds to the initial tweet in order to support her in this troubling moment. In this form of working out loud, tweets again become 'spokesobjects' and take charge of conveying elements that have a strong emotional content. In talking for the workers who write them, they allow for the establishment of relationships across time and space that can then create a cathartic space.

6. Thinking in a reflective manner. Although tweets are short texts that are presumably written quickly between tasks, we found instances where workers take the time to step back, think, and share their considerations with their audience. In these tweets, workers are commenting inwardly about a situation, in that they seem to be talking to themselves, while also opening these inner reflections to others. Hence, these tweets not

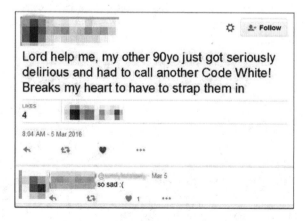

Figure 7. Example of WOL tweet expressing emotions.

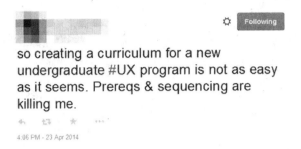

Figure 8. Example of WOL tweet with reflexive thinking.

only have a communicative function, but they also allow workers to be more conscious of their own experience. For example (see Figure 8), a professor in the middle of creating a new curriculum evaluates and recognises the complexity of such an endeavour. Others share their assessment of a situation and communicate how they have faced dilemmas that forced them to make difficult choices. This opportunity for 'reflection in action' and 'a posteriori evaluation' allows workers to make judgments about what happens in their work. Given their textual nature, these tweets facilitate inner dialogue, an effect that has been associated with writing (Fayard & Metiu, 2014). In this case, the short form of tweets may act as an enabling constraint that forces workers to go directly to the heart of the matter.

The performativity of WOL tweets

Based on the repertoire presented in the previous section, all WOL tweets can be understood as creating a trace of what these workers were doing at a specific moment in time. As a communicative practice, working out loud involves producing a variety of tweets. Workers who for various reasons feel an impulse to talk about their work on Twitter produce these tweets. But, as we have also shown, these tweets contribute to the experience of work in specific ways: they do things for the workers and their work. Analytically, we suggest that WOL tweets may emerge from an impulse close to talking (talk directed to oneself or others), but because this impulse leads workers to turn to Twitter to do so (and not to their diary or the phone, e.g.), this talk adopts a textual form. Moreover, in resorting to Twitter, workers engaged in working out loud delegate (in a Latourian sense) the general task of 'talking' about their work to their tweets, which adopt a textual form. Because Twitter, as a social media platform, presents many characteristics, both enabling and constraining, these tweets are able to accomplish more things for these workers, as described in the previous section. Generally speaking, we suggest that WOL tweets have a distinct capacity to render visible elements related to work that otherwise, without the intervention of tweets, tend to remain hidden. In this section, we will begin by highlighting the characteristics that allow for the actions performed by WOL tweets, as summarised in Table 2. We will then discuss the performativity of WOL tweets in more general terms.

These characteristics are not limited to WOL tweets, and have already been described by some researchers (Leonardi & Meyer, 2015; Majchrzak et al., 2013; Treem &

DISCURSIVITY, RELATIONALITY AND MATERIALITY

Table 2. Characteristics of Twitter allowing for the actions performed by WOL tweets.

Form of WOL	Main action done by tweets	Characteristics allowing for these actions
Exposing	Producing traces of work processes	– **Multimodality**: capacity to combine textual and visual elements, materialising work processes, emotions, lessons learned, and reflections, among others.
Contextualising	Creating and maintaining ambient awareness	
Documenting	Planning the course of action	– **Durability of tweets**: once produced, they do not change form (unless users modify them). As durable traces, tweets can distill ambient awareness of knowledge to other Twitter users.
Teaching	Transforming the experience into reusable knowledge	
Expressing	Creating a cathartic space	
Thinking in a reflective manner	Making judgments about what has happened	– **Capacity to transcend time and space**: tweets can reach a broad audience, not limited by geography or time, and establish relationships for the people who produce them.

Leonardi, 2013). They could also be applied to working out loud on other social media, like blogs. However, to date, agency has rarely been extended to tweets, and these characteristics have not been conceptualised as the basis for the tweets' agency. We contend that when WOL tweets are seen as non-human actors, these characteristics do more that simply define these tweets: they are the basis of their agency. Based on our analysis of WOL tweets, we contribute to this ongoing discussion by showing that characteristics that are respectively associated with talk and text meet on Twitter, and that it is this co-presence that allows for specific actions, thus documenting a new form of textual agency (Cooren, 2004; Sergi, 2013; Smith, 1984, 2001).

1) Multimodality. As media, Twitter is considered a 'multimodal communication space' because it can blend 'alphabetic text, hyperlinks, images, and videos' (Wolff, 2015). Such multimodality allows one to express a wide variety of elements through each tweet (such as text, image, video), making the tweet say *more* than the person could have said with words alone. Also, Twitter does not impose or prescribe the tone that should be adopted, leaving open the possibility of making tweets 'talk' with the personal and distinctive voice of each user. In this sense, tweets can be seen as texts that have less of a specific genre than other documents (e.g. a strategic plan; see Vaara, Sorsa, & Pälli, 2010, for a description of this genre), a characteristic that might also enhance the actions they can do. This multimodality may help to go beyond the tweets' brevity, which could be a constraint, as '[t]rying to communicate in the restricted format of 140 characters seems unduly limited to some' (Murthy, 2012, p. 1069). Yet, this multimodality is available to users who can explore it. As such, there is a creativity involved in learning how to make Twitter speak, but, as we propose, when this learning is completed, workers using Twitter to work out loud may then benefit from what this multimodality allows tweets to do.

2) Durability of tweets. WOL tweets are texts that render talk visible, but also more durable. Once 'said' on Twitter, a sentence will not dissipate as talk would: its content does not disappear and remains available to users. It also becomes more stable: once written, it will not change, unless its author deletes it (modifications to tweets are not allowed by Twitter). In this sense, tweets resemble Latour's idea of immutable mobiles (1986). These digital texts are referenced through search engines such as Google and archived by the American Library of Congress (Zimmer, 2015). Their durability, which has been called 'persistence' (Treem & Leonardi, 2013), 'recordability' (Hancock, Toma, & Ellison, 2007),

DISCURSIVITY, RELATIONALITY AND MATERIALITY

or 'permanence' (Murthy, 2012), both enables and constrains actions. On the one hand, it allows for a better awareness of who knows what and whom, which has been shown useful for knowledge sharing (Leonardi, 2014). On the other hand, tweets leave a trace, keeping visible elements that users might want at a later point, to modify or erase.

3) Capacity to transcend time and space. The immediacy and brevity of tweets shape how they are written and read, making it easy to publish and skim large amounts of content quickly. Workers can publish tweets while doing their tasks and others can respond to them immediately. But as noted before, their durability allows them to transcend time as they can be retrieved long after their publication date. This makes tweets 'mobile' not only through time, but also through space, as the retweet capability (i.e. forwarding someone else's tweet to one's own set of followers) and the use of hashtags (i.e. the addition of the '#' sign in front of keywords [e.g. '#work']) can expand their reach beyond the user's initial network. Retweets and hashtags therefore possess 'multicasting' capabilities (i.e. the broadcasting of 'many to many'; Murthy, 2012) that can extend the reach of a conversation by making it visible not only to the worker's organisation or informal network, but also to 'unknown others'. Tweets can therefore establish connections going beyond what the workers might have imagined. However, this result is dependent on the reactions and interactions that the tweet sparks – reactions and interactions that are themselves linked to other factors such as the author's notoriety and Twitter's algorithm that determines which terms are 'trending' at a given moment and in a particular place (Gillespie, 2012). These constraints can undermine the visibilising power of WOL tweets and make it difficult for workers to evaluate the future 'visible' or 'invisible' status that their tweet will attain, since 'the audience range of tweets is not always in congruence with the perceptual range (or indeed intended range) of the original Twitterer' (Murthy, 2012, p. 1068).

As mentioned earlier, our empirical investigation is anchored in the idea that language is performative. WOL tweets are performative because they actively contribute – albeit in a small way – to the individuals' work: they make a difference. Using Twitter in this manner extends what an individual can accomplish. To paraphrase Latour (1994), the person using a Twitter account to work out loud is not the same as the one without an account: he or she can do more, or can do things differently. Working out loud thus adds something to the person's work. Each tweet that belongs to the general WOL practice does things, performing elements for the unfolding process of work, by rendering them visible. Beyond the effects documented in the previous section, these tweets are considered performative because they produce something for the continuation of action. As Table 1 revealed, this contribution is to make visible and to materialise, in texts (in the form of tweets) on a given online platform (Twitter), things mainly related to work that otherwise tend to remain hidden, private, or difficult to reveal in an explicit or formalised way. Because 'work is, in a sense, always invisible to everyone but its own practitioners' (Nardi & Engeström, 1999, p. 2), workers must 'dramatize' their work to make it visible (Leonardi, 2014). This is exactly what workers do when they work out loud on Twitter: they devote effort to the publication of meaningful narratives of work activities that would not 'naturally' be visible to the public in the first place. Therefore, working out loud amplifies the visibility of their works-in-progress, processes, progress, work settings, and inner thoughts. Hence, we suggest that working out loud 'in the open', on a public platform like Twitter, contributes first in performing the work of the individuals who are talking about what they are doing and experiencing and, second, in performing specific professional identities. By engaging in any form of WOL practice, individuals gain something that helps them to go on, to continue their work.

Given the performativity of language, these effects can be ascribed to both talk and text. Our case is interesting not because it reveals such performativity, but because this performativity of talk is intimately linked to its textual form and, more precisely, to the visibilising effects of texts, which in turn give a more durable and mobile basis to these effects. We suggest that the performativity of WOL tweets materialises talk, mainly in the form of text, while helping to perform both work and professional identity. We also suggest that these are the 'extras' to working out loud in itself, generated by the performativity of WOL tweets, and that these extras help workers with the ongoing production and continuation of their work. It is in this sense that WOL tweets can contribute to constituting work in its broader sense.

In many professional domains, some crucial features of work go unnoticed because they are invisible in the physical sense. They do not produce material traces or they happen behind the scenes and are not accessible to people outside of the situation, nor are they part of anybody's job description (and thus they are not formally recognised). These features may also refer to mundane aspects of work that are nonetheless important. In this context, narrating the work in a written form produces material traces of it: it materialises work. It is in this sense that working out loud on Twitter leaves textual traces of the work as it is being performed. Intermediary steps and products of work are thus exposed through their being textualised: work is converted into text through this process of talking about it. At the same time – in a single tweet and over the accumulation of tweets – individuals are presenting themselves as the professionals they are.[5] By making visible what they are doing, experiencing, and struggling with, and how they are solving issues, these individuals are making sense of their work and also making themselves visible as professionals.

However – and contrary to common claims about social media (e.g. Turkle, 2012) – we contend that these people are not solely or mainly exhibiting themselves in a narcissistic manner. Rather, these individuals are constructing their professional self, in order to be better recognised for who they are, what they do, and how they behave. Again, we see that there is a visibility issue behind working out loud, as what is invisible cannot be acknowledged: make something visible is, indeed, making it *matter*. In relation to professional identity and the process of work, we suggest that a form of legitimacy can be constructed as an overall effect of the tweets that present both the person behind the work and the work itself. Based on the size of a tweet, we recognise that the effects created by a single WOL tweet may be limited in scope; yet, by conceptualising tweets as we have done in this article, we have highlighted their potential in terms of action. It is also possible to suggest that an accumulation effect may appear over time as workers engage in WOL practice on a regular basis. These elements remain to be studied in greater detail, through interviews. However, a communication-centred study like ours opens the door to a different line of inquiry, exploring how social media can contribute to performing work and professional identity. The next section explores this idea.

Discussion

Through our CCO-informed investigation of the communicative practice of working out loud on Twitter, we have documented how these tweets constitute work. WOL tweets may represent limited communication events in themselves, based on the limits imposed by Twitter, yet their contributions to work have a clear potential for workers engaging in this practice. The repertoire we have developed of the various forms that the WOL practice can adopt on Twitter shows that these tweets produce actions that each have a contribution in the daily accomplishment of work. Our study has focused on Twitter, but further inquiries on working out loud on other social media platforms could validate and enrich our repertoire, especially given that these platforms present both similarities and differences in their characteristics.

Work is less conceptually preeminent in the CCO perspective. As we have illustrated in this article, starting with a constitutive view of communication allowed us to think of instances of work, even as mundane as WOL tweets, as more than mere micro-texts or micro-conversations. In keeping with the effort of not separating the discursivity and the materiality of phenomena (Cooren, 2015), and by working from a hybrid conception of agency, we accomplished two tasks. First, we revealed how these tweets do things, in a generative way, for the people engaging in working out loud. Second, we reconciled the apparent paradox of the 'talk-text' form. Furthermore, we were able to shed light on the agency of WOL tweets, which contributes to deepening the reflection on this topic. Finally, we began to explore the performative potential of these tweets for the people who work out loud. In addition to the specific actions WOL tweets produce, they also have the potential to contribute to the performance of two things: the work being accomplished and the professional identity of the person who is working out loud. Further studies that would include other tweets could expand on the repertoire presented in this article. Conducting interviews with workers who actively work out loud could also help assess the scale of what they produce through this practice.

With this empirical inquiry, we also pursued a more theoretical reflection. Considering the actions that WOL tweets produce led us to ask what these tweets are in terms of communication. When looking at a tweet categorised as 'working out loud', are we confronted with an instance of talk or conversation – or are we reading a very short form of text? A more conventional approach to working out loud would end up choosing between categorising it as a discursive or material phenomenon, but such a choice would leave out a key facet of working out loud. We suggested that working out loud cannot be fully understood by making such a choice. Therefore, our answer lies between these two possibilities, and the properties exhibited by these tweets led us to this conclusion. We began this article with the idea that WOL tweets may combine talk and text in an unusual manner. We later suggested that these tweets are instances of talk that take on a textual form. However, we recognise that this talk may appear unconventional: it is not a conversation in which talk would be directed towards an identifiable individual or group who could, in turn, respond in a direct fashion. In the various examples published on public Twitter accounts, we see that they resemble a diary entry or a message in a bottle (i.e. they are not addressed to anyone in particular but rather to everyone who might be interested). When these tweets lead to interactions, they have the potential to transform an individual intuition or observation into a point of discussion. In this process of transformation, tweets are not mere transmitters: they actively initiate the transformation. These tweets are thus creating opportunities that would not exist without them.

We also contend, based on the corpus of tweets we analysed, that WOL tweets tend to adopt a specific style, close to the oral form. Working out loud is done in a personal voice rather than being scripted like a press release, promotional link, or formal report. Workers can use Twitter to broadcast work-related information that they would likely not otherwise do through corporate channels, either because such channels with equivalent functions are not available in their work environment, or because they feel that the content and/or tone of their messages would need to be altered. In turn, by creating these WOL tweets, workers' talk is amplified by the specific actions that these tweets produce. As such, new possibilities, perspectives, and feelings can be explored and exposed by workers in voluntary and innovative ways. Moreover, given their characteristics, WOL tweets allow workers to describe and conduct their work, but also to construct their professional identities, which amplifies their action. It is by turning to Twitter, and mobilising its capacity to materialise and reveal elements associated with work that would often remain hidden or private, that such effects can appear and be progressively performed with each WOL tweet.

Concerning these elements, WOL tweets seem to exist between talk and text. First, we discussed that these tweets embody properties and can have effects that are associated with both talk and text. Second, we argued that, depending on what happens after a tweet has been published, it will either lean more towards the textual (if no conversation ensues) or towards the conversational (if exchanges follow). If our inquiry into WOL tweets leads us to suggest that some text can be talk, and some talk, text, this is not a question of equivalence. There are differences between the textual and the talk-like form, and these remain even in cases such as ours where the borders are blurred. Indeed, we can still distinguish them conceptually and empirically. Our case reveals that an oscillation between text and talk is possible, that some communicative instances can be (more or less) both, depending on what follows. Such an oscillation is not commonly seen in more traditional instances of talk (e.g. exchanges during a meeting) or text (e.g. an annual report or a procedure). In organisational contexts, talk and text are intertwined, woven into another, which is one of the fundamental ideas on which CCO's definition of an organisation is based. Among CCO's key empirical focal points are the processes that generate this intertwinement of talk and text, and what arise in and around these processes of intertwinement. With the WOL tweets, we see text that speaks and talk that is written, and – more importantly – the possibility of being more or less both. We thus contend that WOL tweets can be seen as participating in the constitution of work and professional identity, and that such effects derive from the characteristics associated with tweets and, more broadly, with that which Twitter enables or constrains.

Concluding remarks: from tweets to (temporary) organisation?

On a final note, if our study of WOL tweets reveals the links between communication and work, their relationship with organisation is more tenuous, at least based on the evidence accumulated so far. However, if communication is the site for organising/

DISCURSIVITY, RELATIONALITY AND MATERIALITY

organisation (as developed by the CCO stream of studies), what is created, in terms of organisation, by the micro-communicational events that WOL tweets represent? Can an organisation emerge out of recurrent instances of working out loud? Based on what we documented here, we suggest that the visibilising power of the WOL tweets not only contributes to work, but also has the potential to trigger organisation.

Most CCO scholars consider the organisation's perpetuation through action and interaction to be a central mystery still requiring explanation. As stated by Robichaud and Cooren, '[f]rom an ontological standpoint, an organization is thus brought into being as it is performed, acted out, as it becomes literally an event' (2013, p. xiv). But how does an organisation make its first appearance on the stage of interactions? Nicotera (2013) has argued that the birth of organisation has been less focused on by CCO scholarship. She also discusses the idea that it is only when we do move from 'we' to 'it' that an organisation emerges as an entity. As she writes, '[i]f the organisation exists in communication (Taylor & Robichaud, 2004), and is made present in interaction (Brummans, Cooren, & Chaput, 2009), then its moment of conception is the first moment that communication presentifies the entity' (p. 76). Moreover,

> Language unites individuals in collaborative activity. Collaborative activity defines collectivity. Collectivity creates the ground for representation and the emergence of an organisational entity (Nicotera, 2013, p. 84).

Our reflection on WOL tweets' potential to trigger organisations into existence is based on Nicotera's arguments about an organisation's genesis. Working out loud is not primarily located in an organisation; that is, the WOL tweets are not mainly communication whose aim is to presentify, maintain, perpetuate, or transform an organisation whose birth would be a thing of the past. These tweets are voluntarily generated and more closely related to one's work practice, tools used, and preferences. Since each tweet we collected can be seen as a communicative event, small and almost trivial, and as these tweets have the potential to open up conversations, foster interactions, and establish relations, we suggest that, by investigating WOL tweets, we can study the emergence of organisation from its inception. From a CCO point of view, it is communicative practices, in all their variety, that 'scale up to compose an organisation' (Brummans et al., 2014, p. 177). Can focusing on a communicative practice that is accomplished by a single individual without (most of the time) a defined interlocutor or any formal requirement help us identify how an organisation appears, and can it allow us to study this process of scaling up? If we cannot yet answer this question, we still see the seeds of a broader reflection in our analysis. Inspired by CCO's ideas, we suggest that WOL tweets can open up collaborations between people who may not previously have known each other, and that these collaborative endeavours have the potential to be made into work projects – in other words, into temporary organisations.

Not all WOL tweets can have this effect, but our current investigation leads us to suggest that there might be cases in which instances of working out loud open up fortuitous or serendipitous interactions that create conversations about work and draw on properties from both talk and conversation (interactivity, exchange of ideas, decision-making, etc.) and text (multimodality, durability, ability to transcend time and space). The WOL tweets we have collected so far still belong to specific circumstances, located at best within the context of micro-conversations. Yet, the required distanciation and textualisation needed to create an organisation appear close. Recent studies on web collaboration (e.g. Baumer, Sueyoshi, & Tomlinson, 2011; Falgas, 2013) lead us to suspect that such collaborations can be created via practices like working out loud. This could allow us to explore the question of what, exactly, happens before an organisation is made present for the first time. This calls for further empirical work, but our current investigation leads us to suggest that, because language can be conceptualised as performative and because working out loud on Twitter is a communicative practice, WOL tweets have the potential to spark organisations into existence. What remains to be studied more closely is this triggering process, and that which stems from it.

In sum, starting from the individualised practice of working out loud, in the light of a CCO perspective, we suggest that conversations can arise from tweets, that these conversations can create relationships, and that these personal relationships can evolve into professional ties, moving from transient and circumstantial interactions to more formalised collaborative agreements. These agreements can give rise to projects, and at the moment that such a collaboration (what 'we' do together) becomes a common project ('it'), we witness the birth of a temporary or even more permanent organisation. Such exploration could contribute to enriching the reflection began by Dobusch and Schoeneborn (2015), who proposed the concept of 'organizationality', a neologism that expands the definition of an organisation. With this concept they have associated interconnected decision-making, actorhood, and identity as criteria that define what an organisation is. Could witnessing the birth of organisation add to the reflection on organisationality? We will explore these insights in our next round of inquiry into working out loud on Twitter, and further investigate the relationships between work and organisation from a CCO perspective.

Notes

1. The two authors dedicated approximately 1 hour per week to data collection during that period.
2. TweetDeck is a dashboard application that interfaces with the Twitter API in order to facilitate the management of Twitter accounts.
3. It is important to note that Twitter, Inc. makes only a fraction of its content available to the public and researchers through its search engine or APIs (i.e. the tools that can be used to access Twitter data). Indeed, 'It is not clear what tweets are included in these different data streams' (Boyd & Crawford, 2012, p. 669). In sum, no researcher can claim that the data collected on Twitter is representative of all public tweets, regardless of the means or tools used to access it.
4. See Appendix for details on how we distinguish 'talk' and 'conversation', given the specific forms that conversations take on Twitter.
5. The process of fashioning a self-brand on social media (Senft, 2013) can lead people to 'tweak' their identity in order to appear in a better light, or to select only the parts of themselves that they wish to present, to showcase only their best side, as exemplified by the case of the Australian Instagram personality Essena O'Neill, who revealed that everything she posted was edited and/or staged (Hunt, 2015). While acknowledging that these effects could be at play when people work out loud, we are not concerned with the authenticity of what people choose to present in their tweets. However, the issue of authenticity is important on social media and it would be interesting to take it into account in further studies about working out loud.

Disclosure statement

No potential conflict of interest was reported by the authors.

References

Albu, O. B., & Etter, M. (2016). Hypertextuality and social media: A study of the constitutive and paradoxical implications of organizational Twitter use. *Management Communication Quarterly*, *30*(1), 5–31. doi:10.1177/0893318915601161

Anderson, D. L. (2004). The textualizing functions of writing for organizational change. *Journal of Business and Technical Communication*, *18*(2), 141–164. doi:10.1177/1050651903260800

Archambault, A., & Grudin, J. (2012). A longitudinal study of Facebook, LinkedIn, & Twitter use. In J. A. Konstan (Ed.), *Proceedings of the 2012 ACM annual conference on human factors in computing systems — CHI '12* (pp. 2741–2750). New York, NY: ACM Press.

Ashcraft, K. L., Kuhn, T. R., & Cooren, F. (2009). Constitutional amendments: "Materializing" organizational communication. *The Academy of Management Annals*, *3*(1), 1–64. doi:10.1080/19416520903047186

Austin, J. L. (1962). *How to do things with words*. Cambridge, MA: Harvard University Press.

Aytes, A. (2013). Return of the crowds: Mechanical Turk and neoliberal states of exception. In T. Scholz (Ed.), *Digital labor. The internet as playground and factory* (pp. 79–97). Abingdon: Routledge.

Barley, S. R., & Kunda, G. (2001). Bringing work back in. *Organization Science*, *12*(1), 76–95. doi:10.1287/orsc.12.1.76.10122

Baumer, E. P. S., Sueyoshi, M., & Tomlinson, B. (2011). Bloggers and readers blogging together: Collaborative co-creation of political blogs. *Computer Supported Cooperative Work (CSCW)*, *20*(1–2), 1–36. doi:10.1007/s10606-010-9132-9

Boden, D. (1994). *The business of talk: Organizations in action*. London: Polity Press.

Bonneau, C. (2013). Travailler à haute voix sur Twitter: Quand la collaboration informelle emprunte un réseau public [Working out loud on Twitter: Informal collaboration on a public network]. *TIC & Société*, *6*(2), 1–19.

DISCURSIVITY, RELATIONALITY AND MATERIALITY

Boudreau, M. C., Loch, K. D., Robey, D., & Straud, D. (1998). Going global: Using information technology to advance the competitiveness of the virtual transnational organization. *Academy of Management Executive, 12*(4), 120–128.

Boyd, D., & Crawford, K. (2012). Critical questions for big data: Provocations for a cultural, technological and scholarly phenomenon. *Information, Communication & Society, 15*(5), 662–679. doi:10.1080/1369118X.2012.678878

Boyd, D., Golder, S., & Lotan, G. (2010). Tweet, tweet, retweet: Conversational aspects of retweeting on Twitter. In R. H. Sprague Jr. (Ed.), *HICSS 2010 Proceedings of the 2010 43rd Hawaii International Conference on System Sciences* (pp. 1–10). Washington, DC: IEEE Computer Society.

Bozarth, J. (2014). *Show your work: The payoffs and how-to's of working out loud.* San Francisco, CA: Wiley.

Brummans, B., Cooren, F., Robichaud, D., & Taylor, J. R. (2014). Approaches in research on the communicative constitution of organizations. In L. L. Putnam & D. Mumby (Eds.), *Sage handbook of organizational communication* (3rd ed., pp. 173–194). London: SAGE.

Brummans, B. H. J. M., Cooren, F., & Chaput, M. (2009). Discourse, communication, and organisational ontology. In F. Bargiela-Chiappini (Ed.), The handbook of business discourse (pp. 53–65). Edinburg: Edinburgh University Press.

Callon, M. (2002). Writing and (re)writing devices as tools for managing complexity. In J. Law & A. Mol (Eds.), *Complexities: Social studies of knowledge practices* (pp. 191–218). Durham, NC: Duke University Press.

Chaput, M. (2012). *Communiquer la genèse de l'organisation: L'invention rhétorique de Québec solidaire* [Communicating the organization's genesis: The rhetorical invention of Québec solidaire] (Unpublished doctoral dissertation). Université de Montréal, Canada.

Cooren, F. (2004). Textual agency: How texts do things in organizational settings. *Organization, 11*(3), 373–393. doi:10.1177/1350508404041998

Cooren, F. (2006). The organizational world as a plenum of agencies. In F. Cooren, J. R. Taylor, & J. Van Every (Eds.), *Communication as organizing: Practical approaches to research into the dynamic of text and conversation* (pp. 81–100). Mahwah, NY: Lawrence Erlbaum Associates.

Cooren, F. (2010). *Action and agency in dialogue: Passion, incarnation and ventriloquism.* Amsterdam: John Benjamins.

Cooren, F. (2012). Communication theory at the Center: Ventriloquism and the communicative constitution of reality. *Journal of Communication, 62*(1), 1–20. doi:10.1111/jcom.2012.62. issue-1

Cooren, F. (2015). In medias res: Communication, existence, and materiality. *Communication Research and Practice, 1*(4), 307–321. doi:10.1080/22041451.2015.1110075

Cooren, F., & Fairhurst, G. T. (2009). Dislocation and stabilization: How to scale up from interactions to organization. In L. L. Putnam & A. M. Nicotera (Eds.), *Building theories of organization: The constitutive role of communication* (pp. 117–152). New York, NY: Routledge.

Cooren, F., Fairhurst, G. T., & Huët, R. (2012). Why matter always matters in (organizational) communication. In P. M. Leonardi, B. A. Nardi, & J. Kallinikos (Eds.), *Materiality and organizing: Social interaction in a technological world* (pp. 296–314). Oxford: Oxford University Press.

Cooren, F., Kuhn, T. R., Cornelissen, J. P., & Clark, T. (2011). Communication, organizing and organization: An overview and introduction to the special issue. *Organization Studies, 32*(9), 1149–1170. doi:10.1177/0170840611410836

Cooren, F., & Matte, F. (2010). For a constitutive pragmatics: Obama, Médecins Sans Frontières and the measuring stick. *Pragmatics and Society, 1*(1), 9–31. doi:10.1075/ps

Dobusch, L., & Schoeneborn, D. (2015). Fluidity, identity, and organizationality: The communicative constitution of Anonymous. *Journal of Management Studies, 52*(8), 1005–1035. doi:10.1111/joms.2015.52.issue-8

Eisenhardt, M. (1989). Building theories from case study research. *The Academy of Management Review, 14*(4), 532–550.

Ellison, N. B., Steinfield, C., & Lampe, C. (2011). Connection strategies: Social capital implications of Facebook-enabled communication practices. *New Media & Society, 13*(6), 873–892. doi:10.1177/1461444810385389

Falgas, J. (2013). Forme et enjeux de la collaboration autour de la « bédénovela » numérique *Les autres gens* [Form and issues surrounding collaboration in the digital "comic novela" *Les autres gens*]. *TIC&Société, 7*(1), 2–14.

Faraj, S., Jarvenpaa, S. L., & Majchrzak, A. (2011). Knowledge collaboration in online communities. *Organization Science, 22*(5), 1224–1239. doi:10.1287/orsc.1100.0614

Fayard, A., & Metiu, A. (2014). The role of writing in distributed collaboration. *Organization Science, 25*(5), 1391–1413. doi:10.1287/orsc.2013.0893

Flyverbom, M., Leonardi, P. M., Stohl, C., & Stohl, M. (2016). The management of visibilities in the digital age introduction. *International Journal of Communication, 10*, 98–109.

Geertz, C. (1973). *The interpretation of cultures: Selected essays*. New York, NY: Basic Books.

Gillespie, T. (2012). Can an algorithm be wrong? *Limn, 2*. Retrieved from http://limn.it/can-an-algorithm-be-wrong/

Hancock, J. T., Toma, C., & Ellison, N. B. (2007). The truth about lying in online dating profiles. In M. B. Rosson (Ed.), *Proceedings of the SIGCHI conference on human factors in computing systems* (pp. 449–452). New York, NY: ACM.

Hinchcliffe, D. (2015). Watching digital collaboration evolve: Key events over the last year. *ZDNet*. Retrieved from http://www.zdnet.com/pictures/watching-digital-collaboration-evolve-key-events-over-the-last-year/4/

Hine, C. (2015). *Ethnography for the Internet: Embedded, embodied and everyday*. London: Bloomsbury Publishing.

Hobday, M. (2000). The project-based organisation: An ideal form for managing complex products and systems?. *Research Policy, 29*(7–8), 871–893. doi:10.1016/S0048-7333(00)00110-4

Honeycutt, C., & Herring, S. C. (2009). Beyond microblogging: Conversation and collaboration via Twitter. R. H. Sprague Jr. (Ed.), Proceedings from HICSS '09: *42nd Hawaii International Conference on System Sciences* (pp. 1–10). New York, NY: IEEE.

Hunt, E. (2015). Essena O'Neill quits Instagram claiming social media 'is not real life'. *The Guardian*. Retrieved from http://www.theguardian.com/media/2015/nov/03/instagram-star-essena-oneill-quits-2d-life-to-reveal-true-story-behind-images

Kaplan, A. M., & Haenlein, M. (2010). Users of the world, unite! The challenges and opportunities of social media. *Business Horizons, 53*, 59–68. doi:10.1016/j.bushor.2009.09.003

Latour, B. (1986). Visualisation and cognition: Thinking with eyes and hands. In H. Kuklick (Ed.), *Knowledge and society studies in the sociology of culture past and present* (Vol. 6, pp. 1–40). Greenwich, Conn.: Jai Press.

Latour, B. (1994). On technical mediation: Philosophy, sociology, genealogy. *Common Knowledge, 3*, 29–64.

Latour, B. (2005). *Reassembling the social: An introduction to actor-network-theory*. Oxford: Oxford University Press.

Latzko-Toth, G., Bonneau, C., & Millette, M. (in press). Small data, thick data: thickening strategies for trace-based social media research. In A. Quan-Haase & L. Sloan (Eds.), *The SAGE handbook of social media research methods*. London: Sage.

Leonardi, P. M. (2011). When flexible routines meet flexible technologies: Affordances, constraints, and imbrication of human and material agencies. *MIS Quarterly, 35*(1), 147–167.

Leonardi, P. M. (2014). Social media, knowledge sharing and innovation: Toward a theory of communication visibility. *Information Systems Research, 25*(4), 796–816. doi:10.1287/isre.2014.0536

Leonardi, P. M., Huysman, M., & Steinfield, C. (2013). Enterprise social media: Definition, history, and prospects for the study of social technologies in organizations. *Journal of Computer-Mediated Communication, 19*(1), 1–19. doi:10.1111/jcc4.2013.19.issue-1

DISCURSIVITY, RELATIONALITY AND MATERIALITY

Leonardi, P. M., & Meyer, S. R. (2015). Social media as social lubricant: How ambient awareness eases knowledge transfer. *American Behavioral Scientist*, *59*(1), 10–34. doi:10.1177/0002764214540509

Majchrzak, A., Faraj, S., Kane, G., & Azad, B. (2013). The contradictory influence of social media affordances on online communal knowledge sharing. *Journal of Computer Mediated Communication*, *19*(1), 38–55. doi:10.1111/jcc4.2013.19.issue-1

Marwick, A. E. (2014). Ethnographic and qualitative research on Twitter. In K. Weller, A. Bruns, J. Burgess, M. Mahrt, & C. Puschmann (Eds.), *Twitter and society* (pp. 109–122). Bern: Peter Lang.

Miles, M. B., Huberman, A. M., & Saldana, J. (2013). *Qualitative data analysis: A methods sourcebook*. Los Angeles, CA: SAGE Publications.

Murthy, D. (2012). Towards a sociological understanding of social media: Theorizing Twitter. *Sociology*, *46*(6), 1059–1073. doi:10.1177/0038038511422553

Nardi, B. A., & Engeström, Y. (1999). A web on the wind: The structure of invisible work. *Computer Supported Cooperative Work (CSCW)*, *8*(1–2), 1–8. doi:10.1023/A:1008694621289

Nardi, B. A., Whittaker, S., & Schwarz, H. (2000). It's not what you know it's who you know. *First Monday*, *5*(5). Retrieved from http://128.248.156.56/ojs/index.php/fm/article/view/741

Nicolini, D. (2012). *Practice theory, work, and organization: An introduction*. Oxford: Oxford University Press.

Nicotera, A. M. (2013). Organizations as entitative beings: Some ontological implications of communicative constitution. In D. Robichaud & F. Cooren (Eds.), *Organization and organizing: Materiality, agency, discourse* (pp. 66–89). New York, NY: Routledge.

Oostervink, N., Agterberg, M., & Huysman, M. (2016). Enterprise social media: Practices to cope with institutional complexity. *Journal of Computed-Mediated Communication*, *21*(2), 156–176. doi:10.1111/jcc4.12153

Phillips, N., & Lawrence, T. B. (2012). The turn to work in organization and management theory: Some implications for strategic organization. *Strategic Organization*, *10*(3), 223–230. doi:10.1177/1476127012453109

Putnam, L. L., & Nicotera, A. M. (2009). Communicative constitution of organization is a question: Critical issues for addressing it. *Management Communication Quarterly*, *24*(1), 158–165. doi:10.1177/0893318909351581

Robichaud, D., & Cooren, F. (2013). Introduction: The need for new materials in the constitution of organization. In D. Robichaud & F. Cooren (Eds.), *Organization and organizing: Materiality, agency, discourse* (pp. xi–xx). New York, NY: Routledge.

Robichaud, D., Giroux, H., & Taylor, J. R. (2004). The meta-conversation: The recursive property of language as a key to organizing. *Academy of Management Review*, *29*(4), 617–634.

Schoeneborn, D., Blaschke, S., Cooren, F., McPhee, R. D., Seidl, D., & Taylor, J. R. (2014). The three schools of CCO thinking: Interactive dialogue and systematic comparison. *Management Communication Quarterly*, *28*(2), 285–316. doi:10.1177/0893318914527000

Schreier, M. (2012). *Qualitative content analysis in practice*. Thousand Oaks, CA: SAGE Publications.

Senft, T. M. (2013). Microcelebrity and the branded self. In J. Hartley, J. E. Burgess, & A. Bruns (Eds.), *A companion to new media dynamics* (pp. 346–354). Hoboken, NJ: Wiley-Blackwell.

Sergi, V. (2013). Constituting the temporary organization: Documents in the context of projects. In D. Robichaud & F. Cooren (Eds.), *Organization and organizing: Materiality, agency, discourse* (pp. 190–206). New York, NY: Routledge.

Smith, D. E. (1984). Textually-mediated social organization. *International Social Science Journal*, *36*, 59–75.

Smith, D. E. (2001). Texts and the ontology of organizations and institutions. *Studies in Cultures, Organizations and Societies*, *7*, 159–198. doi:10.1080/10245280108523557

Stake, R. E. (2008). Qualitative case studies. In N. K. Denzin & Y. S. Lincoln (Eds.), *Strategies of qualitative inquiry* (pp. 119–150). London: SAGE.

Star, S. L., & Strauss, A. (1999). Layers of silence, arenas of voice : The ecology of visible and invisible work. *Computer Supported Cooperative Work (CSCW), 8,* 9–30. doi:10.1023/A:1008651105359

Stepper, J. (2015). *Working out loud: For a better career and life.* New York, NY: Ikigai Press.

Taylor, J. R. (2009). Organizing from the bottom up? Reflections on the constitution of organization in communication. In L. L. Putnam & A. M. Nicotera (Eds.), *Building theories of organization: The constitutive role of communication* (pp. 153–186). New York, NY: Routledge.

Taylor, J. R., & Robichaud, D. (2004). Finding the organization in the communication: Discourse as action and sensemaking. *Organization, 11*(3), 395–413. doi:10.1177/1350508404041999

Taylor, J. R., & Van Every, E. J. (2000). *The emergent organization: Communication as its site and surface.* Mahwah, NJ: Erlbaum.

Taylor, J. R., & Van Every, E. J. (2011). *The situated organization: Case studies in the pragmatics of communication research.* New York, NY: Routledge.

Treem, J. W., & Leonardi, P. M. (2013). Social media use in organizations: Exploring the affordances of visibility, editability, persistence, and association. *Annals of the International Communication Association, 36*(1), 143–189.

Tufekci, Z. (2014). Big questions for social media big data: Representativeness, validity and other methodological pitfalls In L. Weng, F. Menczer, & Y. Y. Ahn (Eds.), *Proceedings from ICWSM '14: 8th International AAAI Conference on Weblogs and Social Media.* Palo Alto, CA: AAAI Press.

Turkle, S. (2012). *Alone together: Why we expect more from technology and less from each other.* New York, NY: Basic books.

Vaara, E., Sorsa, V., & Pälli, P. (2010). On the force potential of strategy texts: A critical discourse analysis of a strategic plan and its power effects in a city organization. *Organization, 17*(6), 685–702. doi:10.1177/1350508410367326

van Zoonen, W., Verhoeven, J. W., & Vliegenthart, R. (2016). How employees use Twitter to talk about work: A typology of work-related tweets. *Computers in Human Behavior, 55,* 329–339. doi:10.1016/j.chb.2015.09.021

Vásquez, C., & Cooren, F. (2011). Passion in action: An analysis of translation and treason. In P. Quattrone, C. McLean, F. Puyou, & N. Thrift (Eds.), *Imagining organizations: Performative imagery in business and beyond* (pp. 191–212). London: Routledge.

Willis, D. A. (2013). Bring your own device: The facts and the future. *Gartner.* Retrieved from https://www.gartner.com/doc/2422315/bring-device-facts-future

Winer, D. (2009). Narrate your work. *Scripting News.* Retrieved from http://scripting.com/stories/2009/08/09/narrateYourWork.html

Wolff, W. I. (2015). Baby, we were born to tweet: Springsteen fans, the writing practices of in situ tweeting, and the research possibilities for Twitter. *Kairos.* Retrieved from http://kairos.technorhetoric.net/19.3/topoi/wolff/compose.html

Zhang, J., Qu, Y., Cody, J., & Wu, Y. (2010). A case study of micro-blogging in the enterprise: Use, value, and related issues. In E. Mynatt (Ed.), *Proceedings of the 28th international conference on Human factors in computing systems* (pp. 123–132). Atlanta, GA: ACM.

Zimmer, M. (2015). The Twitter archive at the library of congress: Challenges for information practice and information policy. *First Monday, 20*(7). Retrieved from http://firstmonday.org/article/view/5619/4653

DISCURSIVITY, RELATIONALITY AND MATERIALITY

Appendix: Distinctions between 'talk' and 'conversation' on Twitter

We consider 'talk' as a broader category regrouping all instances of communicational events presented in this article. However, we distinguish instances in which talk becomes a conversation. On Twitter, conversations can be detected through specific characteristics, as illustrated in the examples below. WOL tweets can remain in a 'monologue' form, as shown in Figure 9. In this case, 'talk remains talk', since we cannot see any interactions following their publications. Others are retweeted (i.e. they are republished by other users for the benefit of their own audience) or 'favourited' (Figure 10), creating a form of conversation, albeit limited. Finally, some tweets open the door to more conventional conversational exchanges (Figure 11).

Figure 9. Talk without conversation.

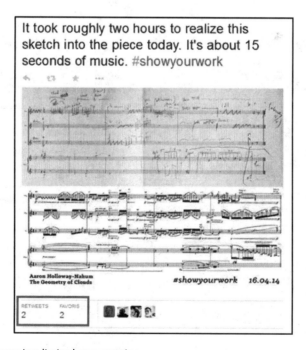

Figure 10. Talk becoming limited conversation.

Figure 11. Talk becoming conversation.

Even though Twitter was not primarily designed for conversation, the marker of addressivity (i.e. the inclusion of '*@username*' to direct a tweet to a specific user) is an example of an innovation by users who wanted to discuss on Twitter. Some authors (Honeycutt & Herring, 2009) even consider that only tweets containing such a marker of addressivity can be categorised as 'conversation'. However, not all Twitter conversations begin with a message including an '@' sign: messages can be broadcast to the user's audience in hopes that they reach appropriate recipients, whether they are known or not. Therefore, it is important to also include tweets that are 'becoming conversation', as shown in Figures 8 and 9. At this point in our research, we hypothesise that these 'conversations to be' may result in serendipitous opportunities for cooperation, whether or not the user intends to cooperate in the first place.

A communication perspective on organisational stakeholder relationships: discursivity, relationality, and materiality

Matthew A. Koschmann

ABSTRACT

The purpose of this research is to rethink the notion of stakeholder communication and articulate a distinct 'communication perspective' on stakeholder relationships, one that takes seriously the constitutive effects of language and human interaction in the ongoing social construction of various connections between and among organisations. This communication perspective involves rethinking three important aspects of stakeholder thinking: (1) stakeholder identification and salience, (2) the false separation of material and symbolic resources, and (3) the political production of meaning involved in stakeholder relationships. The article begins with a critical review of previous literature on stakeholder communication, situated within broader developments of stakeholder research. Key themes and trends in this literature are identified, revealing the need for an alternative notion of communication to ground future thinking about communication and stakeholder relationships. Next, the perspective of communication-as-constitutive is introduced, a meta-theoretical framework that can better capture the complex dynamics of organisational stakeholder relationships. From here, the article describes what a communication perspective of stakeholder relationships entails and how this conceptual shift provides a stronger foundation to understand key aspects of stakeholder thinking. The implications of a communication perspective on stakeholder relationships are explained and theoretical propositions to inform future empirical research are offered.

Over the last 30 years, stakeholder theory has emerged as an important perspective to inform business, management, and organisational studies (Parmar et al., 2010). Beginning as a pragmatic alternative for business strategy and management, stakeholder theory has evolved into a more comprehensive line of research that addresses business–society relations from multiple perspectives (Steurer, 2006), while both complementing and challenging previous theories of the firm (e.g. resource dependency, transaction cost economics, institutional theory, etc.). The central claim of stakeholder thinking is that firms exist within a broad system of interdependent relationships among other organisations and constituents, and therefore should be managed in the interest of all legitimate stakeholders who can affect or be affected by the firm (Laplume, Sonpar, & Litz, 2008). The main ideas of stakeholder thinking have now become established and prevalent assumptions throughout several fields, both in theory and in practice (Agle et al., 2008).

From its foundation as a theory of business strategy (Freeman, 1984), a fundamental premise of stakeholder thinking is some notion of stakeholder management: ways in which focal firms relate with a variety of stakeholders in order to maintain control over their organisational environments. This generally involves various processes to identify and classify the salience of stakeholders and the legitimacy of their claims (e.g. Mitchell, Agle, & Wood, 1997).[1] Furthermore, *stakeholder communication* has emerged as a major area of interest (Andriof, Waddock, Husted, & Rahman, 2003) and represents a potentially key aspect of stakeholder thinking (Kim, 2012; Smith & Arnold, 2005). Despite its practical appeal, the notion of stakeholder communication has had limited impact on the development of stakeholder theory and remains as the periphery of stakeholder thinking. At the root of the problem is a limited view of communication that is not tenable for the complexity of stakeholder relationships that exist in today's organisational landscape, which currently underwrites most thinking about stakeholder communication. This involves static and instrumental notions of communication focused primarily on information exchange, message transmission, and personal expression, but largely ignoring practices of meaning production, identity construction, and the social processes of organisational relationships. The result is a narrow framing that regards communication as a discrete phenomenon that is best explained through other perspectives, particularly financial and economic theories. Yet, stakeholder relationships are inherently communicative, and thus warrant a distinctly communicative conception, especially in terms of understanding how stakes, stakeholders, and stakeholder relationships are constituted by and through processes of social interaction at the intersection of materiality, discursivity, and relationality.

The growing interest in stakeholder communication (Andriof et al., 2003; Smith & Arnold, 2005) cannot be sustained by limited and sterile conceptions of communication grounded in linear models of information exchange. Although this does help us understand how firms and stakeholders send and receive message through various communication channels, it cannot advance knowledge of the social processes that constitute organisational stakeholder relationships, challenge the false dichotomy between material and symbolic resources in stakeholder relationships, uncover the inherent politics within the production of meaning between firms and stakeholders, or explain the dynamism and contingency of stakeholder identification – all of which are important aspects of stakeholder relationships but beyond the logics of conventional stakeholder thinking. However, I argue that an alternative approach to communication provides a path forward. A small, but growing body of research in the business and management literatures does focus on stakeholder communication, in terms of either studying instances of communication among stakeholders or studying management communication from a stakeholder perspective (e.g. Brønn & Brønn, 2003; Crane & Livesey, 2003). Similarly, some communication scholars consider stakeholder relationships as key sites to advance communicative theories of organisational phenomena (e.g. Arnaud & Mills, 2012; Deetz, 1995; Kuhn, 2008). This work offers valuable points of departure to develop a more coherent and impactful contribution to stakeholder thinking. But much more needs to be done to advance the scholarly conversation.

Therefore, the purpose of this research is to rethink the notion of stakeholder communication and articulate a distinct 'communication perspective' on stakeholder relationships, one that takes seriously the constitutive effects of language and human interaction in the ongoing social construction of various connections between and among organisations. The goal here is not just to provide an explanation for a particular communication phenomenon (as important as that is), but rather a more ambitious attempt to provide a communicative understanding of stakeholder relationships that combines discursive, relational, and material aspects of organising into a coherent explanatory framework. I develop a communication perspective to explain three important aspects of stakeholder thinking not adequately addressed in the current stakeholder literature: (1) stakeholder identification and salience, (2) the entanglement of material and symbolic resources, and (3) the political production of meaning involved in stakeholder relationships. This work is needed both to advance the stakeholder literature and to further demonstrate the value of a communication perspective for organisational studies.

The article is structured as follows: the first section presents a critical review of previous literature on stakeholder communication, situated within broader developments of stakeholder research. Key themes and trends in this literature are identified, revealing the need for an alternative approach to communication to ground future thinking about organisational stakeholder relationships. The second section turns to the notion of *communication-as-constitutive*, a meta-theoretical framework to develop a communication perspective on organisational stakeholder relationships. From here, the article describes what a communication perspective on stakeholder relationships entails and how this conceptual shift provides a stronger foundation to understand and explain key aspects of stakeholder thinking. The third section explains the implications of a communication perspective on stakeholder relationships and offers theoretical propositions to inform future empirical research. The central claim of this approach is that stakeholder relationships are best understood as dynamic sites of organisational constitution where negotiation and meaning construction shape how organisational realities are known and experienced.

Literature review: stakeholder communication

Before developing an alternative communication perspective on organisational stakeholder relationships, it is important to understand how communication is conceptualised in the extant stakeholder literature. In their recent review of the stakeholder literature published since Freeman's influential 1984 text *Strategic Management: A Stakeholder Approach*, Laplume et al. (2008) identify five themes marking the development of stakeholder thinking to date: stakeholder definition and salience, stakeholder actions and responses, firm action and responses, firm performance, and various theory debates. Key unanswered questions from their review include issues related to the mechanisms of stakeholder management, the emergence of stakeholder relationships, the symbolic implications of stakeholder management, and conceptions of other-regarding logics in terms of stakeholder relationships. All these unanswered questions

DISCURSIVITY, RELATIONALITY AND MATERIALITY

can be understood as representing a boarder theme of *stakeholder communication* because they entail various aspects of interaction between stakeholders and maintaining constructive stakeholder relationships.

A small, but growing body of research has begun investigating issues of stakeholder communication, though most of this literature was not included within the scope of Laplume et al.'s (2008) otherwise extensive review of stakeholder scholarship. This work on stakeholder communication includes both studies that investigate specific instances of communication within stakeholder relationships (e.g. Patterson & Allen's, 1997 examination of communication between organisational and environmental activist stakeholders) and studies that incorporate a stakeholder perspective to understand broader aspects of business and organisational communication (e.g. Lewis' 2007 stakeholder model of change implementation communication).

For the present study, a review of research involving stakeholder communication was conducted in order to summarise the key themes and trends, as well as to inform subsequent theorising and empirical investigation. This review began with a broad search of the main business, management, organisational, and communication search indices (e.g. Business Source Complete, Business Source Premier, Communication and Mass Media Complete, etc.) using several different search terms to identify any articles having to do with communication and stakeholder relationships (e.g. 'stakeholder theory,' 'stakeholder communication,' 'stakeholder relationships,' 'stakeholder interaction,' etc.). From this initial gathering, stricter criteria were imposed to eliminate certain articles that had limited relevance to the investigation. For example, articles were also excluded that made cursory or generic references to stakeholders and communication but did not seek to advance any particular aspect of stakeholder theory per se, or did not draw from the stakeholder theory literature to inform their investigation. Four scholarly books widely cited in this literature were also included: Phillips' (2003) *Stakeholder Theory and Organizational Ethics*, Parmar et al.'s (2010) *Stakeholder Theory: The State of the Art*, plus the two-volume set *Unfolding Stakeholder Thinking* edited by Andriof, Waddock, Husted, and Rahman (2002, 2003). This resulted in a total of 68 sources to investigate how communication is understood and portrayed in the stakeholder literature, as well as how communication scholars have utilised stakeholder thinking in their research.

This literature review resulted in three primary themes (summarised in Table 1) that illustrate current thinking about stakeholder communication: (1) communication as strategy, (2) communication as interaction, and (3) communication as normative obligation. These themes are not necessarily mutually exclusive, but rather describe

Table 1. Themes of stakeholder communication literature.

Theme	Description	Representative citations
Communication as strategic	Communication as a calculated endeavour that firms engage in to accomplish organisational goals and strengthen firm performance	Lewis (2007); Ulmer (2001)
Communication as interaction	The forms and practices of stakeholder relationships, usually conceived as negotiation or dialogue	Beaulieu and Pasquero (2002); Buchell and Cook (2006, 2008)
Communication as normative obligation	Firms have a responsibility to interact with and involve legitimate stakeholders, usually in relation to some notion of corporate social responsibility (CSR)	Morsing and Schultz (2006); Rasche and Esser (2006)

alternative ways in which stakeholder communication is understood and conceptualised in the literature. Additionally, the literature also reveals an emerging theme related to the social constructionist aspect of stakeholder relationships and language use, but did not fit neatly into either of the above themes or reveal enough coherence to compose a distinct theme. This includes a growing body of work premised on the idea that communication constitutes stakeholder relations that have developed largely outside the mainstream management literature, which suggests an important next step of articulating a robust notion of stakeholder relationships from a communication perspective to advance the literature and guide future theorising and empirical research. These ideas from this emerging theme provide a transition between the summary of the current literature and the argument for a communication perspective of organisational stakeholder relationships, based on a constitutive model of communication.

Theme 1: communication as strategy

The dominant theme in the stakeholder literature is communication as a strategic endeavour that firms engage in to accomplish organisational goals and strengthen firm performance. This theme concentrates mostly on the first half of Freeman's (1984) influential definition of stakeholders: 'those who can affect ... the achievement of the firm's objectives' (p. 25). From this perspective, communication involves a linear (Clark, 2000) flow or exchange of information (Bendell, 2003; O'Riordan & Fairbrass, 2008) as a means of accomplishing strategic ends and achieving various outcomes and benefits, such as organisational learning (Burchell & Cook, 2006) and resource acquisition (Welcomer, Cochran, Rands, & Haggerty, 2003). Much of this work is rooted (implicitly or explicitly) in a linear model of communication as information transmission concerned with message exchanges between senders and receivers (Pfeil, Setterberg, & O'Rourke, 2004) and the need to establish clear channels of communication between firms and their stakeholders (Ulmer, 2001). Communication as strategy is concerned primarily with effectiveness and the proper expression of ideas with stakeholders, especially in terms of promotion and advocacy (e.g. Longest & Rohrer, 2005), as well as minimising threats and concerns from external stakeholders (Miles, Munilla, & Darroch, 2006). Communication is thus conceptualised as a skill (Hornik, Chen, Klein, & Jiang, 2003) to be utilised and perfected in order to increase the likelihood that organisational activities will be successful.

Communication as strategy is also the main theme in the business communication literature, which focuses on the message strategies of numerous parties involved in various organisational relationships and initiatives. For example, Lewis offers an established line of empirical research investigating the strategic implications of stakeholder communication. She demonstrates the importance of stakeholder communication processes during planned organisational change (Lewis, 2007), as well as the significance of communicative attention in relation to strategic resources and the prevalence of information dissemination as a communication strategy in times of organisational change (Lewis, Richardson, & Hamel, 2003), and the potentially negative aspect of change announcements related to perceptions of honesty and trustworthiness of implementers (Lewis, Laster, & Kulkarni, 2013). Other examples include Stephens, Malone, and Bailey's (2005) investigation of message strategies during crisis, Vernuccio's (2014) exploration of corporate branding through social media, Vielhaber and Waltman's (2008) study of crisis communication and changing technology during a strike, and Weber, Thomas, and Stephen's (2015) analysis of communication breakdowns during a failed initiative to change transportation and security regulations of the U.S. Coast Guard. This work exemplifies the main idea that communication with and among stakeholders has important strategic consequences for the achievement of organisational goals and the success (or failure) of various organisational initiatives.

Theme 2: communication as interaction

A different but related theme in the literature on stakeholder communication focuses attention on the forms and practices of stakeholder relationships, and the ways in which organisations and stakeholders engage in relationships via communication. If communication as strategy is concerned primarily with the *why* of stakeholder communication, communication as interaction is more concerned with the *how*. Scholars differ on how they conceptualise stakeholder interactions, whether they assume a traditional hub-and-spoke model with a focal firm and surrounding stakeholders that is assumed in most stakeholder thinking (Frooman, 1999), or a more networked perspective that decentres the notion of a focal firm and highlights patterns of interactions among various stakeholders (Payne & Calton, 2002; Rowley, 1997).

The two most common forms of interaction described in the literature are negotiation and dialogue, though a wide variety of meanings are attributed to both these concepts. Interaction as *negotiation* generally involves a back-and-forth exchange of ideas between organisational representatives in order to reach some level of agreement about some aspect of their relationship. For example, Gregory (2007) describes how firms can involve various stakeholders to negotiate the development of a corporate brand. At a deeper level, negotiation is conceived as the way in which stakeholders order the social reality that forms the basis for their relationships, influences their interpretations of current circumstances, and guides future decisions (Beaulieu & Pasquero, 2002). In this way, communication is seen as patterns of interaction that enable stakeholders to negotiate the stakes of their relationships, as well as the legitimacy of those stakes and the salience of stakeholder claims.

Stakeholder communication in terms of *dialogue* usually involves certain types of interactions where firms and stakeholders engage in a form of reciprocal conversation that enables the parties involved to have their voices heard and where multiple ideas can be shared. Dialogue is usually conceived as a form of interaction that is distinct from 'normal' communication between firms and stakeholders, especially to improve levels of trust (Buchell & Cook, 2006; van Huijstee & Glasbergen, 2008), enhance organisational learning (Burchell & Cook, 2008; Calton & Payne, 2003; Payne & Calton, 2002) and expertise (van Huijstee & Glasbergen, 2008), sustain positive relationships with stakeholders (Kaptein & Van Tulder, 2003), involve stakeholders in decision-making processes (Pedersen, 2006), or develop increased accountability standards (Rasche & Esser, 2006). For other scholars dialogue is a much simpler process, merely equivalent with flows of information (Bendell, 2003); informing and reporting (van Huijstee & Glasbergen, 2008); or a vehicle for sending and exchanging messages (O'Riordan & Fairbrass, 2008). From this perspective, dialogue is merely synonymous with communication, but places more emphasis on listening and involves two-way interaction between stakeholders.

A common assumption across this theme of communication as interaction (negotiation and dialogue) is to see interaction as a type of event, a 'highly structured conversational episode' (Barge & Little, 2002, p. 375) that organisations engage in with their stakeholders and is largely distinct from other organisational practices (and also not a segment of an ongoing stream of practice but something that can be isolated and disconnected from other episodes). Negotiation and dialogue are seen as alternative forms of communication to be utilised in times of crisis or change, but not as ordinary patterns of interaction for everyday organisational occurrences. This perspective separates stakeholder communication from the 'normal' business of the organisation, implying that what generally goes on in organisations is *not* stakeholder communication – stakeholder communication is a special kind of interaction applied in unique circumstances. Yet as I explain later, this is at odds with a constitutive approach to communication, which emphasises the overlapping and intertwined aspect of all organisational communication in the constitution of organisational stakeholder relationships.

Theme 3: communication as normative obligation

A final theme in the literature involves another perspective on the *why* of stakeholder communication. The theme of communication as strategy says the reason why organisations (usually commercial firms in this literature) engage in stakeholder communication is to achieve strategic goals and objectives. Conversely, the theme of communication as normative obligation says the reason why organisations engage in stakeholder communication is because they have a responsibility to involve and interact with legitimate constituencies that have relationships with the organisation and are influenced by its actions. This theme concentrates mostly on the second half of Freeman's (1984) definition of stakeholders: those who are 'affected by the achievement of the firm's objectives' (p. 25). One of the main ideas driving the theme of communication as normative obligation is corporate social responsibility (CSR), the notion that firms are accountable for the broader societal implications of their actions, not just their financial performance. CSR is a larger trend in stakeholder thinking beyond communication, as many scholars see stakeholder thinking as a valuable perspective to underwrite ethical arguments that advance ideas of CSR (e.g. Basu & Palazzo, 2008). Accordingly, much of the recent stakeholder literature is published in journals such as *Business Ethics Quarterly* and *Journal of Business Ethics*.

In contrast to seeing communication with stakeholders as a means to accomplishing some broader strategic ends, literature within this theme of normative obligation sees communication with stakeholders as a moral end in and of itself. This is because ethical standards of communication suggest that information should be shared with those who are impacted by the firm's activities, and that they have a right to be involved in certain decision-making processes (Morsing & Schultz, 2006). A Habermasian theory of discourse ethics is common in much of this literature (e.g. Reed, 1999). Broadly stated, Habermas' (1981) discourse ethics emphasises the notion of 'communicative action' where firms and stakeholders engage in mutual deliberation and argumentation in order to reach an intersubjective consensus about the status of their relationships. These ideas are foundational for Phillips (2003) theory of stakeholder fairness and his identification of normative and derivative stakeholders. Similarly, Rasche and Esser (2006) argue from a Habermasian perspective to claim that stakeholder communication is a necessary precondition (not just an outcome) for stakeholder accountability standards. Furthermore, Zakhem (2008) demonstrates that a mere transactional account of stakeholder relationships cannot provide direction for normative stakeholder claims, arguing instead that relationships between firms and stakeholders should involve a discursive process with an illocutionary goal of working towards mutual understanding (versus strategic action).

When stakeholder communication is viewed as a normative obligation, it then becomes an indicator to evaluate the relationships between firms and stakeholders, not just an instrument to achieve other strategic ends (van huijstee & glasbergen, 2008). The notion of responsibility becomes a key consideration from this perspective, such that firms and stakeholders share responsibility for the social reality they construct (Beaulieu & Pasquero, 2002) and that firms understand the relational responsibility (Payne & Calton, 2002) that exists when they embark on activities that affect other stakeholders. Overall, the theme of stakeholder communication as normative obligation arises from a particular understanding of what it means for firms to exist within an interdependent network of stakeholder relationships, and that communicating with these stakeholders is an ethical responsibility, especially in terms of sharing information and involvement in decision-making.

To summarise, the literature reviewed in this section suggests three primary ways in which scholars understand stakeholder communication: as a strategic means, as a form of interaction, or as a normative obligation. These themes are distinct but not mutually exclusive. For example, Burchell and Cook (2006) combine ideas from all these themes to discuss stakeholder dialogue as a CSR strategy, Morsing (2006) talks about strategic CSR communication with external stakeholders, and O'Riordan and Fairbrass (2008) explain CSR in relation to models of stakeholder dialogue in order to enhance firm strategy implementation. Though drawing from each of the three themes identified here, these studies still maintain a conceptual difference between strategy, interaction, and normative obligations.

Emerging theme: social construction and constitutive communication

A small number of articles and book chapters question the instrumental and informational view of communication that is assumed in the vast majority of the stakeholder literature and thus do not fit within one of the primary themes mentioned above. Rather than seeing communication as a linear process of message transmission between firms and stakeholders, some scholars argue that stakeholder thinking needs a much more dynamic conception of communication in order to understand and explain the complexity of stakeholder relationships that exist in today's organisational landscape. Simply put, the stakeholder literature has not adequately considered the constitutive effects of language (Crane & Livesey, 2003) and the co-construction of social reality (Beaulieu & Pasquero, 2002). To be sure, these ideas are not completely absent from the broader stakeholder literature, but they are on the periphery and have yet to make a

DISCURSIVITY, RELATIONALITY AND MATERIALITY

substantive contribution to mainstream stakeholder thinking. That is the goal of this study – build upon the ideas from this emerging theme of literature to develop a distinct communication perspective on organisational stakeholder relationships to advance stakeholder scholarship in the key areas noted earlier (i.e. stakeholder identification and salience, symbolic and material resource, and political production of meaning).

A limited number of articles and book chapters in the stakeholder literature have moved beyond inadequate notions of information transmission and are more in line with a constitutive approach to communication, though not necessarily using this terminology. Rowley (1997) was one of the first to move 'beyond dyadic ties' of stakeholder relationships in order to understand the interactions of multiple influences within the domain of stakeholder environments, and how these interactions shaped an organisation's relationship to a network of stakeholders. Beaulieu and Pasquero (2002) explain how organisations and stakeholders create a social reality of negotiated order, which is a co-construction between various stakeholders and the interdependent issues that define them. Brønn and Brønn (2003) introduce a model of co-orientation as a framework for understanding the communication processes that influence perceptions of stakeholder relationships. Crane and Livesey (2003) advocate a form of stakeholder communication that involves genuine symmetric practice between organisations and stakeholders in a joint negotiation of meaning, which entails communicating *with* stakeholders in contrast to merely communicating *to* stakeholders. Sedereviciute and Valentini (2011) develop a more holistic model of identification for online stakeholders, recognising that stakeholder attributes change across time and situations. Finally, Friedman and Miles (2004) argue that stakeholder communication must go beyond organisations' internal views of their stakeholder relationships, and that communication practice should be 'decentred' from the notion of a focal organisation.

Communication scholars writing from a more explicitly constitutive perspective discuss implications for stakeholder relationships, though not necessarily with the intention of contributing to the development of stakeholder theory per se. This includes Kuhn's (2008) communicative theory of the firm, which has important implications regarding the process of organisational change in relation to governance and competence theories of stakeholder relations; Arnaud and Mills' (2012) analysis of interfirm collaboration, which demonstrates how coordinated actions among stakeholder through micro-level conversations enable the formation of a stable collection competence that constitutes and interorganisational relationship among manufacturing companies; Deetz's (1992, 1995, 2005) critical model of stakeholder engagement, communication, and corporate governance; and Kuhn and Ashcraft (2003) communicative theorising about corporate scandals and stakeholder claims. Accordingly, the perspective developed in this study has its roots in organisational communication scholarship, proposing further alignment and eventual integration of stakeholder scholarship with an organisational communication perspective.

Despite important insights provided by these studies, the above-mentioned work remains relatively fragmented and has yet to make a definitive, coherent contribution to shape thinking about stakeholder communication (especially in the mainstream stakeholder literature). But taken together, these studies –from both the stakeholder literature that turn towards an alternative understanding of communication and studies from the communication literature that have implications for stakeholder thinking – move us closer to the nexus of discourse, relationality, and materiality and the articulation of a distinct communication perspective on stakeholder relationships. More than just an attempt to investigate particular instances of stakeholder communication, the goal is to conceptualise stakeholder relationships from a communicative perspective. To accomplish this, the article now turns to the literature on communication-as-constitutive, which provides a meta-theoretical framework to explain how discursive, relational, and material aspects of organising combine to constitute stakeholder relationships, with several important implications for subsequent research on stakeholder communication.

Specifically, three key areas are not adequately addressed (and perhaps cannot be) within current stakeholder thinking: (1) the process of stakeholder identification and the constitution of stakeholder salience, (2) the connection between material and symbolic resources between stakeholders, and (3) the political production of meaning in stakeholder relationships. These are key areas for rethinking stakeholder communication, but they are not well understood if stakeholder relationships are assumed to only involve the linear exchange of information and pre-existing meaning.

Developing a communication perspective towards stakeholder relationships

Having reviewed how communication has been studied in the stakeholder literature and how communication scholars have utilised stakeholder thinking, we are now in position to articulate a distinct contribution that communication can make to enhance stakeholder research. To begin, the main tenets of a constitutive approach to communication are summarised. From there three key implications of communicative constitution are explained, all of which involve a rethinking of communication and stakeholder relationships – especially at the intersections of discursivity, relationality, and materiality. Together, these ideas form an overall 'communication perspective' that can advance our understanding of stakeholder theory.

Communication as constitutive

The common view of communication in much of the stakeholder literature is that of *transmission*, rooted in informational models of messages exchanged between senders and receivers (Axley, 1984; Shannon & Weaver, 1949). From this perspective, communication involves the expression of already formed realities, and the primary concern is with the effectiveness of these expressions. Not that a transmission model of communication is necessarily wrong, but rather incomplete. Alternatively, over the last 25 years, communication scholars have developed a *constitutive* view of communication that focuses on the power of language in the production of meaning and how social realities are known via symbolic interaction (see Carey, 1989; Craig, 1999; Deetz, 1994a, 1994b; Pearce, 1989; Shepherd, 1993). This way of thinking is rooted in the linguistic turn in social theory (Rorty, 1967), where language is actively involved in the production and creation – not just the reflection or expression – of social realities. Communication acts on the world, it does not merely describe it. From this perspective, communication is a dynamic, interactive process that involves constant negotiation

DISCURSIVITY, RELATIONALITY AND MATERIALITY

over interpretation and meaning, not just the transmission of information. Social realities are not fixed such that they can be reflected or expressed unproblematically, and things often taken for granted in the social world – organisations, institutions, and relationships – only maintain their existence through sustained patterns of interaction. Communication can thus be defined as a dynamic, interactive process of meaning negotiation and interpretation through symbol use involving contextualised actors who coordinate and control their own and others' activity and knowledge (combining definitions from Ashcraft, Kuhn, & Cooren, 2009; Kuhn, 2008).

In a seminal essay published in *Communication Theory*, Craig (1999) articulated the notion of *communicative constitution* (or communication as constitutive) as a meta-theoretical framework to encompass all communication scholarship. As Craig explains, 'Communication, from [a constitutive] perspective is not a secondary phenomenon that can be explained by antecedent psychological, sociological, cultural, or economic factors; rather, communication itself is the primary, constitutive social process that explains all these other factors' (p. 126). In fact, Ashcraft et al. (2009) call communicative constitution the 'overarching principle that guides the discipline [of communication] today.' This constitutive view of communication has gained particular traction among scholars in the subfield of organisational communication, who have long incorporated constitutive ideas in their research, but more recently have coined the term communicative constitution of organisation (CCO) to connote a more explicitly constitutive approach to communication and organisational ontology (see Ashcraft et al., 2009; Putnam, Phillips, & Chapman, 1999). This work moves away from conceiving organisations as containers *within* which communication happens, to a more profound claim that organisation exists *as* communication, and thus seeking to explain all aspects of organisational existence and operation in distinctly communicative terms – what Kuhn (2008) simply refers to as 'taking communication seriously.'

Over the last few years, three schools of CCO scholarship have emerged as the main articulation of communicative constitution in the field of organisational communication. These include the Montreal School, which foregrounds the distanciation and imbrication of text-conversation dialectics that scale up to organisational forms; McPhee's Four Flows model, a structuationist approach that foregrounds distinct communication processes necessary for social structures to exist as organisations; and Luhmann's general theory of social systems, which foregrounds self-organisation (autopoiesis) and paradoxical decision events that enable organisations to distinguish themselves from their environments. Extensive reviews of these lines of scholarship exist elsewhere (see Ashcraft et al., 2009; Bisel, 2009; Brummans, Cooren, Robichaud, & Taylor, 2014; Cooren, Kuhn, Cornelissen, & Clark, 2011; Kuhn, 2012; Schoeneborn, 2011; Schoeneborn et al., 2014), and my purpose here is not to align with a particular school of CCO thinking. Instead, I want to step back from any specific articulation of CCO in favour of a broader perspective that emphasises the general principle of communicative constitution they all share, thus developing a foundation for a distinct communication perspective of organisational stakeholder relationships (that subsequently could be advanced by proponents of any particular school of CCO thinking in more targeted investigations, e.g. Kuhn, 2012). As Cooren et al. (2011, p.) state in their summary of CCO scholarship:

151

DISCURSIVITY, RELATIONALITY AND MATERIALITY

The general claim is that if communication is indeed constitutive of organization, it cannot be considered to be simply one of the many factors involved in organizing, and it cannot be merely the vehicle for the expression of pre-existing 'realities'; rather, it is the means by which organizations are established, composed, designed, and sustained. Consequently, organizations can no longer be seen as objects, entities, or 'social facts' inside of which communication occurs.

From this broad orientation towards a constitutive model of communication, we are able to construct what Craig (1999) calls a 'communicational perspective on social reality,' specifically organisational stakeholder relationships. Therefore, we can move beyond seeing organisations as pre-existing, independent entities that 'have' stakeholders, and instead focus on how organisations are embedded within a dynamic, relational landscape consisting of various stakeholder relationships. These relations make organisations what we consider them to be – they have no reality outside of these networks of relations. To develop these ideas further, I next explain how a communication perspective contributes to three key areas of organisational stakeholder relationships: (1) stakeholder identification and salience, (2) the entanglement of material and symbolic resources, and (3) the political production of meaning involved in stakeholder relationships – all of which are essential to the development of stakeholder thinking but beyond the logics of conventional stakeholder literature.

Stakeholder identification and salience

One of the most fundamental topics in the stakeholder literature is 'stakeholder identification and salience' (Freeman, Harrison, Wicks, Parmar, & De Colle, 2010; Mitchell et al., 1997). This involves labelling different stakeholder groups and classifying various stakeholder relationships, and then deciding which stakeholders managers should pay attention to (Andriof & Waddock, 2002). The most established and widely cited model in the literature to date is Mitchell, Agle, and Wood's (1997) theory of stakeholder identification and salience. In an attempt to explain Freeman's (1994) principle of 'who and what really counts,' they proposed that stakeholder salience will be positively related to the 'cumulative number of stakeholder attributes – power, legitimacy, and urgency – perceived by mangers to be present' (Mitchell et al., 1997, p. 873). High, low, and moderate levels of stakeholder salience would then depend on the number of attributes thought to be present by managers. A subsequent study of Chief Executive Officers from 80 companies by Agle, Mitchell, and Sonnenfeld (1999) found empirical support for this typology, with urgency as the best predictor of executive response. Following the lead of Mitchell et al. (1997), several ensuing articles and books in the stakeholder literature sought to identify stakeholders based on various attributes and characteristics. Table 2 provides a summary of this research, showing both the salient attributes and resulting stakeholder identities.

It is this area of stakeholder identification and salience that draws the most attention and criticism in current stakeholder research (Laplume et al., 2008). Some claim that the area of stakeholder identification is under-theorised and under-researched (Stoney & Winstanley, 2001); others say that the lack of specificity around stakeholder identification is a severe barrier for further development of stakeholder theory and application (Dunham, Freeman, Liedtka, & Arnold, 2006). A communication perspective of

DISCURSIVITY, RELATIONALITY AND MATERIALITY

Table 2. Summary of stakeholder identification research.

Citation	Stakeholder attributes	Stakeholder identities
Brickson (2005)	Identity orientations	Individualistic, relational, and collectivist
Carroll (1989)	Moral legitimacy	Stakeholders identity based on moral obligations
Clarkson (1994)	Bearing of risk in an organisation	Legitimate and non-legitimate stakeholders
Clarkson (1995)	Claim, ownership rights, or interests in an organisation	Primary, public, and secondary stakeholders
Clarkson Centre for Business Ethics – Consensus Statement (University of Toronto)	Risk bearing in value creation	Intentional and consequential stakeholders
Friedman and Miles (2002, 2004)	Nature of contracts with organisations (explicit/implicit, recognised/unrecognised	Compatible/incompatible stakeholders, necessary/contingent stakeholders
Frooman (1999)	Resource dependency	Direct/indirect influence pathway strategies and withholding/usage resource control strategies
Hill & Jones, 1992	Moral legitimacy	Stakeholder identities based on moral claims
Hitt, Harrison, and Ireland (2001)	Potential for value creation	Capital market, product market, and organisational stakeholders
Kaler (2002)	Moral obligations or ability to affect an organisation	Claimant, influencer, or combination stakeholders
Mitchell et al. (1997)	Power, legitimacy, and urgency	Dormant, discretionary, demanding, dominant, dangerous, dependent, definitive, and non-stakeholder
Preble (2005)	Contractual relationships	Primary/public stakeholders
Phillips (2003)	Legal and moral obligations	Normative/derivative stakeholders
Sedereviciute and Valentini (2011)	Positional power, content relevance, and discussion frequency/intensity	Based on member inter-connectivity and content shared
Whysall (2000)	Inputs contributed and costs incurred	Internal, marketplace, and external stakeholders

stakeholder identification and salience offers a way forward by rethinking the notion of identification in terms of relational association (versus classification) and also by recognising the contingent and discursive character of salient attributes (versus stable properties).

The primary understanding of identification across nearly all the stakeholder literature is that of classification and categorisation: identification *of*. This approach involves decisions by management to classify various stakeholders and the legitimacy of their claims on the firm. But a communication perspective suggests a different understanding of identification, namely a process of relational association: identification *with*. In this regard, identification is the perception of oneness or sense of belonging with another, where an organisation defines itself in terms of its relationality with others (Mael & Ashforth, 1992). Identification relates to communication, as Cheney and Tompkins (1987) explain, because 'the *process* of identification is conducted primarily with language, and the *product* of identification is expressed primarily with language' (p. 11; emphasis added). Rather than merely classifying stakeholders in terms of various roles (employees, suppliers, etc.), identifying with stakeholders involves an ongoing process of association via shared interests and goals. This understanding of identification is rooted in Burke's (1950) concept of *consubstantiation*, a process whereby individuals (or organisations) connect to elements in the social world to consider shared interests.

DISCURSIVITY, RELATIONALITY AND MATERIALITY

The assumption in most of the previous stakeholder literature is that stakeholders 'exist' and then they need to be identified by managers. But an alternative way of thinking about this would be to think of stake-holding as emerging from a relational process of identification, where the legitimacy of stakes are established to the extent that firms and other constituencies identify with each other in relation to common targets. The notion of a stakeholder does not come into being apart from this process of identification; a constituent does not have a separate status as 'stakeholder' apart from identifying *with* a particular organisation, versus being identified *by* the organisation.

Some might argue that this relational approach to stakeholder identification is relatively unimportant (immaterial), since once stakeholder identities have emerged as are understood as fairly stable, they can be treated as having a separate status and existence by organisational actors – and thus no real explanatory power is lost. However, this ignores the contingency and social constructedness of stakeholder attributes. Forms of conversation among stakeholders actually construct – not merely represent – the realities of stakeholder relationships (Barge & Little, 2002); they do not exist apart from interaction. Thus, stakeholder salience is better understood as a discursive property of communication practice, not a stable property of managerial attribution. Rather than managers deciding whether a particular stakeholder (and its claims on the firm) is salient or not, organisational members can instead consider salient features of their relationships with stakeholders and the social construction of stakes that constitute these relationships. A communication perspective towards stakeholder relationships is less concerned with labelling and categorising different stakeholders versus assessing (by both scholars and practitioners) the quality of the relationships among stakeholders in terms of how salient properties emerge from certain patterns of interaction and association.

When a shift is made from identification *of* stakeholders to identification *with* stakeholders, several possibilities arise. First, the process of identification becomes decentred from the management of a focal organisation. This opens up the identification process to include the participation of multiple voices, which is an important aspect of organisational adaptation and landscape fit (Ashmos, Huonker, & McDaniel, 1998). Second, it creates an opportunity frame from which organisations can develop novel and creative solutions. Conceptualising stakeholder identification in terms of classification and categorisation implicitly puts organisations in a defensive frame where the goal is to mitigate the impact of stakeholder claims on organisational performance. But this narrows the possibility that firm–stakeholder relationships can result in new ideas that can be mutually beneficial for all parties involved. Finally, conceiving stakeholder identification as a communication process of association enables a shift away from homogenous role-based identities, which has received nearly 'unanimous adoption' in previous stakeholder literature (Wolfe & Putler, 2003, p. 66). Instead, stakeholder identification involves more attention to intra-group diversity (Winn, 2001) and the ways in which stakeholder identities shift in relation to changing organisational circumstances. Thus, a communication perspective towards stakeholder relationships entails the following proposition:

DISCURSIVITY, RELATIONALITY AND MATERIALITY

Proposition 1: Stakeholder relationships involve a relational process of identification whereby organisations discursively construct their identities in relation to common points of association with internal and external constituent groups.

Stakeholder communication research can examine the validity of this claim by investigating how stakeholder identities are embedded in certain relational practices, and how these identities compare to managerial classifications of stakeholder identification. Key questions for this line of research include how it is that various stakeholder groups come to have certain identities, what communication practices help sustain these identities, and how these identities evolve in relation to various stakeholder interactions. Managerial decision-making is certainly an important aspect of the identification process, but a communication perspective on stakeholder relationships goes beyond managerial interests to include the entire range of stakeholder interactions that could influence identification.

The entanglement of material and symbolic resources

A second area where a communication perspective towards stakeholder relationships has important implications is with regard to the dichotomy between material and symbolic resources that prevails throughout stakeholder research. Previous stakeholder literature has long acknowledged a broad understanding of resource dependency in firm–stakeholder relationships (Kochan & Rubinstein, 2000; Post, Preston, & Sachs, 2002), meaning that organisations depend on resources provided by stakeholders, and vice versa. In this literature, these resources are perceived as either material *or* symbolic, presuming an opposition between materiality and symbolism and thus confusing how these elements combine to constitute stakeholder relationships. Previous stakeholder literature tends to privilege the supposed material aspect of resources, usually implying some notion of financial capital, labour, or physical infrastructure, with less attention given to theorising so-called (and separate) symbolic resources. For example, Laplume, et al.'s (2008) extensive review of the stakeholder literature argues that a key area for future stakeholder research is the development of symbolic resources (e.g. legitimacy and reputation), investigating whether 'symbolic management' is adequate for firm performance or if 'concrete' actions through [material] resources are necessary for improved performance. Despite the call for increased attention to symbolism, a dichotomy between materiality and symbolism is still assumed. Yet is this dichotomy justified? After all, the symbolic dimensions of various resources must be embodied somewhere somehow, and the material dimensions of various resources are only meaningful to the extent they are animated or "brought to life" though certain beliefs, ideas, motivations, or feelings (Cooren, 2012).

In contrast, a communication perspective on stakeholder relationships provides the latitude to question the prevailing distinction that is made between material and symbolic resources, and to think instead of the relationship of between materiality and symbolism as one of *inextricable entanglement*. Ashcraft et al. (2009) express this idea in their recent efforts to 'materialise' organisational communication. They argue that 'communication is the mechanism whereby the material and [symbolic] co-mingle and transform accordingly. In communication,

DISCURSIVITY, RELATIONALITY AND MATERIALITY

symbol becomes material; material becomes symbol; and neither stay the same as a result' (p. 34). This 'mutual constitution' (p. 31) of materiality and symbolism prevents overly structuralist or naively constructionist explanations of stakeholder relationships. Instead, the complexities of both material and symbolic are realised in communication – where symbolic dimensions are embodied and material dimensions are animated.

For example, when firms rely on investors to provide financial capital for their operations, or workers to provide physical labour, or repeat customers to provide legitimacy, material and symbolic resources are always co-present and should not be understood apart from each other – they are sociomaterial (Orlikowski, 2007). Things such as 'legitimacy' or 'reputation' always have a material dimension – they have to be materialised in some way in order to make a difference. Legitimacy or reputation must be embodied somehow somewhere if they are to have any sort of meaningful existence, such as in the way people talk about the organisation or the way it is described in the media. Likewise, supposedly material resources such as 'buildings' or 'labour' have no inherent meaning or value in themselves – they must be animated by various beliefs, feelings, traits, objectives, and the like. For them to even exist *as resources* (versus mere raw physical elements) already suggests the presence of symbolism, a material manifestation of a symbolic dimension that can be uncovered through a constitutive approach to communication. Legitimacy, reputation, labour, and buildings are always both material and symbolic – materiality and symbolicity are two constitutive aspects of their mode of existence, all of which is realised communicatively. The contribution of materiality and symbolism is not a consequence of their separate attributes or some sort of dialectical relationship between them. Rather, they operate as an integrated entity in a mutually constitutive relationship.

A communication perspective of stakeholder relationships eliminates a false dichotomy between material and symbolic resources, showing that in interaction, symbolic dimensions are embodied materially and material dimensions are animated symbolically (see Cooren, 2012). If stakeholder relationships entail resource-dependent associations, then theories of stakeholder relationships must account for the ways in which materiality *and* symbolism implicate each other in the way stakeholder relationships unfold. Current stakeholder thinking does not do this, but a communication perspective can provide such an explanation, demonstrating that communication is the way in which material and symbolic shape each other through a reciprocal process of mutual constitution. This is especially true at the boundaries of organisational relationships, as organisational members negotiate the extent of their stakeholder associations. An organisation's relationship with a particular supplier, for example, is not merely a sterile exchange of products and financial capital at the intersection of supply and demand, but rather a dynamic interplay among organisational boundary spanners who negotiate the sociomateriality of various resources in relation to each other. Decisions about various resources are shaped by what those decisions *mean* or *represent* to a firm, not simply what materials *are* or *do*. This leads to a second proposition for a communication perspective of stakeholder relationships:

Proposition 2: Stakeholder relationships consist of resource-dependent associations that are realized communicatively through the mutual constitution of materiality and

DISCURSIVITY, RELATIONALITY AND MATERIALITY

symbolism – in communication, symbolic dimensions are embodied materially and material dimensions are animated symbolically.

This means that stakeholder communication research should investigate the co-presence of materiality and symbolism in the resource-dependencies that compose stakeholder relationships. This could involve demonstrating how presumed symbolic resources (such as legitimacy or reputation) only exist to the extent they are materialised in interaction. Additionally, this line of research could reveal how seemingly material resources (such as physical infrastructure or communication technologies) are in fact animated by various ideas, beliefs, emotions, and motivations, which can be uncovered by investigating their communicative constitution (and not privilege their taken-for-granted materiality).

Political production of meaning

A final implication of a communication perspective includes the ways in which political interests are involved in the formation and development of stakeholder relationships. The notion of stakeholder power is widely accepted as a key attribute of stakeholder salience in previous stakeholder literature (i.e. Agle et al., 1999; Mitchell et al., 1997), but previous stakeholder research does very little to theorise power itself. Power is almost universally understood in terms of resource dependence, meaning that stakeholder power involves the ability to provide/withhold key resources to/from other organisations. Yet little research shows how or why it is that power is attributed to certain resources and not others, or how power is constituted in stakeholder relationships.[2]

In contrast, a communication perspective recognises that power relations are produced and reproduced discursively, and that communication is the process by which certain power relationships are realised. As Deetz and Mumby (1990) explain, 'Power is most successfully exercised when an individual or group has the ability to frame discursive and non-discursive practices within a system of meanings that is commensurate with that individual's or group's own interests' (p. 32). The implication for stakeholder relationships is that attributions of power should be understood in terms of the social processes that produce contingent and intersubjective meanings, and the political interests that are included (or excluded) in decision-making. With its origins in strategic management, the stakeholder literature overwhelmingly locates the ability to frame discursive practices in stakeholder relationships at the level of management, which privileges certain interests over others. However, the social processes by which power is produced and attributed should not be accepted uncritically, but rather opened up to investigate how it is that stakeholders come to know and experience other stakeholders as powerful, and how these processes produce (versus merely transmit) meaning.

This idea is rooted in the Foucault (1972) argument that there is power *in* knowledge, not just power *of* knowledge. In organisational contexts, the issue is the arbitrary privileging of certain managerial interests that distorts decisions and suppresses meaningful conflicts (Deetz, 1992). The question for stakeholder thinking is who is making decisions about attributions of power among other stakeholders, and how these decisions serve to further constitute the firm. A communication perspective theorises power in terms of stakeholder participation in the discursive construction of meaning and attributions of power. Accordingly, the following proposition is offered:

> **Proposition 3:** Attributions of stakeholder power are produced discursively within ongoing and contested representational practices and are a function of the participatory processes involved in stakeholder relationships.

Thus, the power dynamics in stakeholder relationships can be assessed as a matter of participation in the discursive processes of meaning production, not simply in the managerial designation of power as a stakeholder attribute. Stakeholder communication research should question the way attributions of power are embedded within participatory (or exclusionary) processes. Additionally, stakeholder communication research can ask whether various stakeholder interests are substantively included in strategic decisions among stakeholders (versus merely expressed in meetings or forums), and what processes of meaning construction shape the power dynamics between stakeholders.

Discussion

The purpose of this research was to develop a communication perspective towards stakeholder relationships, taking seriously the constitutive effects of language and human interaction in the ongoing social construction of various connections between and among organisations. To that end, the article provided a critical review of the stakeholder communication literature in order to demonstrate the need for an alternative conception of communication to underwrite future stakeholder communication research. In order to advance thinking about stakeholder communication, we do not just need more investigations of isolated communication phenomena (though that is valuable), but rather a perspective where stakeholder relationships are explained in distinctly communicative terms (cf. Kuhn, 2012).

This involves focusing on what stakeholder relationships are and what stakeholder relationships do – all at the nexus of discursivity, relationality, and materiality. To that end, three propositions are offered for a communication perspective of stakeholder relationships regarding (1) stakeholder identification and salience, (2) the entanglement of material and symbolic resources, and (3) the political production of meaning. As organisations become sites of increasing participation and conflict over fundamental meanings (Deetz, 1992), communication theories of message transmission and information exchange are less valuable. A communication perspective helps explain stakeholder relationships as dynamic sites of organisational constitution where negotiation and meaning construction shape how organisational realities are known and experienced.

In their extensive review of the last 25 years of stakeholder research, Laplume et al. (2008) claim that stakeholder thinking would benefit from including additional theoretical perspectives. A constitutive approach to communication is one such theoretical perspective that provides a broad foundation from which to advance stakeholder thinking. Constitutive communication enables the development of a distinct perspective of stakeholder relationships, with important implications for stakeholder thinking. First,

DISCURSIVITY, RELATIONALITY AND MATERIALITY

a communication perspective of stakeholder relationships shifts the unit of analysis from focal firms or stakeholder networks to the discursive and relational sociomaterial *processes* of relationship constitution. A communication perspective does not take the existence of organisations or networks as given, but rather suggests that firms and networks are achieved and only exist meaningfully in communication. Therefore, stakeholder relationships could be studied in terms of the instances of sociomaterial engagement when stakeholders produce and negotiate the meanings that constitute their relationships, not just the economic factors that give rise to stakeholder relationships or the structural parameters of those relationships.

Second, a communication perspective of stakeholder relationships goes beyond simply acknowledging *that* stakeholders interact to examining interaction per se, what Taylor and Van Every (2000) refer to as the conversational modality of communication. This brings needed attention to how stakeholders sociomaterially co-construct the social worlds that constitute their relationships, not just the antecedent conditions or outcomes of their associations. If stakeholder relationships literally exist in the interactions between stakeholders, then it is critically important to understand how certain patterns of interaction influence the emergence of certain properties (i.e. trust, legitimacy, collective identity, etc.) that are valuable for stakeholder relationships – these properties exhibit a relational ontology (Benjamin, 2015) that cannot be understood apart from communicative constitution.

Finally, a communication perspective opens up the development of stakeholder relationships to include alternative voices beyond narrow managerial interests. The locus of stakeholder identification, for example, no longer privileges managerial decisions (though these still play an important role) because there are additional voices that participate in the process of identifying with other organisational constituents and affected parties. A communication perspective towards stakeholder relationships recognises that multiple voices do (and should) participate in the constitution of stakeholder relationships, even though some of these voices have not been acknowledged in the past. When we accept the notion that communication has the power to create the organisational realities of stakeholder relationships (not merely express or transmit pre-existing realities), we are in a much better position to understand the dynamic sociomaterial process of organisational constitution. A communication perspective directs attention away from limited conceptions of stakeholder relationships, instead seeing stakeholder relationships as constituted in and by communication at the nexus of materiality, discursivity, and (stakeholder) relationality. In doing so, it opens the way to greater alignment between the stakeholder and organisational communication literatures.

Notes

1. Even recent stakeholder thinking that challenges the corporate-centric assumptions of most previous stakeholder research in favour of decentring the conception of a focal firm (e.g. Friedman & Miles, 2002), recognises the simultaneous influence of multiple interdependent stakeholders (e.g. Rowley, 1997), and questions the idea of homogeneous stakeholder interests within role-based groups (e.g. Winn, 2001; Wolfe & Putler, 2003) is still very much concerned with relationships between stakeholders and how these relationships are managed.
2. Mitchell et al. (1997) do acknowledge that stakeholder attributes (such as power) are socially constructed, but they do little to explain *how* it is that power is socially constructed

DISCURSIVITY, RELATIONALITY AND MATERIALITY

or the implications of this process. They also provide a discussion of Etzioni's (1964) concept of normative power, which involves power based on symbolic resources. But again, there is little discussion of *how* these symbolic resources come to constitute power.

Disclosure statement

No potential conflict of interest was reported by the author.

References

Agle, B., Donaldson, T., Freeman, R., Jensen, M., Mitchell, R., & Wood, D. (2008). Dialogue: Toward superior stakeholder theory. *Business Ethics Quarterly, 18*(2), 153–190. doi:10.5840/beq200818214

Agle, B. R., Mitchell, R. K., & Sonnenfeld, J. A. (1999). Who matters to CEOs? An investigation of stakeholder attributes and salience, corporate performance, and CEO values. *The Academy of Management Journal, 42*(5), 507–525. doi:10.2307/256973

Andriof, J., & Waddock, S. (2002). Unfolding stakeholder engagement. In B. H. J. Andriof, S. Waddock, & S. S. Rahman (Eds.), *Unfolding stakeholder thinking* (pp. 19–42). Sheffield: Greenleaf.

Andriof, J., Waddock, S., Husted, B., & Rahman, S. (2002). *Unfolding stakeholder thinking: Theory, responsibility, engagement.* Sheffield: Greenleaf.

Andriof, J., Waddock, S., Husted, B., & Rahman, S. (2003). *Unfolding stakeholder thinking 2: Relationships, communication, reporting and performance.* Sheffield: Greenleaf.

Arnaud, N., & Mills, C. E. (2012). Understanding interorganizational agency: A communication perspective. *Group & Organization Management 37.* doi:1059601112451125.

Ashcraft, K., Kuhn, T., & Cooren, F. (2009). Constitutional amendments: "Materializing" organizational communication. *The Academy of Management Annals, 3*(1), 1–64. doi:10.1080/19416520903047186

Ashmos, D. P., Huonker, J. W., & McDaniel, R. R. (1998). Participation as a complicating mechanism: The effect of clinical professional and middle manager participation on hospital performance. *Health Care Management Review, 23*(4), 7–20. doi:10.1097/00004010-199802340-00002

Axley, S. (1984). Managerial and organizational communication in terms of the conduit metaphor. *The Academy of Management Review, 9*(3), 428–437.

Barge, J., & Little, M. (2002). Dialogical wisdom, communicative practice, and organizational life. *Communication Theory, 12*(4), 375–397. doi:10.1111/comt.2002.12.issue-4

Basu, K., & Palazzo, G. (2008). Corporate social responsibility: A process model of sensemaking. *Academy of Management Review, 33*(1), 122–136. doi:10.5465/AMR.2008.27745504

Beaulieu, S., & Pasquero, J. (2002). Reintroducing stakeholder dynamics in stakeholder thinking: A negotiated-order perspective. *Journal of Corporate Citizenship, 6*, 53–69. doi:10.9774/GLEAF.4700.2002.su.00007

DISCURSIVITY, RELATIONALITY AND MATERIALITY

Bendell, J. (2003). Talking for change? Reflections on effective stakeholder dialogue. In B. H. J. Andriof, S. Waddock, & S. S. Rahman (Eds.), *Unfolding stakeholder thinking 2* (pp. 53–69). Sheffield: Greenleaf.

Benjamin, A. (2015). *Towards a relational ontology: Philosophy's other possibility*. Albany: State University of New York Press.

Bisel, R. S. (2009). A communicative ontology of organization? A description, history, and critique of CCO theories for organization science. *Management Communication Quarterly*. doi:10.1177/0893318909351582

Brickson, S. (2005). Organizational identity orientation: Forging a link between organizational identity and organizations' relations with stakeholders. *Administrative Science Quarterly, 50* (4), 576–609.

Brummans, B., Cooren, F., Robichaud, D., & Taylor, J. R. (2014). Approaches in research on the communicative constitution of organizations. In L. L. Putnam & D. Mumby (Eds.), *SAGE handbook of organizational communication* (3rd ed., pp. 173–194). Thousand Oaks, CA: Sage.

Brønn, P. S., & Brønn, C. (2003). A reflective stakeholder approach: Co-orientation as a basis for communication and learning. *Journal of Communication Management, 7*(4), 291–303. doi:10.1108/13632540310807430

Burchell, J., & Cook, J. (2006). Assessing the impact of stakeholder dialogue: Changing relationships between NGOs and companies. *Journal of Public Affairs, 6*(3–4), 210–227. doi:10.1002/(ISSN)1479-1854

Burchell, J., & Cook, J. (2008). Stakeholder dialogue and organisational learning: Changing relationships between companies and NGOs. *Business Ethics: A European Review, 17*(1), 35–46. doi:10.1111/j.1467-8608.2008.00518.x

Burke, K. (1950). *A rhetoric of motives*. Berkeley, CA: University of California Press.

Calton, J., & Payne, S. (2003). Coping with paradox: Multistakeholder learning dialogue as a pluralist sensemaking process for addressing messy problems. *Business & Society, 42*(1), 7–42. doi:10.1177/0007650302250505

Carey, J. W. (1989). *Communication as culture: Essays on media and society*. Winchester, MA: Unwin Hyman.

Carroll, A. B. (1989). *Business & society*. Cincinnati, OH: South-Western Pub.

Cheney, G., & Tompkins, P. (1987). Coming to terms with organizational identification and commitment. *Central States Speech Journal, 38*(1), 1–15. doi:10.1080/10510978709368225

Clark, C. (2000). Differences between public relations and corporate social responsibility: An analysis. *Public Relations Review, 26*(3), 363–380. doi:10.1016/S0363-8111(00)00053-9

Clarkson, M. B. E. (1994, May). *A risk based model of stakeholder theory*. Paper presented at the Center for Corporate Social Performance and Ethics, Toronto, ON.

Clarkson, M. B. E. (1995). A stakeholder framework for analyzing and evaluating corporate social performance. *Academy of Management Review, 20*, 92–92.

Cooren, F. (2012). Communication theory at the center: Ventriloquism and the communicative constitution of reality. *Journal of Communication, 62* (1),1–20.

Cooren, F., Kuhn, T., Cornelissen, J. P., & Clark, T. (2011). Communication, organizing and organization: An overview and introduction to the special issue. *Organization Studies, 32*(9), 1149–1170.

Craig, R. T. (1999). Communication theory as a field. *Communication Theory, 9*(2), 119–161

Crane, A., & Livesey, S. (2003). Are you talking to me? Stakeholder communication and the risks and rewards of dialogue. In B. H. J. Andriof, S. Waddock, & S. S. Rahman (Eds.), *Unfolding stakeholder thinking 2*. Sheffield: Greenleaf.

Deetz, S. (1995). *Transforming communication, transforming business: Building responsive and responsible workplaces*. Cresskill, NJ: Hampton Press.

Deetz, S. (2005, May). *Keynote address: Stakeholder engagement, corporate governance, and communication*. Paper presented at the Governance without Government: New Forms of Governance in the Knowledge Economy Conference, Cardiff University (Whales).

Deetz, S., & Mumby, D. K. (1990). Power, discourse, and the workplace: Reclaiming the critical tradition. *Communication Yearbook, 13*, 18–47.

DISCURSIVITY, RELATIONALITY AND MATERIALITY

Deetz, S. A. (1992). *Democracy in an age of corporate colonization: Developments in communication and the politics of everyday life.* Albany, NY: State University of New York Press.

Deetz, S. A. (1994a). Future of the discipline: The challenges, the research, and the social contribution. In S. A. Deetz (Ed.), *Communication yearbook* (Vol. 17, pp. 565–600). Thousand Oaks, CA: Sage.

Deetz, S. A. (1994b). The micro-politics of identity formation in the workplace: The case of a knowledge intensive firm. *Human Studies, 17*(1), 23–44. doi:10.1007/BF01322765

Deetz, S. (1994c). Representational practices and the political analysis of corporations: Building a communication perspective in organizational studies. In B. Kovacic (Ed.), *New approaches to organizational communication* (pp. 211–244). Albany: State University of New York Press.

Dunham, L., Freeman, R., Liedtka, J., & Arnold, D. G. (2006). Enhancing stakeholder practice: A particularized exploration of community. *Business Ethics Quarterly, 16*(1), 23–42. doi:10.5840/beq20061611

Etzioni, A. (1964). *Modern organizations.* Englewood Cliffs, NJ: Prentice-Hall.

Foucault, M. (1972). *The archaeology of knowledge* (A. M. Sheridan Smith, Trans.). New York, NY: Pantheon Books.

Freeman, R. E. (1984). *Strategic management: A stakeholder approach.* Boston, MA: Pitman Publishing.

Freeman, R. E. (1994). The politics of stakeholder theory: Some future directions. *Business Ethics Quarterly, 4*, 409–421.

Freeman, R. E., Harrison, J. S., Wicks, A. C., Parmar, B. L., & De Colle, S. (2010). *Stakeholder theory: The state of the art.* New York: Cambridge University Press.

Friedman, A., & Miles, S. (2002). Developing stakeholder theory. *Journal of Management Studies, 39*(1), 1–21. doi:10.1111/1467-6486.00280

Friedman, A. L., & Miles, S. (2004). Stakeholder theory and communication practice. *Journal of Communication Management, 9*(1), 89–97.

Frooman, F. (1999). Stakeholder influence strategies. *Academy of Management Review, 24*(2), 191–205.

Gregory, A. (2007). Involving stakeholders in developing corporate brands: The communication dimension. *Journal of Marketing Management, 23*(1–2), 59–73. doi:10.1362/026725707X178558

Habermas, J. (1981). *The theory of communicative action.* London: Beacon Press.

Hill, C. W. L., & Jones, T. M. (1992). Stakeholder-agency theory. *Journal of Management Studies, 29*(2), 131–154. doi:10.1111/j.1467-6486.1992.tb00657.x

Hitt, M. A., Harrison, J. S., & Ireland, R. D. (2001). *Mergers and acquisitions: A guide to creating value for stakeholders.* New York: Oxford University Press.

Hornik, S., Chen, H., Klein, G., & Jiang, J. (2003). Communication skills of IS providers: An expectation gap analysis from three stakeholder perspectives. *IEEE Transactions on Professional Communication, 4*(1), 17–34. doi:10.1109/TPC.2002.808351

Kaler, J. (2002). Morality and strategy in stakeholder identification. *Journal of Business Ethics, 39* (1/2), 91–100. doi:10.1023/A:1016336118528

Kaptein, M., & Van Tulder, R. (2003). Toward effective stakeholder dialogue. *Business and Society Review, 108*(2), 203–224. doi:10.1111/basr.2003.108.issue-2

Kim, J.-N. (2012). From relational quality to communicative actions of publics and stakeholders: Understanding causality loops between behaviors of organizations and behaviors of publics in strategic communication. *International Journal of Strategic Communication, 6*(1), 1–6. doi:10.1080/1553118X.2012.652010

Kochan, T. A., & Rubinstein, S. A. (2000). Toward a stakeholder theory of the firm: The Saturn partnership. *Organization Science, 11*(4), 367–386.

Kuhn, T. (2008). A communicative theory of the firm: Developing an alternative perspective on intra-organizational power and stakeholder relationships. *Organization Studies, 29*(8–9), 1227–1254. doi:10.1177/0170840608094778

Kuhn, T. (2012). Negotiating the micro-macro divide: Thought leadership from organizational communication for theorizing organization. *Management Communication Quarterly, 26*(4), 543–584. doi:10.1177/0893318912462004

DISCURSIVITY, RELATIONALITY AND MATERIALITY

Kuhn, T., & Ashcraft, K. L. (2003). Corporate scandal and the theory of the firm: Formulating the contributions of organizational communication studies. *Management Communication Quarterly, 17*(1), 20–57. doi:10.1177/0893318903253421

Laplume, A. O., Sonpar, K., & Litz, R. A. (2008). Stakeholder theory: Reviewing a theory that moves us. *Journal of Management, 34*(6), 1152–1189. doi:10.1177/0149206308324322

Lewis, L. (2007). An organizational stakeholder model of change implementation communication. *Communication Theory, 17*(2), 176–204. doi:10.1111/comt.2007.17.issue-2

Lewis, L. K., Laster, N., & Kulkarni, V. (2013). Telling'em how it will be: Previewing pain of risky change in initial announcements. *International Journal of Business Communication, 50*(3), 278–308. doi:10.1177/0021943613487072

Lewis, L. K., Richardson, B. K., & Hamel, S. A. (2003). When the "stakes" are communicative: The Lamb's and the Lion's Share During Nonprofit Planned Change. *Human Communication Research, 29,* 400–430.

Longest, B., Jr., & Rohrer, W. (2005). Communication between public health agencies and their external stakeholders. *Journal of Health and Human Services Administration, 28*(2), 189–217.

Mael, F., & Ashforth, B. (1992). Alumni and their alma mater: A partial test of the reformulated model of organizational identification. *Journal of Organizational Behavior, 13*(2), 103–123. doi:10.1002/(ISSN)1099-1379

Miles, M., Munilla, L., & Darroch, J. (2006). The role of strategic conversations with stakeholders in the formation of corporate social responsibility strategy. *Journal of Business Ethics, 69*(2), 195–205. doi:10.1007/s10551-006-9085-6

Mitchell, R., Agle, B., & Wood, D. (1997). Toward a theory of stakeholder identification and salience: Defining the principle of who and what really counts. *Academy of Management Review, 22,* 853–886.

Morsing, M. (2006). Corporate social responsibility as strategic auto-communication: On the role of external stakeholders for member identification. *Business Ethics: A European Review, 15*(2), 171–182. doi:10.1111/beer.2006.15.issue-2

Morsing, M., & Schultz, M. (2006). Corporate social responsibility communication: Stakeholder information, response and involvement strategies. *Business Ethics: A European Review, 15*(4), 323–338. doi:10.1111/beer.2006.15.issue-4

O'Riordan, L., & Fairbrass, J. (2008). Corporate social responsibility (CSR): Models and theories in stakeholder dialogue. *Journal of Business Ethics, 83*(4), 745–758. doi:10.1007/s10551-008-9662-y

Orlikowski, W. J. (2007). Sociomaterial practices: Exploring technology at work. *Organization Studies, 28*(9), 1435–1448.

Parmar, B. L., Freeman, R. E., Harrison, J. S., Wicks, A. C., Purnell, L., & De Colle, S. (2010). Stakeholder theory: The state of the art. *The Academy of Management Annals, 4*(1), 403–445. doi:10.1080/19416520.2010.495581

Patterson, J. D., II, & Allen, M. W. (1997). Accounting for your actions: How stakeholders respond to the strategic communication of environmental activist organizations. *Journal of Applied Communication Research, 25,* 293–316. doi:10.1080/00909889709365482

Payne, S., & Calton, J. (2002). Towards a managerial practice of stakeholder engagement: Developing multi-stakeholder learning dialogues. In B. H. J. Andriof, S. Waddock, & S. S. Rahman (Eds.), *Unfolding stakeholder thinking* (pp. 121–136). Sheffield: Greenleaf.

Pearce, W. B. (1989). *Communication and the human condition.* Carbondale, IL: Southern Illinois Press.

Pedersen, E. (2006). Making corporate social responsibility (CSR) operable: How companies translate stakeholder dialogue into practice. *Business and Society Review, 111*(2), 137–163. doi:10.1111/j.1467-8594.2006.00265.x

Pfeil, M., Setterberg, A., & O'Rourke, J. (2004). The art of downsizing: Communicating lay-offs to key stakeholders. *Journal of Communication Management, 8*(2), 130–141. doi:10.1108/13632540410807600

Phillips, R. (2003). *Stakeholder theory and organizational ethics*. San Francisco, CA: Berrett-Koehler.

Post, J., Preston, L., & Sachs, S. (2002). Managing the extended enterprise: The new stakeholder view. *California Management Review*, 45(1), 6–28. doi:10.2307/41166151

Preble, J. F. (2005). Toward a comprehensive model of stakeholder management. *Business and Society Review*, 110(4), 407–431. doi:10.1111/basr.2005.110.issue-4

Putnam, L., Phillips, N., & Chapman, P. (1999). Metaphors of communication and organization. In S. Clegg, C. Hardy, & W. R. Nord (Eds.), *Managing organizations: Current issues* (pp. 375–408). Thousand Oaks, CA: Sage.

Rasche, A., & Esser, D. (2006). From stakeholder management to stakeholder accountability. *Journal of Business Ethics*, 65(3), 251–267. doi:10.1007/s10551-005-5355-y

Reed, D. (1999). Stakeholder management theory: A critical theory perspective. *Business Ethics Quarterly*, 9(3), 453–483. doi:10.2307/3857512

Rorty, R. (Ed.). (1967). *The linguistic turn: Recent essays in philosophical method*. Chicago, IL: University of Chicago Press.

Rowley, T. (1997). Moving beyond dyadic ties: A network theory of stakeholder influences. *Academy of Management Review*, 22(4), 887–910.

Schoeneborn, D. (2011). Organization as communication: A Luhmannian perspective. *Management Communication Quarterly*, 24(4), 663–689.

Schoeneborn, D., Blaschke, S., Cooren, F., McPhee, R. D., Seidl, D., & Taylor, J. R. (2014). The three schools of CCO thinking: Interactive dialogue and systematic comparison. *Management Communication Quarterly*, 28, 285–316. doi:10.1177/0893318914527000

Sedereviciute, K., & Valentini, C. (2011). Towards a more holistic stakeholder analysis approach. Mapping known and undiscovered stakeholders from social media. *International Journal of Strategic Communication*, 5(4), 221–239. doi:10.1080/1553118X.2011.592170

Shannon, C. E., & Weaver, W. (1949). *The mathematical theory of information*. Urbana: University of Illinois Press.

Shepherd, G. J. (1993). Building a discipline of communication. *Journal of Communication*, 43(3), 83–91. doi:10.1111/jcom.1993.43.issue-3

Smith, J., & Arnold, D. G. (2005). Fairness, communication, and engagement: New developments in stakeholder theory. *Business Ethics Quarterly*, 15(4), 711–721. doi:10.5840/beq200515434

Stephens, K. K., Malone, P. C., & Bailey, C. M. (2005). Communicating with stakeholders during a crisis: Evaluating message strategies. *Journal of Business Communication*, 42(4), 390–419. doi:10.1177/0021943605279057

Steurer, R. (2006). Mapping stakeholder theory anew: From the "stakeholder theory of the firm" to three perspectives on business-society relations. *Business Strategy and the Environment*, 15(1), 55–69. doi:10.1002/(ISSN)1099-0836

Stoney, C., & Winstanley, D. (2001). Stakeholding: Confusion or Utopia? Mapping the conceptual terrain. *Journal of Management Studies*, 38(5), 603–626. doi:10.1111/1467-6486.00251

Taylor, J. R., & Van Every, E. J. (2000). *The emergent organization: Communication as its site and surface*. Mahwah, NJ: Lawrence Erlbaum Associates.

Ulmer, R. (2001). Effective crisis management through established stakeholder relationships: Malden Mills as a case study. *Management Communication Quarterly*, 14(4), 590–615. doi:10.1177/0893318901144003

van Huijstee, M., & Glasbergen, P. (2008). The practice of stakeholder dialogue between multi-nationals and NGOs. *Corporate Social Responsibility and Environmental Management*, 15(5), 298–310. doi:10.1002/csr.v15:5

Vernuccio, M. (2014). Communicating corporate brands through social media: An exploratory study. *International Journal of Business Communication*, 51(3), 211–233. doi:10.1177/2329488414525400

Vielhaber, M. E., & Waltman, J. L. (2008). Changing uses of technology: Crisis communication responses in a faculty strike. *Journal of Business Communication*, 45(3), 308–330. doi:10.1177/0021943608317112

Weber, M. S., Thomas, G. F., & Stephens, K. J. (2015). Organizational disruptions and triggers for divergent sensemaking. *International Journal of Business Communication, 52*(1), 68–96. doi:10.1177/2329488414560281

Welcomer, S., Cochran, P., Rands, G., & Haggerty, M. (2003). Constructing a web: Effects of power and social responsiveness on firm-stakeholder relationships. *Business & Society, 42*(1), 43–82. doi:10.1177/0007650302250502

Whysall, P. (2000). Addressing ethical issues in retailing: A stakeholder perspective. *The International Review of Retail, Distribution and Consumer Research, 10*(3), 305–318. doi:10.1080/095939600405992

Winn, M. I. (2001). Building stakeholder theory with a decision modeling methodology. *Business & Society, 40*(2), 133–166. doi:10.1177/000765030104000202

Wolfe, R., & Putler, D. (2003). How tight are the ties that bind stakeholder groups? *Organization Science, 13*(1), 64–80. doi:10.1287/orsc.13.1.64.544

Zakhem, A. (2008). Stakeholder management capability: A discourse–theoretical approach. *Journal of Business Ethics, 79*(4), 395–405. doi:10.1007/s10551-007-9405-5

Index

Note: **Boldface** page numbers refer to tables & italic page numbers refer to figures. Page numbers followed by "n" refer to endnotes.

activity theory 3, 45, 46, 48–50, *49*
actor-network theory 7, 8, 69, 72, 76
affordances, social media 114
agency/structure dualism 1
Amin, A. 85, 91, 92
Annin, P. 72
ANT *see* actor-network theory
AntConc software program 75, 82n5
Arnaud, N. 2, 149
Ashcraft, K. 149, 155
authoritative mode: instructional mode *vs.* 64; of model-drawing 57–60, **60**; projective mode *vs.* 63

Bailey, C. M. 145
Barad, K. 81
Beaulieu, S. 149
Beaux Arts style 50, 52
Bechky, B. 47–8
Bencherki, Nicolas 2
Beyes, T. 88
'bifurcation of nature' 8
Bigville Tenants' Association, "things do things with words": Charles' case 14, 15, 17; community workers 14, 15, 17; moisture meter 15, *15, 16*; objectivity of spokesthings 9–11; perspectives of 11–13; Rental Board 14; Sylvia's case 14–16; Tamara's case 14, 16–17; thermometer 17
Bonneau, Claudine 3
Bring Your Own Device (BYOD) policies 114
British politics, geographical analysis of 91–2
Brønn, C. 149
Brønn, P. S., 149
Burchell, J. 148
Burke, K. 153
Business Ethics Quarterly 147
Buttny, R. 75

Castor, Theresa 3
CCO *see* communicative constitution of organisation
Cheney, G. 153
Chilean scientific outreach programme 3, 82n1, 85, 94, 99
coexistent trajectories, space as 103–5
'colonial space' 99
communication: breakdowns 146; constitutive 143, 148–52, 158; conversational modality of 159; crisis 146; scholarship 90; symbol and material in 155–6
'communicational perspective on social reality' 152
communication-centred approach 89–91, 105, 106
communication perspective, stakeholder relationships 150–2, 155, 156; discussion 158–9; material and symbolic resources 155–7; political production of meaning 157–8; stakeholder identification and salience 152–5
Communication Theory 151
communicative constitution of organisation (CCO) 1, 2, 24, 29, 68, 69, 89, 113 130, 132; communication, organisation and work 115–17; communication scholarship 90; grammar of relations 92; Luhmannian trend of 6; materiality in conversation 36–7; open question 90; scholarship 151; scholarship studies communication events 89–90; stakeholder communication 3 *see also* Montreal School studies
communicative theory of the firm 149
community workers 14, 15, 17
computerisation 28
conceptual drawing 54
Concertación de Partidos por la Democracia 93
ConCiencia 85, 86; coexistent trajectories 103–5; Easter Island's exclusion from 104; fieldwork 92–3; mission 93; network, space as 95–9; as outreach organisation 98; in region Sur 99, *100*, 102–4; showpiece event 93; space as region 99–103; spatial grammar 103, 106; spatial imaginary 87, 94, 95, 106

INDEX

constitutive communication 143, 148–52, 158–9
consubstantiation 153
Cook, J. 148
Cooren, F. 70, 71, 74, 81, 82n1, 116
co-orientation model 149
corporate scandals, communicative theorising and 149
corporate social responsibility (CSR) 147, 148
Craig, R. T. 152
Crane, A. 149
Crutzen, P. J. 69
CSR *see* corporate social responsibility
Czarniawska, B. 72, 77, 81

Deetz, S. 149, 150, 157
Demer, Christiane 3
design tools 46–8 *see also* modes, of design tools
digital technology: human-centred perspective 27; as sociomateriality 24, 27–8; techno-centric perspective 26–7
discourse ethics 147–8
'division of labour' 49
drawings: conceptual 54; Corner's study of 63; projective qualities of 47
Dryzek, J. S. 70, 82n2

Easter Island 104
Enfield, N. J. 71
enterprise social media (ESM) 114
Esser, D. 148

Fairbrass, J. 148
Fairhurst, G. T. 69
Fauré, Bertrand 2
Fehr, B. J. 71
Foucault, M. 157
Four Flows approach 6
Freeman, R. 143, 145, 152
French style garden 52
freshwater controversy, relational positioning in 3, 68–9, 82; compact as mediator 79–80; data gathering 74–5; discussion 80–1; Great Lakes of North America 72–4; Lake Michigan 78–9; materiality and matter 70; method of analysis 75–6; radium 76–7; relational ontology 70–2
Friedman, A. 149

'geosocial environment' 1
Giddens, A. 4, 69
'grammar of relations' 85
Great Lakes of North America 68; Compact 72–3, 81; discussion 80–1; Lake Michigan as matter of concern 78–9; materiality of freshwater and radium 76–7; mediator, compact as 79–80; method of analysis 75–6; physical materiality 69; public hearing 74–5; Waukesha's water diversion request 73–4; *see also* Waukesha city

Great Whale River controversy 74
Gregory, A. 146
Groleau, Carole 3
'grounded-in-action' approach 69

Habermas, J. 147–8
heterogeneity of, (organisational) spaces 103
horticultural project, sociomaterial dynamics of: authoritative mode 57–60, **60**, 63, 64; conceptual drawing 54; garden styles 52, 54; instructional mode 60–2, **62**, 64; interactional patterns 47–8; investigation of 50–1; 'Islands in the City' concept 50, 57; landscape architecture 51, 55–6, 58–9; model-drawing *55*; modes, concept of 54; projective mode 54–7, **57**, 63; stages of design process 52, **53**; working drawings *60, 61*
housing workers, machines of 13–17, *15, 16*

inextricable entanglement 155
information technology 24 *see also* digital technology
instructional mode: authoritative mode *vs.* 64; of working drawings 60–2, **62**
interactional patterns 47–8
interfirm collaboration 149
inter-organisational relationships 37; and organisational transformations 38–9

Jefferson, G. 95
Journal of Business Ethics 147

Koschmann, Matthew 3
Kuhn, T. 149, 151

Lake Michigan 69, 73, 74, 76–9, 81
landscape architecture: design process 51–2; garden styles 52, 54; notion of 51
Laplume, A. O. 143, 144, 155, 158
Latour, B. 69, 70, 80, 88, 89, 99
Law, J. 102–3, 105
Lefebvre, H. 88; framework 88; heuristic 88, 89
Lewis, L. 145
Livesey, S. 149
Luhmann's general theory of social systems 151

Malone, P. C. 145
Manuf.Co (French manufacturer) 29, **31**, 32–4, 37
Massey, D. 85, 91, 99, 103, 105
materiality: actions and consequences 71; and discourse 2; of freshwater and radium 76–7; matter and 70, 71
'material semiotics' 8
'matters of concern' 70
'matters of fact' 70
McPhee's Four Flows model 151

INDEX

mediation, concept of 48
Miles, S. 149
Mills, C. E. 149
model-drawing 55; authoritative mode of 57–60,
  60; projective mode of 54–7, **57**
modes, of design tools: authoritative 57–60, **60**;
  comparative analysis 62–4; concept of 54;
  instructional 60–2, **62**; projective 54–7, **57**
moisture meter 15, *15, 16*
Montreal School (TMS) studies 68, 69, 115–16,
  151; actor-network theory 7, 8; bifurcation
  of nature 8; materiality perspective 7–9;
  methodological approach 7; participative
  ethnographic approach, 11; 'plenum of
  agencies' 7, 8; social *vs.* technical subsystem 9
Morsing, M. 148
Mumby, D. K. 157

nature, bifurcation of 70
network, net and 72
normative power concept 160n2

objectivity of spokesthings 9–11
O'Neill, Essena 133n5
online stakeholders 149
organisational communication 1, 28–9; analysis
  of interactions 33–4, **34**; CCO perspective
  24, 29, 36–7, 115–17, 132; conversation
  analysis 30–2, **31**; data collection 29–30,
  40n1; emergent communicative skills 37–8;
  entanglement of practice 27, 32–3, 35;
  interfirm information system 32–3; inter-
  organisational relations and 38–9; materiality
  of information 25, 36–7; operational managers'
  daily interactions 30, **30,** 33; OuesTranport–
  Manuf.Co. collaboration 29; perspectives on
  sociomateriality 28–9; poor communication
  32, 35; 'presence/absence,' notion of 25–8,
  36–7; problem-solving interactions 34–5;
  qualitative data collection 29–30; responses
  to heterogeneity 35–6; social and material
  resources 34; Twitter 114
organisational relationships 69, 142, 145, 156
organisational spaces, communicative
  constitution of 85, 106–7; bringing space
  back in 87–9; coexistent trajectories
  103–5; communication-centred approach
  86–7, 89–91, 105; conceptions of space
  87; literature on 86–7; methodology 93–5;
  network, space as 95–9; research context 92–3;
  space as region 99–103; spatial grammar of
  organising 91–2
organisational stakeholder, communication
  perspective 141, 152; discussion 158–9;
  material and symbolic resources 155–7;
  political production of meaning 157–8;
  stakeholder identification and salience 152–5

organisational transformations 38–9
organising stresses, notion of 91
'organizationality,' concept of 133
O'Riordan, L. 148
OuesTranport (European transport company)
  29–30, **31,** 32–4, 37

Parmar, B. L. 144
Pasquero, J. 149
Pentland, B. T. 71
Phillips, R. 144, 148
'plenum of agencies' 7, 8
political production of meaning 157–8
Pomerantz, A. 71
prairie style garden 52
Production of Space, The (Lefebvre) 88
projective mode: authoritative mode *vs.* 63; of
  model-drawing 54–7, **57**
Putnam, L. L. 69

quantum physics, philosophical analysis of 81

radium, freshwater and 76–7
Rasche, A. 148
relational ontology 3, 81; Lake Michigan; in
  communication 68; ideas of 69, 81–2; matter
  and materiality 71; nature of entities 72;
  overview 70–2; *see also* Great Lakes of North
  America
representational logic 88
Robinson's four-stage methodology 52, **53**
Rowley, T. 149

Schoeneborn, D. 90
Science Week 96, 98, 99, 102, 104
Sedereviciute, K. 149
Sergi, V. 3, 90
shadowing 107n2
Sidnell, J. 71
Simondon, Gilbert 12
Singh, H. 71
snowball sampling approach 120
social construction, constitutive communication
  and 148–50
social 'gatherings 70
social media 114; affordances 114; corporate
  branding through 146; issue of authenticity
  133n5; working out loud 113–15
social reality: co-construction of 148;
  communicational perspective on 152
sociomateriality 1, 2; activity theory 48–50,
  49; design tools 46–8; digital technology
  as 24, 27–8; interactional patterns 47–8;
  notion of 27; organisational communication
  28–9; and relationality 45–6; *see also*
  horticultural project, sociomaterial
  dynamics of

INDEX

'spatial grammar of organising' 3, 86, 91–2;
coexistent trajectories 103–5; space as network
95–9; space as region 99–103
spatial imaginary 85, 106; ConCiencia 87, 94, 95,
103, 106; political effects of 92
'spatial sensibility' 94–5
Spicer, A. 87
spokesthings, objectivity of 9–11
stakeholder attributes 149, 152, **153,** 159n2
stakeholder communication 3; dialogue 146–7;
growing interest in 142; as interaction
146–7; investigating issues of 144; message
strategies during crisis 145; negotiation 146;
as normative obligation 147–8; notion of 143;
review of research 144; as strategy 145–6;
themes of **144;** thinking about 149
stakeholder identification and salience 152–5;
communication research 155; identification
research 152, **153,** 154; locus of 159; process
of identification 153; product of identification
153; relational approach to 154
stakeholder literature: discursive practices 157;
extensive review of 155
stakeholder relationships 142, 144, 148, 149;
attributions of power 157; communication
perspective towards 150–9; power dynamics
in 158
stakeholder research 143, 150, 152, 155, 158, 159n1
stakeholder salience 150, 152, 154, 157
stakeholder scholarship 144, 149
stakeholder theory 141, 142, 144, 149, 152
Stakeholder Theory and Organizational Ethics
(Phillips) 144
Stakeholder Theory: The State of the Art (Parmar) 144
stakeholder thinking 150, 156, 158; central claim of
141–2; question for 157–8; themes marking 143
Stephens, K. J. 146
Stephens, K. K. 145
Steyaert, C. 88
Strategic Management: A Stakeholder Approach
(Freeman) 143
structuration theory 7, 27, 48
subjective world 70

Tarde, Gabriel 10
Taylor, J. R. 159
Taylor, S. 87
textual agency 7, 11, 18, 113, 120
theory of stakeholder fairness 148
theory of stakeholder identification 152
"things do things with words" 11–13
Thomas, G. F. 146
Thrift, N. 85

Tompkins, P. 153
tools, activity system 46; mediation 48;
multivoicedness 50; social nature of 49;
types of 48
transduction, Simondon's notion of 12
TweetDeck 120, 133n2
tweets, working out loud 113, *119,* 130–2;
characteristics 126–7, **127;** contextualising
121, **122,** *123;* documenting 121, **122,** 124,
124; durability 127–8; exposing 121, **122,**
123; expressing emotions **122,** 125, *125;*
multimodality 127; Nicotera's arguments 132;
performativity of 126–9; reflexive thinking
122, 125, 126, *126;* teaching **122,** *124,* 124–5;
time and space 128–9
Twitter 3, 133n3; asymmetrical attribute
of connections 115; coding process 120;
digital ethnography 119; features 114–15;
organisational communication 114; qualitative
textual analysis 120; snowball sampling
approach 120; talk and conversation *139,*
139–40, *140;* TweetDeck 120, 133n2; tweets
119, 120, 126–9, **127;** use of hashtags 115, 120;
working out loud 117–18

Unfolding Stakeholder Thinking 144

Valentini, C. 149
Van Every, E. J. 159
Vásquez, C. 3, 90
Vernuccio, M. 145
Vielhaber, M. E. 146
Vygotsky, L. S. 48

Waltman, J. L. 146
Waukesha city 72, 82; freshwater and radium
76–7; public briefing 74, 79, 80; purchasing
water 73; water diversion request 74, 77, 80
Waukesha Water Utility 82n6
Weber, M. S. 146
Weick, K. E. 91, 92, 105
Whitehead, Alfred 70
Wisconsin Department of Natural Resources 76
WOL *see* working out loud
working drawings *60, 61;* instructional mode of
60–2, **62,** 64
working out loud (WOL) 3, 113; on social media
113–15 *see also* tweets, working out loud;
Twitter

Yanow, D. 94

Zakhem, A. 148